Social Research

Also from Polity

Approaches to Social Enquiry, 2nd edition, Norman Blaikie (2007)

Designing Social Research, 2nd edition, Norman Blaikie (2010)

Norm... ...ie and Jan Priest

polity

Copyright © Norman Blaikie and Jan Priest 2017

The right of Norman Blaikie and Jan Priest to be identified as Author of this Work has been asserted in accordance with the UK Copyright, Designs and Patents Act 1988.

First published in 2017 by Polity Press

Polity Press
65 Bridge Street
Cambridge CB2 1UR, UK

Polity Press
350 Main Street
Malden, MA 02148, USA

All rights reserved. Except for the quotation of short passages for the purpose of criticism and review, no part of this publication may be reproduced, stored in a retrieval system, or transmitted, in any form or by any means, electronic, mechanical, photocopying, recording or otherwise, without the prior permission of the publisher.

ISBN-13: 978-0-7456-7184-0
ISBN-13: 978-0-7456-7185-7(pb)

A catalogue record for this book is available from the British Library.

Typeset in 10.5pt on 12pt Plantin by
Servis Filmsetting Ltd, Stockport, Cheshire
Printed and bound in Great Britain by Clay Ltd, St. Ives PLC

The publisher has used its best endeavours to ensure that the URLs for external websites referred to in this book are correct and active at the time of going to press. However, the publisher has no responsibility for the websites and can make no guarantee that a site will remain live or that the content is or will remain appropriate.

Every effort has been made to trace all copyright holders, but if any have been inadvertently overlooked the publisher will be pleased to include any necessary credits in any subsequent reprint or edition.

For further information on Polity, visit our website:
politybooks.com

Contents

Detailed Contents		vii
List of Figures and Tables		xiii
Acknowledgements		xv
Introduction		1
1	Fundamental Choices in Social Research	6
2	Road Maps for Research	23
3	Principles of Neo-Positive Research	53
4	The Neo-Positive Research Paradigm in Action	72
5	Principles of Interpretive Research	99
6	The Interpretive Research Paradigm in Action	127
7	Principles of Critical Realist Research	168
8	The Critical Realist Research Paradigm in Action	195
9	Multiple Paradigm Research	220
10	And Another Thing . . .	229
Appendix: Review Questions		244
Notes		251
References		257
Index		269

Detailed Contents

List of Figures and Tables	xiii
Acknowledgements	xv

Introduction   **1**
   What kind of book is this?   1
   What are its key themes?   2
   Why is the book structured this way?   4

1 Fundamental Choices in Social Research   **6**
   Chapter summary   6
   Introduction   6
   What are the book's philosophical and methodological foundations?   7
   Worldviews are everywhere   15
   Generating new knowledge   18
   Why the choice of research paradigm is more important than the choice of research methods   19
   Choosing a research paradigm   21
   Conclusion   22

2 Road Maps for Research   **23**
   Chapter summary   23
   Introduction   23
   Road maps   24
   Different roads to travel with different stops along the way   25

An Illustration of the Three Paradigms in Action: Sexual Abuse of Children and Young People in the Catholic Church	**40**
Introduction	40
The research problem	40
Regularities	42
Further research questions	43
Choice of research paradigms	44
Research paradigms in action	45
Comment	47
Conclusion	47
Further reading	52
3 Principles of Neo-Positive Research	**53**
Chapter summary	53
Introduction	53
Origins	54
An alternative: Neo-Positivism	55
Main characteristics	59
A different logic of inquiry: from pattern explanations to deductive theories	60
Limitations of the Neo-Positive paradigm	62
Review	64
Characteristic steps of the paradigm	65
Review questions	70
Further reading	70
4 The Neo-Positive Research Paradigm in Action	**72**
Chapter summary	72
1 Age and Environmentalism	**72**
Introduction	72
The problem	73
Research questions	73
Review of extant literature	74
A possible explanation for the regularity	75
Concepts	76
Testing the theory	78
Summary	79
2 The Impact of Leaders' Experience on the Effectiveness of First-responder Actions: Background to Crisis Leadership Illustrations in Chapters 4, 6 and 8	**80**
Leadership in natural disaster crises	80

Contents

3 Crisis Leadership in Australia's 2009 East Kilmore Fire — 84
  Problem and regularity — 84
  Characteristics of the problem — 86
  Research questions — 86
  The 'maverick theory' about leading in a crisis — 87
  Theory simplified — 88
  Context, data and concepts to test the theory — 89
  Sources of data to test the theory: population and sampling — 90
  Testing the theory — 91
  Concepts and their formal and operational definitions — 92
  More about testing the theory — 97

5 Principles of Interpretive Research — 99
  Chapter summary — 99
  Introduction — 99
  Origins — 100
  Main characteristics — 103
  Description and beyond: the use of typologies — 104
  Limitations of the Interpretive paradigm — 114
  Characteristic steps of the paradigm — 116
  And what about grounded theory? — 124
  Summary — 125
  Review questions — 125
  Further reading — 125

6 The Interpretive Research Paradigm in Action — **127**
  Chapter summary — 127
  1 Technology Management — 127
    Introduction — 127
    Road map for this illustration — 128
    The phenomenon, problem and regularity — 128
    Literature — 129
    Research questions — 130
    Research design — 131
    The population — 131
    The sample — 132
    Data generation — 132
    Data analysis — 133
    Analysis that led to the braided-work type — 134
    Analytic work that identified 'left-brain' and 'right-brain' types of work — 135

Contents

Deriving sociological constructs from the analytic notes	137
Findings: a typology to help answer the 'what' question	138
Conclusion	138
2 First-Responder Leaders' Experiences and Perceived Effectiveness of Agency Response Effort	**139**
Road map for this illustration	139
Study's focus and scope	140
Analysis and types	143
Analysis and understanding	151
Answering the 'what' question with more than one typology	154
Analysis and theorizing	159
Findings: typology-based answers and theory-based answers	164
Conclusion: a critique of the study, practice implications and further research	167
7 Principles of Critical Realist Research	**168**
Chapter summary	168
Introduction	168
Origins	170
Main characteristics	171
Relationship to critical theory	182
The critic's standpoint	184
Limitations of the Critical Realist paradigm	186
Conclusion	187
Characteristic steps of the paradigm	187
Review questions	193
Further reading	193
8 The Critical Realist Research Paradigm in Action	**195**
Chapter summary	195
1 Gender and Environmentalism	**195**
Introduction	195
The problem	196
Research questions	196
Review of extant literature	197
A possible explanation	197
Possible explanatory mechanisms	199
Concepts	201
Establishing and confirming the model	202

Contents   xi

    Summary   203
  2 Why Leaders' Broader Experiences Support Better Outcomes of First Responders in Crises   204
    Introduction   204
    Road map for this illustration   205
    The phenomenon of interest and the research problem   206
    Context and regularity   206
    Purpose and population   207
    Relevant literature   208
    Construct a causal mechanism   208
    Evidence from data and analysis   213
    When to stop   218

9 Multiple Paradigm Research   220
  Chapter summary   220
  Introduction   220
  Two types of multi-paradigm research   222
  Two illustrations   223
    1 Sexual Abuse of Children and Young People in the Catholic Church   223
    Introduction   223
    Research questions   223
    Choice of paradigms to answer three research questions   224
    2 Crisis Leadership: A Multi-Paradigm Research Programme   225

10 And Another Thing . . .   229
  Chapter summary   229
  Introduction   229
  The neglected craft of theory construction   229
  Creative theoretical imagination   237
  A porous paradigm boundary   238
  Influences on choice of research paradigm   238
  Conclusion   242

Appendix: Review Questions   244
  Starting questions relevant to all three research paradigms   244
  Questions peculiar to the Neo-Positive research paradigm   245
  Questions peculiar to the Interpretive research paradigm   247
  Questions peculiar to the Critical Realist research paradigm   249

Concluding questions common to all three research paradigms	250
Notes	251
References	257
Index	269

Figures and Tables

Figures

7.1	Realist explanations of regularities	176
8.1	A causal mechanism in context	210
8.2	Five types of interrelated reasoning resources	210

Tables

2.1	Differences and similarities between the typified research paradigms	26
2.2	Differences and similarities between the three research paradigms in the investigation of institutional sexual abuse of children and young people	48
6.1	Opposite types of work combined for a common purpose	135
6.2	Illustration of coding that identified 'left-brain' and 'right-brain' types of work	136
6.3	Deconstruction of abstracted categories and their everyday typifications of experience-based influences on leaders' repertoire	148
6.4	Typology of experienced-based influences on leaders' repertoire as a result of abductively constructing types from components of meaning	149
6.5	Co-frequency of types of experiential influences referred to by leaders in 'well-handled' and 'poorly handled' responses to bushfire emergencies	152
6.6	Co-occurrence of types of influences that are most distinct or most similar across 'well-handled' and 'poorly handled' responses to bushfire emergencies	153

6.7	Signature characteristics of types of leader orientation	158
6.8	Co-frequencies of leader orientations in 'well handled' and 'poorly handled' responses	160
6.9	Co-occurrences of experiential influences and leader orientations in cases of 'well-handled' and 'poorly handled' responses	161
6.10	Co-frequency of leader orientations in each sampled bushfire emergency	163
6.11	Type characteristics most and least suited to leadership of effective bushfire responses	166
7.1	Domains of reality	178

Acknowledgements

Any work of this kind is based on intellectual influences, inputs and contributions from a variety of sources over many decades. We are grateful to countless methodologists and social researchers, students and colleagues, research participants and sponsors, who, over the years, have provided useful ideas and intellectual resources, stimulation and challenges, opportunities and support which have proven valuable in shaping our orientations towards, knowledge of, and skills for doing social research.

We are particularly indebted to Erica Hallebone who travelled with us during the planning phase and in the early stage of writing this book. She made significant contributions to the setting of its aims and provided insightful comments on early drafts. In particular, the selection of the illustration on the institutional sexual abuse of children and young people was hers, and she was responsible for its initial draft.

We also wish to acknowledge the material support provided by the Graduate School of Business and Law at Melbourne's RMIT University and the support of InfoServ Pty Ltd for access to its research and practice files.

Introduction

'[T]he purpose of social enquiry is to produce ever more adequate knowledge ... [and] ever more powerful explanations of social phenomena.'

Layder 1998: 9

What kind of book is this?

The aim of this book is to contribute to what Layder has identified as the purpose of social inquiry. While this purpose may be regarded as uncontroversial, its achievement is a constant challenge – 'to produce ever more adequate knowledge' and 'ever more powerful explanations'. The ultimate challenge for social researchers is to go beyond description to explanation; to be able to say *why* something is as it is or is happening that way, not just *what* exists or is going on. This book presents and illustrates three major ways in which this can be achieved in the social sciences.

It is important to state at the outset that this is not a standard research methods textbook. It differs from such books in a number of important ways. First, it makes only passing references to the techniques that are currently used to collect, generate or analyse data. Secondly, it deals with a range of decisions that have to be made before a researcher gets to the point of needing to think about data. It is our view that there is a tendency in many social research methods textbooks to neglect or not deal adequately with many if not most of these decisions.

What this book does is pick up and develop themes that have been expounded in its two forerunners, *Approaches to Social Enquiry*

(Blaikie 2007) and *Designing Social Research* (Blaikie 2010). Both of these books identified a number of research paradigms, classical and contemporary, which have dominated the social sciences from their beginnings. However, what these two books did not do was to show what roles these paradigms play in social research. The unique feature of this third book is that it makes this connection and explains, with illustrations, how research paradigms can be used in practice.

What are its key themes?

There are two key themes: that successful social research requires much more than collecting, generating and analysing data; and that moving beyond description to explanation is the most challenging aspect of social research.[1]

While social researchers must have the skills to be able to produce and manipulate data, many prior steps and decisions have to be taken before an appropriate selection of methods can be made. In particular, a researcher has to be clear about the research question(s) to be investigated, a choice has to be made between different assumptions about the nature of the social reality being studied, and a decision has to be made about how knowledge of that reality can be generated – about which logic of inquiry will be used to answer the research question(s).

The foundation of an investigation of any social phenomenon is an adequate description of what exists, of what is going on and, maybe, of how it is changing. Description requires taking an array of specific pieces of data and producing generalizations from them. For example, a research topic may be concerned with the nature and extent of homelessness, and the problem to be investigated may be who these people are and the circumstances that led them to this situation. Hence, the research requires descriptions of the characteristics of these people and of their biographies and contexts.

Achieving appropriate descriptions can be challenging and requires a great deal of background knowledge and research skills. For some research problems, description may be all that is required. This is the case in the above example. However, if the researcher added another research question – Why have these people become homeless? – the complexity of the research will have been considerably elevated. The ultimate challenge for a social researcher is to be able to explain what exists or what is happening. Furthermore, without adequate explanations, it is not possible to begin to find solutions to social problems. Description alone may help to make a problem more intelligible but cannot suggest reliable solutions.

We believe that a major weakness in much contemporary social research is that the nature of social explanation, and how it can be achieved, is not well understood. It is for this reason that this book explores social research through the prisms of three alternative research paradigms. Each paradigm provides a strategy for explaining social phenomena. The main task for a researcher is to select the paradigm that is judged most likely to produce the desired explanation to answer a 'why' research question.

A choice of paradigm entails making a set of fundamental philosophical assumptions. While this might sound like an unnecessary part of social research, we believe that all researchers make such assumptions, whether or not it is recognized. These assumptions need to be made explicit and all elements of a research design made consistent with them. When they are not articulated, consumers of the research do not have the whole story and cannot readily compare the findings with other research on the same topic. Hence, it is our conviction that to be able to make important and useful contributions to knowledge of social life *it is necessary to conduct research with eyes philosophically wide open*. This requires researchers to be fully aware of the assumptions that they are making, and have to make.

Another vital aspect of arriving at explanations of social life is the need for a creative theoretical imagination. This cannot be achieved by following a set of rules or procedures. Like all forms of creativity, it requires a great deal of background knowledge and an ability to make connections and to see possibilities. In fact, bringing together ideas that are not normally related can stimulate creative thinking. In social research, this creativity is disciplined by the use of different logics of inquiry for moving beyond descriptions to explanations. Because theories start out as untested ideas, a process is necessary to establish whether a particular theory is an adequate explanation. The three paradigms that we discuss entail the use of very different logics of inquiry, different ways of producing potential explanations and testing them. The role of creativity in social research is noted with references in chapter 10. The intervening chapters elaborate the principles, procedures and practical use of the research paradigms.

Why is the book structured this way?

As well as dealing with these themes, the book takes the reader through a discussion of research planning and practice. It focuses particularly on the characteristics of, and differences between, the three research paradigms, including the ways in which they lead to different research processes and outcomes. In order to deal with these complexities in an intelligible and manageable way, the book is structured as a set of logically distinct but interrelated steps.

- Chapters 1 and 2 introduce important social research issues, challenges and themes that are developed throughout the book.
- Chapters 3 to 8 form three pairs. The first of each pair outlines and discusses the principles of one of the typified research paradigms, including historical, philosophical and theoretical elements, and then highlights how the paradigm is used. The second chapter in the pair provides two illustrations of the paradigm in action, one basic and one more advanced. As the aim of the illustrations is to indicate how the research paradigms can be used in practice, they are presented schematically rather than using an academic-journal structure. All are based on the authors' research but modifications have been made to satisfy this aim, and some parts are research designs rather than research reports.
- Chapter 9 discusses how the research paradigms can be used in combinations, either in parallel or in sequence, and then provides two brief research illustrations of multi-paradigm research.
- By way of review, the final chapter returns to the issues of theory construction and paradigm choice: it discusses the complex and creative processes involved in both constructing testable theories and in developing theory in a bottom-up manner; it refers to a source of ideas that can stimulate creativity in social research; it raises questions about the relationships between two of the research paradigms; and returns to the influences and processes that lead to the choice of a particular research paradigm.
- The book concludes with an Appendix of review questions, chapter endnotes and the usual bibliography and index.
- Readers wanting to further explore the three paradigms in action or aspects of the crisis leadership illustrations may go to www.InfoServ.com.au and select appropriate menu items.

Throughout this book, the reader will be alerted to specific additional content at this website wherever the address www.InfoServ.com.au appears.

Because of its structure, this book should be read, at least initially, like a novel, by starting at the beginning and working through the chapters systematically.

1
Fundamental Choices in Social Research

Chapter summary

- The book's philosophical and methodological foundations are outlined using the following questions.
  - What is social research?
  - What is a research paradigm?
  - What have research paradigms got to do with social research?
  - Why these three paradigms?
  - What are logics of inquiry?
  - What is the relationship between research paradigms and logic of inquiry?
- The ubiquitous role of social actors' and social researchers' worldviews is elaborated, particularly how social researchers should regard social actors' worldviews.
- Weaknesses in current approaches to the processes by which new knowledge is generated are briefly discussed.
- Arguments are presented in support of the core theme: the choice of research paradigm is more important than the choice of research methods, and that this choice needs to be conscious and explicit.

Introduction

A superficial glance at popular research methods texts, and published research, reveals that there is an underlying concern about whether quantitative or qualitative methods should be used. Over recent decades, there has been a movement from the defence of one type of method to a willingness to use either type where appropriate. Now the trend is to deliberately use both types together, as mixed methods, and researchers are encouraged to triangulate a variety of methods (see Blaikie 1991 for a critique of naive uses of triangulation).

An appropriate form of mixed methods is to be encouraged. Throughout the book, we support the idea of using a variety of methods in social research. However, we propose to shift the primary consideration to research paradigms and how they can be used singly or in combination. To make this shift it is necessary to recognize the role that worldviews play, not only in everyday life but also in social research.

What are the book's philosophical and methodological foundations?

What is social research?

Social research is about solving problems, which include both intellectual puzzles and practical problems. As Robert Merton stated many years ago, 'every problem in a science involves a question' (Merton 1959b: x). Social scientists want to be able to describe, understand and explain puzzling aspects of social life. They may also want to try to influence or change some features of a social situation. We want to know *what* is going on, *why* it is happening and, maybe, *how* it could be different (see Blaikie 2010: 10–11 for a 'manifesto of social research').

In order to research a problem, it must be translated into one or more research questions – 'what', 'why' and/or 'how' questions. (For a detailed discussion of research questions, see Blaikie 2010: 58–69). Some studies may only require one research question while others may need a set of questions. Some studies may concentrate on 'what' questions while others may also include 'why' questions. It is also possible to include all three types of research questions. Just how many and what types of questions will be entertained depends on the nature and complexity of the research problem and, more importantly, how much of it the researcher wishes to investigate.

Once a research problem is defined, and research questions established, it is then necessary to begin to think about all the other decisions that have to be made in order to answer the research questions. These include:

- the research paradigm or paradigms to be adopted, including the logic or logics of inquiry;
- the context in which the research will be conducted;
- the concepts and theories that will be used;
- who or what will be the sources of data;
- how selections will be made from these sources;
- what kind(s) of data will be required;
- how the data will be collected/generated and analysed; and
- how the findings will be communicated (see Blaikie 2010).

It is important to stress that, while this series of decisions is set out here as a linear sequence, in practice the research problem, research questions and the context of the research may emerge, or need to be revisited, as work proceeds. Whether this happens depends to a large extent on which research paradigm is adopted. Therefore, the most important decision in this list is the point of view from which the research will be conducted. This involves the selection of one or more research paradigms, with their philosophical assumptions and associated logics of inquiry.

What is a research paradigm?

Thomas Kuhn (1962) is responsible for introducing the concept of 'paradigm' into philosophical, scientific and everyday discourse. It found its way into sociology in the 1970s (Friedrichs 1970) and debates about the relative merits of paradigms continued for decades (see e.g. Lincoln and Guba 1985; Guba 1990; see also Lakatos 1970; Masterman 1970; Barnes 1982).

Kuhn (1970a) argued that scientific communities share a paradigm, or 'discipline matrix', which consists of views of the *nature of reality* (ontological assumptions), concepts, theories and *techniques of investigation* that are regarded as appropriate (epistemology), and *examples* of previous scientific achievements that provide models (exemplars) for scientific practice. Our use of 'paradigm' is consistent with Kuhn's views.

According to Kuhn, the adherents to rival paradigms live in different worlds. As their concepts, theories and practices are based on different ontological and epistemological assumptions, it is difficult for adherents to different paradigms to communicate effectively; there is no common vocabulary with shared meanings, and there is no neutral ground from which to adjudicate the merits of the paradigms or their products. While Kuhn may have somewhat overstated

Philosophical and methodological foundations

the case for the incommensurability of paradigms, the relevance of paradigms to research cannot be overstated.

The role of paradigms in the natural sciences has been well demonstrated by Kuhn. He saw disciplines in the natural sciences as being dominated by a single paradigm that, over time, is replaced by another, usually in a slow revolution. However, the social sciences are characterized by concurrent, competing research paradigms. It is the research paradigms that currently dominate the social sciences, and that we believe to be the most useful for social researchers, that are the focus of this book.

The idea that social theories can be seen as adopting different points of view is now well established. Consult any review of social theories and you will be confronted by an array of philosophical and theoretical perspectives. The defining characteristics of these perspectives are the assumptions made about the nature of social reality (ontology) and the basis of social order.

The key point is that different theoretical perspectives provide different kinds of explanations of social life. However, social researchers have to go further than this; they need another set of assumptions; *epistemological* assumptions that indicate how knowledge of this (assumed) social reality can be obtained. Social researchers have to select and argue for assumptions that are judged to be the most appropriate for investigating the problem at hand. They have to decide on the best way to obtain the knowledge necessary to answer research question(s).

To reiterate, the key feature of a research paradigm is its ontological and epistemological assumptions. In any attempt to produce new knowledge about social life, it is vital that the choice of these assumptions be made explicit. Then the descriptions, understanding and explanations produced from the point of view of a particular research paradigm can be evaluated in terms of those assumptions and sense made of different findings from research conducted from different points of view.

Two important arguments that run through the book are: *paradigms are unavoidable in research*; and *loyalty to one paradigm is both unnecessary and undesirable*. Research paradigms offer alternative ways of addressing research problems; they are like different tools for different tasks. Rather than declaring allegiance to only one, and using it to address every research problem, research paradigms provide a range of possible ways of approaching and investigating a research problem. This choice is not about methods of investigation but about ontological and epistemological assumptions and logics of inquiry. The challenge is to select a paradigm that will provide the greatest chance of answering a research question, given the entailed assumptions.[1]

What have research paradigms got to do with social research?

In spite of all the arguments and claims made that researchers should be 'objective', and that research is used to produce truths about the social world, it is our view that it is not possible to adopt a neutral point of view to achieve this; there is no alternative but to view the social world from somewhere. As a consequence, all knowledge generated by social research is tentative because it is conducted from a particular point of view. This has an influence on:

- the kinds of problems that are selected for research;
- how they are defined;
- how they are investigated; and
- how the products of investigation may be understood and used.

The question arises as to whether the need for researchers to adopt a point of view in social research jeopardizes the possibility of making useful contributions to knowledge. The purists might argue that to allow such a subjective element to enter into the research process is to destroy the credibility of the findings. It is certainly true that adopting a point of view affects the value of contributions to knowledge by putting limits on their utility; limits on what is seen and discovered, on what is included and excluded from consideration. However, the critical question is: have we any alternative?

When complex problems are researched, it is likely that more than one research paradigm will need to be used. While the notion of a single truth must be abandoned in the social sciences, what a multi-paradigm approach produces is the possibility of increasing the comprehensiveness of knowledge.

There is a close relationship between how the social world is viewed and the choices available for advancing knowledge of that world, i.e. between ontological and epistemological assumptions. Blaikie (2010: 92–5) has set out six dominant types of both ontological and epistemological assumptions and has shown how they are related. Not all of these are relevant to the three research paradigms being considered here.

It should now be obvious that the decisions about methods of data collection and analysis occur late in the research design process and

Philosophical and methodological foundations 11

are largely determined by the research question(s) and the context of the research. However, as we shall see, the extent to which the choice of methods is influenced by the ontological and epistemological assumptions adopted is an open question.

Another aspect of the role of these assumptions needs to be highlighted here. Users of social research approach findings from a point of view and they will 'appropriate' findings for their own purposes, within their point of view. Users are bound to pay attention to different things; to 'see or not see' particular outcomes. Also, their interpretation of the findings may be rather different from what the researcher intended or assumed would occur. If the aim is to use research findings for policy development, they may be interpreted and applied in quite different ways.

In adopting a point of view, we need to have reasons for what is included and excluded. When research paradigms are adopted explicitly, rather than taken for granted, they expose this.

Why these three paradigms?

The literature on theoretical perspectives (e.g. Ritzer and Stepnisky 2013) and, more particularly, on research paradigms, reveals a wide array of alternatives. For example, Blaikie (2007, 2010) has discussed four classical paradigms (positivism, critical rationalism, classical hermeneutics and interpretivism) and six contemporary paradigms (critical theory, ethnomethodology, social/critical realism, contemporary hermeneutics, structuration theory and feminism). Baronov (2015) has also reviewed a similar range of paradigms, including embryonic positivism, logical positivism, post-positivism, structuralism, hermeneutics, anti-foundationalism and pragmatism. However, it should be noted that not all these paradigms can be regarded as 'research' paradigms; they have philosophical and theoretical components but are not generally articulated into research practice.

Given that the core idea in this book is how to put research paradigms into practice, we have reduced these paradigms to just three. The aim has been to create a user-friendly set of paradigms that relate to current research traditions and that are also practical and manageable while still being scholarly. However, these three paradigms can be traced back to the approaches to social inquiry advocated by the three main founders of sociology, Durkheim, Weber and Marx, and this provides some legitimacy for working with them.

The classic positivist paradigm has been dropped but an updated version, with some of the same elements modified to overcome its deficiencies, is included. The second paradigm incorporates elements of the classic version of interpretivism advocated by Weber, as well as contributions from hermeneutics and structuration theory. The third paradigm draws mainly on the more recent developments in realist social science and is also known as 'scientific realism'.

These three paradigms must be regarded as typifications, as abstractions that bring together similarities and recognize differences. They are not intended to be prescriptive. Readers who wish to use other paradigms are encouraged to apply our scheme and template to elaborate them into research practice. However, it is necessary to ensure that the philosophical assumptions adopted (ontological and epistemological) are compatible and are made explicit, and that other research design decisions are consistent with them.

We recognize that other paradigms are likely to emerge and are being advocated (see, for example, the 'new materialism' advocated by Fox and Alldred (2015) and others, with its machine ontology and the behaviour and affects of impersonal assemblages). However, an examination of the fashions in social theory over the past seven decades indicates that many do not last very long. We believe that the traditions on which our three are based have persisted long enough to be taken seriously.

We also recognize a current trend to adopt an eclectic and pragmatic approach to social research, be it in the use of mixed methods or in this 'new materialism'. (This is discussed in more detail later in this chapter, pp. 20–1) This trend seems to be designed to avoid any consideration of many of the things we argue for in this book, particularly the recognition of the role of philosophical assumptions.

What are logics of inquiry?

In order to answer research questions, a decision has to be made about where to start and what steps to follow. The different starting points and steps are referred to here as 'logics of inquiry' and have been discussed elsewhere as 'research strategies' (see Blaikie 2007: 8–10; 2010: 80–92).

Four main *logics of inquiry* are available: *inductive*, *deductive*, *abductive* and *retroductive*. *Inductive* logic produces generalizations from data; *deductive* logic involves the construction of theories and the testing of them by gathering and analysing data; *abductive* logic generates social scientific accounts from everyday accounts of social life; and *retroductive* logic proposes underlying explanatory mechanisms and/or structures and tries to establish their existence.

Philosophical and methodological foundations 13

1. *Inductive* logic starts with data about the characteristics associated with some phenomenon of interest; general descriptions, including patterns (as regularities or associations between concepts), are derived from these data, and used particularly to answer 'what' research questions.
2. *Deductive* logic begins with regularities that have previously been identified and that need to be explained; a theory that might offer an explanation is either borrowed or constructed, one or more hypotheses are deduced, and these are then tested by matching them against some data.
3. *Abductive* logic starts by discovering the lay concepts, meanings and motives that social actors use in the area of social life under investigation and, from the recording of these everyday accounts, technical or social scientific accounts are produced by an iterative process of typification[2] and abstraction, each of which can involve other logics, such as iterations using induction and deduction. The movement is from lay descriptions and explanations to social scientific descriptions and explanations.
4. In *retroductive* logic, characteristics of a regularity are documented and modelled, using a combination of *inductive* and *deductive* logic; a possible mechanism is developed and hypothesized, its context of operation defined and efforts made to establish whether the mechanism exists. It is a case of inferentially working back from a known regularity to an unknown explanatory mechanism.

What is the relationship between research paradigms and logics of inquiry?

The choice of a particular research paradigm entails a choice of a particular logic of inquiry. However, there are four logics and only three paradigms. This brings us to the key role that paradigms play in social research. Each research paradigm provides a particular way of explaining social phenomena by answering 'why' research questions, and this is largely determined by its dominant logic of inquiry.

Neo-Positivism principally uses *deductive* logic
Interpretivism principally uses *abductive* logic
Critical Realism principally uses *retroductive* logic

The reason why each research paradigm is not exclusively associated with just one logic of inquiry is that steps in the processes involved in producing explanations can involve the informal use of more than one logic. This informal use is part of a researcher's thinking processes, particularly during the stages when creativity is required. For example, an explanatory idea may tentatively be entertained and its consequences explored in mental experiments, requiring the use of both *inductive* and *deductive* thinking. Hence, these two logics of inquiry can stand in their own right as ways of answering research questions, and they can also play the role of under-labourers in the use of both *abductive* and *retroductive* logics. However, in the end, a dominant logic is used in the formal process of knowledge generation. We shall come back to these issues in later chapters.

It is important to note that the research paradigms are not required to answer 'what' research questions, although both ontological and epistemological assumptions are involved. 'What' questions need descriptions to answer them; descriptions of some characteristic of, or regularity in, some social phenomenon. A logic of inquiry is needed to do this and the predominant logic here is *induction*. However, as we shall see, in certain circumstances, *abductive* logic can also be used to produce descriptions as well as to generate theory.

'Why' questions are posed about some established regularity, most likely one that was discovered in answering a prior 'what' question. 'Why' questions need some form of theorizing to answer them, and this is where the logics of *deduction, abduction* and *retroduction* come into their own.

To anticipate an illustration that will be presented in chapter 4, a research project might begin with the question: '*What* is the form of the relationship between age and environmentalism?' (This question presumes there is one.) Let us assume that an investigation found the relationship to be linear and negative, with the highest level of environmental concern and action being amongst youth, and the lowest level amongst the elderly. This relationship between these two concepts, *age* and *environmentalism*, is a regularity or pattern.

How do we answer this 'what' question? One way is to translate these two concepts into variables, measure them quantitatively and then look for a statistical relationship between them. A logic of inquiry is involved here – it is *induction* – as the pattern of association between these two concepts is derived from data collected, say, from a sample of individuals. From a set of particulars about a number of individuals, a generalization is produced that summarizes the results obtained from these individuals into a pattern or an association between the two concepts.

Another way to answer this question would be to do in-depth

interviews with a sample of people covering all ages. Assuming that the data remain qualitative, as text rather than numbers, statistical generalization is not possible. Any patterns in the data will be discursively described using *abductive* logic. An elaboration of this logic will be provided in later chapters.

Then we come to the more difficult question: '*Why* does this relationship exist?' To answer this, we need to choose one of the research paradigms, each of which entails a different combination of ontological and epistemological assumptions.

To reiterate: choice of research paradigm is definitely required for answering 'why' research questions, but is not required to answer 'what' questions. However, choice of assumptions is required in both cases. 'What' questions can be answered using *inductive* logic, and also *abductive* logic, and answering 'why' questions requires a choice to be made between *deductive*, *abductive* and *retroductive* logics. The choice of research paradigm will determine which assumptions are adopted (see Table 2.1).

Worldviews are everywhere

Social actors' worldviews

Human beings view and interpret the world around them, as well as their place in it, from a variety of points of view or perspectives. We cannot avoid doing so. How an individual views the social world is determined by a complex set of factors that can include: family, community and society of origin; life trajectory and experiences; level of self-awareness; the occupations and career(s) that we take up; the social relationships that we develop; and, of course, the period of history in which we live. The extent to which we freely choose the view of the world we adopt is an interesting question, but it is probably less free than we might like to think.

These everyday points of view are sometimes called 'worldviews', although the 'world' that is 'viewed' may be quite limited. Over time, our worldview can change as a result of new and different influences.

Social actors invariably take their view of the world for granted and may defend it in the face of others as being objectively true and legitimate. Social researchers are not immune from these tendencies!

How should researchers regard social actors' worldviews?

The social worlds studied by social researchers were inherited from the research participants' predecessors and are continually reconstructed and maintained by them. Social researchers have a choice as to how much attention they give to the way research participants view their social world and their place in it. Researchers have two fundamental alternatives: to conduct research from the *outside* or the *inside* – *top-down* or *bottom-up*.

In the outside/top-down position, participants' points of view are largely ignored and research is conducted using the researcher's chosen or assumed point of view. This latter position might be supported by an argument that, as a result of their education and training, and their capacity for detachment, social researchers are in a much better position than social participants to be able to describe and explain what is happening in any social world. Social participants only have their limited, perhaps distorted, points of view to go on, while researchers have the benefit of being able to draw on a large body of social scientific knowledge.

In the other major alternative, the inside/bottom-up position, a social researcher endeavours to view a social world from the participants' points of view, at least in the early stages of the research. The understanding gained can then be used as an ingredient in the accounts that a researcher produces. However, the ability of any outsider to grasp the participants' points of view is a matter of degree. It requires intensive engagement with them, usually over an extended period of time. The only sure way to fully achieve this is to become part of that social world. The key point is that participants' points of view are taken seriously as being what their social world is for them; and the researcher does not prejudge it.

Regardless of whether social researchers adopt a top-down or bottom-up stance, what they produce are social constructions, perhaps more correctly sociological constructions. These differ from everyday social constructions in their nature and purpose but are constructions nevertheless. When the top-down stance is adopted, the construction will be entirely from the researcher's point of view. When the bottom-up stance is adopted, the construction will have the participants' social constructions as its fundamental ingredients. The researcher cannot simply report participants' points of view; the reporting process is also an interpretive one, from a point of view. However, a researcher has considerable control over the balance of influence of the two points of view.

Therefore, the extremes in the choice that social researchers make about how to deal with participants' points of view range from complete detachment to complete immersion. The three research paradigms differ in the way they deal with this issue, each sitting somewhere along this continuum. Hence, the choice of research paradigm determines the researcher's stance *vis-à-vis* participants' points of view.

The traditional view of 'the scientific method' is that everything should be done to eliminate researchers' 'subjective' influences. As we shall see in later chapters, this is just not possible. The alternative is to accept that social scientists approach research from some point of view; they have to stand somewhere. The point of view adopted should be made explicit and the role that this plays should be acknowledged.

Of course, social researchers are also social actors, and they also live in specialized social worlds that can have dominant points of view. However, unlike in everyday life, social researchers can consciously choose to adopt one or more points of view, i.e. research paradigms, as they endeavour to answer research questions.

Current attempts to recognize the role of researchers' worldviews

While philosophical assumptions (ontological and epistemological), as worldviews or paradigms, are referred to in some textbooks, what is generally missing is an explicit recognition and understanding of the role they play not only in the framing of research problems but also in how research problems are investigated.

Creswell (2014) has referred to four worldviews, three of which resonate with ours, but he and Plano-Clark (Creswell and Plano-Clark 2011) have a preference for a fourth, the pragmatic worldview. They argued (2011: 50) that researchers need to acknowledge the worldview they bring to a research project, identify its components and relate them to the mixture of methods being used. This is a tall order for novice researchers, particularly when no guidance is offered as to how this is to be done. In fact, the authors reveal their own insecurities about this aspect of social research: 'One of the most confusing issues for individuals designing a mixed-method study is whether to discuss the philosophical foundations and assumptions that provide a framework for conducting their studies . . . and their proposals and reports' (2011: 278). Yes, it can be confusing, and we are here to help!

Punch (2015) identified two paradigms: *positive* and *interpretive/constructivist*. This oversimplified classification may be attractive to researchers who prefer not to be overwhelmed with more complex categories and a more nuanced discussion, but this type of oversimplification is highly unsatisfactory to say the least. In the end, Punch, like so many other authors, discussed social research in terms of the crude quantitative/qualitative dichotomy and associated the former with the positive paradigm and the latter with the interpretive/constructive.

Over many editions, Neuman (2014) has also made a gesture in this direction by proposing three approaches to social research: *positive* social science, *interpretive* social science and *critical* social science. For Neuman, the positive approach emphasizes the discovery of causal laws involving careful observation and value-free research, the interpretive approach emphasizes meaningful social action, socially constructed meaning and value relativism,[3] and the critical approach places emphasis on combating surface-level distortions, while also recognizing multiple levels of reality and value-based activism for human empowerment.

Neuman claimed that few academic researchers adopt the critical approach. He also proposed two more embryonic approaches, which he regarded as not yet fully-fledged paradigms; *feminist* research and *post-modern* research. Apart from being broader classifications, these latter two categories are not mutually exclusive from the other three; amongst other things, feminist research is explicitly critical, and post-modernism just takes the relativizing element, which Neuman attributes to the interpretive approach, much further. If these two categories are to be included, then other candidates should be considered as well.

Our solution is to regard what we call research paradigms as typifications, as abstractions from the wide range of philosophical and methodological approaches discussed in the literature (see e.g. Blaikie 2007: 109–205; 2010: 96–104) and used in practice. This range has been reduced to three to facilitate understanding of the complexities and to make their use manageable. In the process, we are quite explicit about the principles on which each paradigm is based and how they can be used in practice.

Generating new knowledge

The major weakness in most if not all research methods textbooks is a lack of attention to the processes by which new social science knowledge is produced and tested and, in particular, the logics of inquiry that are used to bring explanatory ideas and data together. In this regard, Neuman referred to *deduction* as characteristic of the positive approach, and abduction gets a brief mention in the critical approach, but just why and what role they play is unclear; the other two logics that we regard as essential – *induction* and *retroduction* – are not mentioned.

Neuman (2014) devoted the whole of chapter 4 to the elaboration and discussion of these approaches, but that is as far as it goes; they are not connected with or used in the following discussion of research methods; the qualitative/qualitative dichotomy takes over. The same is true for the discussion of theory and research in chapter 3. While stating that top-quality research needs theory (2014: 88), the researcher is left to her or his own devices to work out the connections of research approaches (paradigms) and theory to research practice.

Neuman's books on social research methods have much to commend them (some years ago, one author thought an earlier edition was worthy of being set as a text in his research methods course), particularly in giving a place to philosophical assumptions and theory in social research. However, there are a number of important missing links in his research chain. In contrast, many textbooks on social research methods just ignore these issues, and even the best of them do not go far enough in making the connections and helping researchers build these fundamental elements into their research practice.

While the classification of research paradigms used by us has a superficial resemblance to Neuman's approaches to social research, we elaborate a full spectrum of characteristics of each paradigm, including philosophical and methodological positions, and pay particular attention to how the paradigms can be used. Apart from an earlier work in business and management research by Hallebone and Priest (2009), no other book on the market contrasts research practice in terms of paradigmatic differences in ontology and epistemology, logic of inquiry and methods.

Why the choice of research paradigm is more important than the choice of research methods

The now common practice of characterizing social research as being either *quantitative* or *qualitative* (see, e.g. Bryman 1988; Kaplan 2004; Denzin and Lincoln 2011; Neuman 2014; Punch 2014) has, more recently, had a third *mixed* category added (e.g. Brannen 1992, 2005; Tashakkori and Teddlie 1998, 2010; Bryman 2006b, 2007; Teddlie and Tashakkori 2009; Creswell and Plano-Clark 2011; Creswell 2013, 2014, 2015; Plano-Clark and Ivankova 2015). Some writers go even further and refer to the three categories of methods – qualitative, quantitative and mixed – as research paradigms. In other words, what began as a choice between working with words or numbers, or working with both, is now used to distinguish fundamentally different approaches to social research (e.g. Bryman 1988; Brannen 1992, 2005).

What this trend has done is to elevate to a fundamental level a feature of data collection and analysis that is secondary when compared with the fundamental choice between research paradigms, between ontological and epistemological assumptions and logics of inquiry. It is our view that decisions about the latter have to be made before a choice of methods can be made.

The move to promote the use of mixed methods arose in the wake of the paradigm wars that raged in sociology, particularly in the last quarter of last century (such as between positivism, interpretivism, Marxism, and the like), and sometimes between related theoretical perspectives (such as structural-functionalism, symbolic interactionism, conflict theory and exchange theory). This move towards a focus on the legitimacy of all types of social research methods was seen as providing some kind of rapprochement between positions that had been vehemently defended and were regarded by some as being incompatible (e.g. Bryman 2006a, 2014: 121; Greene 2007). However, it is difficult to see how encouraging researchers to use both kinds of methods, either singly or in some combination, provides a way of dealing with the much more fundamental choices that need to be made.

What this move seems to have encouraged is a pragmatic approach to research in which philosophical and methodological complexities are downplayed or sidestepped entirely. This can be seen, for example, in Onwuegbuzie and Leech (2005), when they argued that using both quantitative and qualitative methods makes for pragmatic researchers, and in Creswell (2014) and Creswell and Plano-Clark (2011) when they introduced a pragmatic worldview (read 'research paradigm' in our parlance) alongside post-positive (read Neo-Positive), social constructivist (read Interpretive paradigm) and advocacy and participation (partly related to our Critical Realist paradigm). They expressed a preference for this pragmatic position, so it would seem, to avoid the complexities of having to address the fundamental differences between these other paradigms when methods are mixed within a research project. Greene (2007) went a step further and argued that mixed-method research should be guided by pragmatism, as traditional paradigms are no longer relevant. Pragmatism is seen as a new emerging paradigm along with 'scientific or critical realism' and 'transformative emancipation'. (As we shall see in chapter 7, the latter is associated with critical theory, which is not a research paradigm as such, and is also present in some versions of Critical Realism.) We totally reject this trend.

Rather than follow any of the traditions that dominate the social research literature at present, particularly those that conflate all aspects of social research into the quantitative/qualitative dichotomy, and that downplay or fudge their way through fundamental issues in the philosophy and methodology of the social sciences, we focus attention on the differences between research paradigms. This might be seen by some as a retrograde step, back to the era of paradigm wars. However, our intention is just the opposite. By identifying the differences, we wish to highlight the fundamental choices that researchers now have in how they attempt to generate new knowledge and, in particular, how they can offer explanations for puzzling aspects of social life.

While particular methods may have come to be associated with particular research paradigms, even if implicitly, our position is that there is considerable flexibility in the pairing of research paradigms and methods. For example, while qualitative methods may be commonly used within the assumptions of the Interpretive paradigm, they can also be used with the other two paradigms. There is not a one-to-one correspondence between paradigms and methods. Most methods can serve more than one master; we want to make clear who these masters are or can be!

In short, it is the research paradigms that provide particular types of philosophical assumptions and particular logics of inquiry. That is why this book presents the choice between different research paradigms, rather than between quantitative and qualitative methods, as the key-defining characteristic of approaches to social research.

Choosing a research paradigm

A theme that runs throughout this book is that choice of research paradigm should be conscious, justified and made explicit. This allows researchers to be fully aware of what they are trying to do, rather than leaving the philosophical assumptions and choice of logic of inquiry implicit and unexamined, as so often happens. We argue that the choice of research paradigm, or paradigms, should be made essentially with the research problem and research questions in mind. The paradigm selected should be the one that the researcher considers will provide the greatest likelihood of being able to answer the research questions satisfactorily.

Choice of research paradigm is made in the context of many and often competing influences on how research problems are defined and investigated, and against the background of personal preferences and many external pressures. A discussion of the influences on choice of research paradigm, or multiple paradigms, can be found in chapter 10. By this time, the reader will be familiar with the three paradigms, their differences, strengths and limitations, and should be in a better position to think about how to choose the best one for the task at hand.

Conclusion

By elaborating the book's philosophical and methodological foundations, by stressing the fundamental role that both social actors' and social researchers' worldviews play in social research and considering the lack of attention usually given to the processes by which new knowledge is generated, a start is made to distinguish the approach taken in this book from most other textbooks in the field.

Two other key arguments are introduced that also add to the distinguishing features: that the choice of research paradigm, or paradigms, is much more fundamental and important than the choice of techniques to collect, generate or analyse data; and that, in focusing on the central role of research paradigms, each with its characteristic assumptions and associated dominant logic of inquiry, the choice between them, or in combination, needs to be deliberate, explicit and justified.

2
Road Maps for Research

Chapter summary

- The first part of the chapter sets out the steps involved in using each research paradigm, in particular, their characteristic:
  - starting point;
  - intermediate stages; and
  - end point.
- Road maps for each research paradigm are compared and contrasted.
- The second part of the chapter introduces an illustration and explores how each paradigm might be used to provide a way to answer one of the research questions.

Introduction

The journey through a research project can be tortuous and it is easy to get lost. One way to counter these difficulties is to have a road map. However, each research paradigm has its own road map and the choice of paradigm largely determines the kind of journey that the researcher takes.

In the first part of this chapter, we identify many of the elements or steps that a social researcher will usually encounter, and we provide signposts to aid navigation through the three research paradigms.

Road maps

Apprehending an important research problem, and then formulating questions and designing and conducting rigorous and informative research, is demanding, intellectually and practically. Demands arise in relation to the twin and often competing requirements for intellectual rigour and insight on the one hand, and the need for practical and self-conscious development and progress on the other.

Maintaining a road map, to guide the research process through the planning and doing aspects, helps a researcher preserve a cogent 'big picture' while also attending to unfolding complexities and practicalities. Road maps help readers of a study's reports to better apprehend and understand its importance, rigour, conduct and, ultimately, its contribution to knowledge and/or problem solution.

Important elements of a typical road map are:

- developing clear statements about specific aspects of the problem and corresponding particular questions (and sub-questions) against which all later work is designed, done, reviewed and reported;
- choosing and justifying one or more research paradigms that best suit the particular problem and have the best chance of providing answers to the research question(s); and
- providing an overall logic that is consistent with the chosen paradigm(s).

These three elements inevitably involve reference to appropriate literature in order to highlight debates, identify gaps and explain and justify choices about the research focus and the paradigmatic and logical architecture of the intended study. Consistent with the products of these elements, the researcher then selects with justification, samples, data, analytic procedures and specific methods to be used to produce, verify and report answers to the research questions. The diverse administrative aspects of the study also need to be prepared and commonly include a formal research proposal, ethics issues and arrangements, intellectual property agreements, resource requirements and arrangements, work scheduling, accountability and progress reporting, quality reviews and performance agreements.

Different roads to travel with different stops along the way

Social research has a number of critical decision points along the road. Each paradigm has a different starting point and takes quite a different route to the destination of answered research questions. Hence, we need three road maps, one for each paradigm.

These different routes will first be discussed under a set of universal characteristics of social research design and conduct, and then, in Table 2.1, the different routes taken by each research paradigm are contrasted.

Starting points

The starting point for the Neo-Positive and Critical Realist research paradigms is a pattern or regularity that needs to be explained. A pattern or regularity is a description of some state of affairs that is associated with a social problem or phenomenon and that has been established by systematic research. It may have been established in previous research or may come out of the first stage of a new research project; it is commonly an answer to a 'what' research question. In the Neo-Positive paradigm, 'what' questions are answered by identifying regularities in the form of relationships between concepts. In the Critical Realist paradigm, a regularity is in the form of a model that incorporates a detailed, discursive description that can be elaborated in diagrams or images.

For example, after collecting data on a wide variety of cases of juveniles who have been convicted of a crime, a researcher may have discovered that they tend to have one important thing in common; they grew up in a dysfunctional family or, perhaps, lacked a 'normal' family upbringing. A generalization may be arrived at that there is an association between juvenile delinquency and family background. It is important to note that such generalizations are limited in time and place; they only apply to a particular social location at a particular time.

The Interpretive paradigm may have the same kind of starting point but it is also possible to start out without a clear answer to a 'what' question. Research may proceed for some time before such a question emerges, and the answer may be in the form of a discursive description of some social phenomenon.

In order to establish a generalization that identifies a regularity or relationship, *inductive* logic will be required. Just which methods of data collection/generation and analysis are used to do this is not

Table 2.1 Differences and similarities between the typified research paradigms

Part A: Initial decisions and actions

Paradigm	Neo-Positive	Interpretive	Critical Realist
Starting point	An observed regularity or pattern that needs an explanation.	A social phenomenon that needs to be better understood.	An observed regularity or pattern that needs a causal explanation.
Purpose	To find or produce a theory and test it as a possible explanation for an observed regularity or pattern.	To develop typified descriptions and interpretation-based understanding of everyday concepts and meanings.	To establish the existence of underlying explanatory structures and mechanisms.
Assumptions	*Ontology*: cautious realist. *Epistemology*: falsificationism.	*Ontology*: idealist. *Epistemology*: constructionism.	*Ontology*: depth realist. *Epistemology*: neo-realism.
Using extant literature	As a source of an existing theory or idea that can be used to construct a new theory.	To develop sensitizing concepts and identify possible ideas to help generate understanding.	To help sensitize researchers' recognition and imaginative theorizing as part of identifying possible underlying causal mechanisms.
Type of research design	Linear.	Iterative.	Linear and iterative.
Researcher's stance	Top-down; outsider. Detached observer.	Bottom-up; insider. Any or all of: empathetic observer; faithful reporter; mediator of languages.	Both bottom-up & top-down; insider & outsider. Reflective partner.

Part B: Logic, concepts, theory and hypotheses

Logics of inquiry	*Inductive* to establish the regularity. *Deductive* to produce a possible explanation.	*Inductive* or *abductive* to produce thematic descriptions and abstracted typifications.	*Inductive* or *abductive* to model the regularity. *Retroductive* to produce a possible underlying causal explanation.
Initial process	Select or construct a theory to explain the observed regularity or relationship between concepts. Deduce hypotheses from the theory to test it.	Explore an everyday social world to develop typified concepts and interpreted understanding.	Model both the regularity and possible underlying explanatory structures and causal mechanisms.
Later process	Corroborate, reject or modify the theory for further testing.	Use emerging hypotheses as a way of developing more comprehensive understanding and explanation.	Search for evidence of the existence of the hypothesized causal structures and mechanisms.
Role of concepts	To identify observable phenomena. Concepts are formally defined and then operationalized.	Sensitizing concepts provide an orientation to the phenomenon. These give way to everyday concepts that provide the basis for typified descriptions and understanding.	Used to model both the regularities and explanatory structures and mechanisms.
Role of theory	A theory in deductive form is necessary at the outset to provide a possible explanation.	Theory emerges from the iterative process in the interplay between ideas and data.	Theoretical ideas may emerge and be embedded in the description of hypothetical causal structures and mechanisms.

Table 2.1 (cont.)

Part B: Logic, concepts, theory and hypotheses

Paradigm	Neo-Positive	Interpretive	Critical Realist
Role of hypotheses	As statements of relationships between concepts that are deduced from a theory for testing.	Micro-working hypotheses play a role in the emergence of interpretive understanding and explanation.	Explanatory mechanisms are hypothesized as potential causal explanations.

Part C: Data generation/collection and analysis

	Neo-Positive	Interpretive	Critical Realist
Use of data	To describe regularities and relationships about social phenomena and to test hypotheses.	To generate concepts, descriptions and understanding from everyday concepts and interpretations.	To model regularities in social phenomena and find strong evidence for the existence of hypothesized causal structures and mechanisms.
Main types and forms of data	Primary, secondary and tertiary. Predominantly numerical.	Primary and individual case studies. Predominantly textual. Researchers' cognitive data.	Primary, secondary and tertiary. Numerical and textual. Researchers' cognitive data.
Main data sources	Semi-natural and artificial settings; social artefacts.	Natural and semi-natural social settings.	Natural, semi-natural and artificial social settings; social artefacts.
Main types of data selection	Populations, probability and non-probability samples.	Populations and non-probability samples.	Populations, probability and non-probability samples.
Main methods of data collection & generation	Mainly quantitative. Collected rather then generated.	Qualitative. Generated.	Quantitative and qualitative. Collected and generated.

Different roads and stops along the way

Purpose of data analysis	To corroborate, reject or modify a theory according to evidence obtained.	To iteratively (or even reflexively) produce typified concepts, understanding and explanation.	To reflexively model regularities and relationships. To evaluate evidence for the existence of the hypothesized causal structures and mechanisms.
Main types of data analysis	Measures of distribution, association or difference and, if appropriate, tests of significance.	*Abductive* generation of typifications, understanding and explanation.	Iterative modelling of contexts and causal mechanisms. Evaluate evidence for the presence or absence of causal structures and mechanisms.

Part D: Status and use of results

Establishing status of research findings	'Validity' and 'reliability' established by accepted methods. 'Objectivity' a goal.	Authenticity established by use of 'member checking'.	Depends on domain of reality. Strength of argument from evidence for the existence of proposed causal structures and mechanisms.
Generaliz-ability of results	From probability sample to population. Beyond a population: methods of 'transferability' and 'relatability'.	The use of analytic induction to generalize. Methods of 'transferability' and 'relatability'.	Where appropriate, methods of 'transferability' and 'relatability'.
Reporting	See relevant section above.	See relevant section above.	See relevant section above.

important, although in the Neo-Positive paradigm they are likely to be quantitative. *Inductive* logic may be used in the Interpretive paradigm but *abductive* logic may be more appropriate. The only requirement is that the pattern or regularity needs to be convincing before further research is undertaken. Research paradigms only come into play when there is something that needs to be explained or better understood.

Returning to the example, once the regularity has been established, the obvious question is: '*Why* is this so?' Why do certain kinds of family experiences lead these young people into criminal activities? The problem with such research questions is to know where to start and then what to do to arrive at an answer.

Purpose

The research paradigms set out to answer 'why' research questions in very different ways. The Neo-Positive paradigm seeks answers by finding and testing a theory that might explain a regularity in a particular context. The purpose of the Interpretive paradigm is not only to identify and describe the typifications that social actors use with regard to the research problem, but also to produce social scientific typifications that can form the basis of a theoretical account. The Critical Realist paradigm approaches the task of explanation differently again. It seeks to discover and establish the mechanism that produces a described regularity in a particular context. While this causal process could be elaborated in theoretical propositions, this paradigm concentrates on trying to imagine what mechanism or mechanisms are operating and then sets out to find evidence for their existence and mode of operation.

Assumptions

It is their particular combination of ontological and epistemological assumptions that readily distinguish the research paradigms. While the Neo-Positivist and Critical Realist paradigms both work with realist ontological assumptions, their realist notions are different. Both paradigms assume that social reality has an existence that is independent of the social actors who inhabit it, but they differ in their view of the extent to which social activity has a bearing on the nature of that reality.

The Neo-Positivist paradigm adopts a *cautious realist* ontology that recognizes the limitations and unreliability of our senses as

Different roads and stops along the way 31

'observational' tools and the limiting role of researcher's worldviews. This is then associated with the epistemological assumptions of *falsificationism*, in which a process of trial and error is used to propose and test theories against empirical evidence. It is assumed that knowledge produced by this process must always be regarded as tentative. (The ontological and epistemological categories used in this section are derived from Blaikie [2007: 12–27; 2010: 92–5] and are discussed here in chapters 3, 5 and 7.)

The Interpretive paradigm adopts quite different assumptions; its ontological assumptions are *idealist* and this is associated with the epistemological assumptions of *constructionism*. Social reality is considered not to have an independent existence from either social actors or researchers. It is made up of shared interpretations that social actors produce and reproduce as they go about their everyday lives. Just what exists apart from these interpretations, and how these interpretations relate to this, is a matter of some dispute.

In the Critical Realist paradigm, reality is assumed to be stratified and to consist of different domains or layers. At the surface is the 'empirical' domain that can be observed, however imperfect this may be. At a deeper level is the 'real' domain, not readily observable and consisting of the structures and mechanisms that produce what is observed in the 'empirical' domain. Both domains are assumed to be independent of the observer but, unlike natural realities, social realities are not regarded as being independent of the conceptions or activities of social actors in that social context. The ontological assumptions are *depth realist* and this is associated with the epistemological assumptions of *neo-realism*. It is important to note that the ontological assumptions of one version of Critical Realism overlaps with those of the Interpretive paradigm. We will return to this in chapter 7.

Using extant literature

In the Neo-Positivist paradigm, literature can be used in different ways. One set of literature can provide evidence for the existence of a research problem, and maybe answers to 'what' questions, particularly if research on them has already been conducted. Another set of literature can provide possible explanations or be a source of theoretical ideas that could be ingredients in a new theory. Of course, answers to 'what' questions can also come from the research itself. These are the prime functions of literature in this research paradigm and, if viewed in this way, can provide direction to the 'review of the literature'.

Literature can also be used in the Critical Realist paradigm both to establish the problem and as a possible source of ingredients for the modelling of a regularity; other ingredients may need to come from new research. Literature can also provide ideas for possible explanatory mechanisms.

The role of literature in the Interpretive paradigm is rather different. Yes, a research problem has to be documented, but its characteristics may emerge more from the early stages of the research than from the literature. However, to begin this type of research, sensitizing concepts may be needed to provide some focus and starting points. However, it is in the search for answers to 'why' questions that this research paradigm most strongly diverges from the other two. At least initially, answers are not sought in the literature but from research participants, from the way they conceptualize and interpret the aspects of their social life of interest to the researcher. As the researcher's account begins to emerge from the investigation of everyday accounts, some help may be needed from the literature to support the process of abstracting social scientific typifications.

Types of research design

A Neo-Positive research design is presented as a linear series of steps. While some steps, such as the formulation of the research problem, or the development of a new theory, may require some iterations to complete, only when this is done is it possible to move on to the next step. Whether or not this is actually the way research is conducted within this paradigm, the emphasis is on systematic and logical steps and procedures. In the Interpretive paradigm, the process is very different. Research is more like a spiral with each stage evolving out of previous stages; it can also involve many iterations. Stages overlap and/or can get out of sequence; it is a messy process with no consistent steps. The Critical Realist paradigm involves both linear and iterative processes, depending on the type of research problem and the stage of the research. Modelling a regularity or explanatory mechanism is a creative and typically iterative process that cannot be reduced to logical steps; this kind of creativity is discussed in chapter 10. Determining confirming or disconfirming evidence for the existence of a proposed explanatory mechanism is a more linear process.

Researcher's stance

As we have seen, social researchers have no choice but to adopt a position in relationship to research participants and to substantive content. We have to stand somewhere and the stance adopted influences the way the research problem is framed, designed and conducted, and the outcomes that the research produces. The basic choice is between conducting research from the researcher's point of view or, at least initially, from the participants' points of view; top-down versus bottom-up. Another way of looking at this is whether a researcher views social life from the outside or whether they become involved, to some degree, in the area of social life under investigation; outsider versus insider. A combination of these two choices produces a number of stances (see Blaikie 2010: 50–4 for a discussion of the typical stances identified here).

The Neo-Positive researcher works top-down and as an outsider. This has been typified as the *detached observer*. The interpretive researcher's stance is the opposite; bottom-up and as an insider. However, these choices can be a matter of degree and have been typified as *empathetic observer*, *faithful reporter* and *mediator of languages*. The common element here is of a researcher endeavouring to reveal some area of social life in a way that reflects how it is experienced and understood by the participants. In the Critical Realist paradigm, researchers are likely to adopt a range of stances depending on the nature of the research problem and on which part of the research they are working.

Logic of inquiry

All three research paradigms need to first describe what it is that they wish to explain or understand. In the Neo-Positivist paradigm, this requires some kind of limited generalization based on evidence. The logic appropriate for this is *inductive*, to examine a number of specific instances and then derive a general statement of a relationship between concepts. The same logic may be used in the Interpretive paradigm, but *abductive* logic is more consistent with the paradigm's assumptions. The Critical Realist paradigm may also use both of these logics, depending on the nature of the phenomenon being investigated.

It is in the task of going beyond description to explanation that the paradigms differ. *Deductive* logic is appropriate in the Neo-Positive paradigm to test the relevance of a particular theory. *Abductive* logic is appropriate in the Interpretive paradigm to generate social scientific understanding and explanations based on everyday concepts and meanings. *Retroductive* logic is used in the Critical Realist paradigm to go from the observed regularity to the construction of a possible explanatory mechanism.

Initial process

In the Neo-Positive paradigm, one or more hypotheses are derived from an existing or new theory and the concepts in the hypotheses are turned into variables by selecting or devising measures for them. Immersion in an everyday social world, to discover the concepts and interpretations used by social actors, which are relevant to the research problem and questions, is the initial stage of the Interpretive paradigm. The Critical Realist paradigm requires the modelling of both the regularity and possible explanatory mechanisms.

Later process

The measurement of variables, and subsequent data analysis, constitutes the testing of the Neo-Positivist's chosen explanation. In the Interpretive paradigm, hypotheses may also be involved in the *abductive* process used to generate a social scientific account. However, these are micro-working hypotheses that are tentative answers to emerging 'small' questions and help to give direction to the iterative process that characterizes the use of *abductive* logic. Once a hypothetical explanatory mechanism has been identified and envisaged (modelled) in the Critical Realist paradigm, the key task is to find evidence for its existence. Such evidence may be indirect and fragmented but, whatever its form, it will provide the basis for an argument in favour of this rather than some other possible mechanisms.

Role of concepts

In the Neo-Positive paradigm, researchers use concepts to identify phenomena and establish links with the observable world. However, the status of these concepts is a matter of dispute. Some argue that every social phenomenon can be identified with unique concepts, while others regard concepts as somewhat arbitrary tools that are devised as a way of viewing social reality rather than having a one-to-one correspondence with it.

The Interpretive paradigm uses concepts in various ways. Fundamentally, it takes everyday concepts, in the language of the

Different roads and stops along the way 35

participants, very seriously and endeavours to locate and elaborate them and their meanings. It then sets out to use these concepts as ingredients in the production of social scientific concepts and accounts. Concepts can also be used in the initial stages of research to orient or sensitize researchers to the phenomenon and possible areas of exploration.

In the Critical Realist paradigm, the primary role of concepts is in the language used to model both the regularities to be explained and the explanatory mechanisms themselves.

Role of theory

In their various attempts to produce explanations, i.e. to answer 'why' questions, the role of theory is different in the three paradigms. In the Neo-Positivist paradigm, a well-articulated theory, in the form of a *deductive* argument, is required at the outset, from which one or more hypotheses can be deduced for testing. Theoretical ideas are also needed early on in the use of the Critical Realist paradigm, but these are embedded in the descriptions of mechanisms that are considered to produce the observed regularity rather than in the form required in the Neo-Positivist paradigm. Theory plays a very different role in the Interpretive paradigm where, if it is present at all, it will emerge out of the research process.

Role of hypotheses

It is only in the Neo-Positive paradigm that hypotheses play a formal role. They are necessary as an essential part of the process of testing whether a selected theory provides an adequate explanation. The use of *abductive* logic in the Interpretive paradigm involves exploring micro hypotheses that a researcher thinks might help answer the continuous barrage of minor 'why' questions that emerge during the research process. Exploring answers to such questions is the way that understanding is produced. Again, hypotheses do not have a formal role in the Critical Realist paradigm. However, mechanisms that are proposed as possible explanations for observed regularities start out as hypothetical.

Use of data

In all three paradigms, evidence for a research problem, and descriptions related to it, may take many forms; they may be numerical or discursive and they may have been produced by various methods. However, once research moves beyond the establishment of patterns or regularities, data are used differently. In the Neo-Positive paradigm, data can both describe social phenomena and be used to test hypotheses. In the Interpretive paradigm, data are generated and described as everyday concepts and then abstracted into social scientific concepts that constitute understanding. In the former, data are collected to measure concepts; in the latter, data *are* the concepts, both everyday and social scientific. In the Critical Realist paradigm, various forms of data can be used both to model social phenomena and as evidence for the existence of causal mechanisms.

Main types and forms of data

The Neo-Positive paradigm uses mostly data in numerical form and of any type; primary (produced by the researcher), secondary (produced by other researchers) and tertiary (produced *and* analysed by other researchers). In the Interpretive paradigm, data are almost exclusively textual (e.g. transcripts of interviews or field notes) and primary, with individual case studies being very common. The Critical Realist paradigm is eclectic in both the form and type of data used; this will depend on the nature of the research problem, the nature of the causal model or mechanism and the preferences of the researcher.

Main data sources

The Neo-Positive paradigm is used mainly in semi-natural settings (getting respondents to report on what has happened in natural settings, usually with questionnaires or structured interviews), but also in artificial setting (experiments). Social artefacts (official statistics and documents) may also be used. In the Interpretive paradigm, research is conducted exclusively in natural (observation of various kinds) and semi-natural (in-depth or unstructured interviews) settings. Again, the Critical Realist paradigm uses data from any of these sources. (See Blaikie 2010: 160–71 for discussion of types, forms and sources of data.)

Main types of data selection

The Neo-Positive paradigm normally uses data from large populations and, particularly, from probability samples. Non-probability

Different roads and stops along the way 37

samples are usually used as a last resort. In the Interpretive paradigm, small populations and non-probability samples predominate. While the Critical Realist paradigm selects data by any of these methods, evidence for the existence of explanatory mechanisms may be fragmentary and less systematic than more formal methods of data selection.

Main methods of data collection and generation

The contrast here is between the Neo-Positive and Interpretive paradigms. While not exclusive, the predominant methods in the former are used to collect quantitative data, while in the latter they are used to generate qualitative data. As discussed above, the Critical Realist paradigm is eclectic.

Purpose of data analysis

In the Neo-Positive paradigm, data analysis is used to test hypotheses and, hence, to corroborate, reject or modify the theory for which they were derived. In the Interpretive paradigm, data analysis occurs in conjunction with data generation and is used to produce typified, social scientific concepts and understanding. Data analysis has a variety of purposes in the Critical Realist paradigm; to model a regularity, to help imaginatively construct a hypothetical mechanism and then to produce evidence for the presence or absence of that mechanism.

Main types of data analysis

The Neo-Positive paradigm normally uses any of the range of quantitative methods of data analysis; measures of distribution, association or difference and, if appropriate, tests of significance. With its main logic of abduction, data analysis in the Interpretive paradigm is a creative process that goes on in the mind of the researcher as attempts are made to generate typical concepts and understanding from a variety of everyday concepts and understanding. Data generation and analysis occur together. In the Critical Realist paradigm, one form of data analysis is the iterative modelling of social contexts and explanatory mechanisms, and the other is the search for evidence of the presence or absence of mechanisms in such contexts. Any method of analysis that contributes to this creative and investigative process can be employed.

Status of research findings

In the Neo-Positive paradigm, attention is given to the 'validity' and 'reliability' of the measures of concepts. Followers of this paradigm have devised methods that they believe can establish both. There is also a concern with the 'objectivity' of measurement and analysis, and there are shared ideas on how this can be achieved. The ideas behind these procedures are consistent with the paradigm's assumptions but may be regarded as illegitimate by followers of the other paradigms, particularly the Interpretive paradigm.

In the Interpretive paradigm, the emphasis is on demonstrating that a social scientific account is an authentic account of these actors' social lives. This is achieved by getting social actors to respond to social scientific accounts, to the typifications a researcher has produced about them and their social world (perhaps translated back into their language). If social actors cannot recognize themselves and others in the account of their social world produced by the researcher, some revision will be necessary. In the ethnomethodological tradition, this is known as 'member checking' (Garfinkel 1967) and, in the interpretive tradition, as 'retaining the integrity of the phenomenon' (Schütz 1963a, 1963b). Depending on the approach taken in the Critical Realist paradigm, the status of research findings may be defended by a variety of strategies. However, the main one will be argument based on whatever evidence is available.

Generalizability of results

Concern with generalizing results in the Neo-Positive paradigm focuses on using data derived from probability samples as evidence for what is happening in the population from which the sample was drawn. It is in this that tests of significance have their main role. When the concern is to generalize these kinds of results, or those obtained from a population itself, beyond that population, say, to other social contexts, quite different methods have to be used, and they are the same as those used in other paradigms. In other words, the process is one of 'analytic induction' rather than 'statistical generalization'. Various methods have been proposed for the former, such as 'transferability' and 'relatability' (see Blaikie 2010: 192–7). In the Critical Realist paradigm, the method used will depend on what is appropriate in that context.

Reporting

The way research results are reported will depend on the context in which the research is conducted, e.g. academic institutions, independent research organizations, government departments or business organizations. It is helpful to start report writing with clear statements about the purpose of the report, the nature of the intended audience as well as distinctive messages about important as well as counter-intuitive features of the study and the implications of its findings. With this in place, it is then useful to devise a storyline that reveals these messages in a way that is coherent and interesting. A good storyline will be logical, intriguing, plausible and informative.

- A *logical* storyline traces a study's context and problem focus followed by the study's research questions, overall reasoning, operating assumptions and scope, design and conduct, analyses and findings and finally the study's limitations and implications. While this is not the only logical form, it is certainly very common.
- An *intriguing* storyline is inviting and even surprising. Pinpointing dilemmas, contradictions and gaps within critical elements of the study, and then revealing reasoned choices arising from these, can help establish this element of the storyline.
- A *plausible* storyline will be persuasive – especially where critical assumptions, argument, evidence, interpretation and judgement are concerned. Evidence and its clearly expressed critical evaluation are important here.
- An *informative* storyline will include insightful and nuanced descriptions and explanations that are also crisp, clear and instructive and that support each of the study's key messages.

All of the above elements can be systematically developed regardless of the paradigm used in the research. However, the research report's language, imagery and style will be distinctive for the way it reflects consistency between the study's purpose, its ontological and epistemological assumptions, logic of inquiry and choice of methods.

An Illustration of the Three Paradigms in Action: Sexual Abuse of Children and Young People in the Catholic Church

Introduction

The purpose of this illustration is to 'put some flesh on the bones' of Table 2.1; to translate the general statements about the differences in the principles of the three research paradigms into the paradigms in action. In this chapter, the illustration will focus on only one research question from a set of six. Three of the questions will be taken up in chapter 9 to illustrate multi-paradigm research, with a different paradigm being used for each question. The other two questions address aspects of the research problem but are not examined.

The illustration will not attempt to present fully developed research designs for each research paradigm but will sketch out how each paradigm could be used to answer the same question. In the process, the principles of each paradigm, and the differences between them, will be highlighted.

A research topic has been chosen that is highly controversial at the time of writing and is being exposed and discussed around the world. For centuries, physical, mental and sexual abuse has been present in various institutions, such as military, religious and educational, as well as government and charity welfare organizations. This illustration is restricted to religious institutions and to the Roman Catholic Church in particular. The reason for this is that evidence for the nature and extent of the sexual abuse of children and young people in this church is becoming increasingly evident around the world through reports from investigative journalism and official inquiries.[1]

The research problem

Over the past five decades, worldwide reports of the sexual abuse of children and young people, whilst under the care of government, NGO and religious institutions, have proliferated, yet these institutions have resisted recognizing the extent of the problem, let alone dealing appropriately with it. Institutional responses have been predominantly legalistic and have been typified by chronic secrecy. In addition, there has been systematic protection of perpetrators with tacit if not explicit approval of arrangements to protect the reputation of institutions at the expense of adequate responses to deal with the needs of victims.

An illustration of paradigms in action 41

Recently, there has been an increasing exposure of these activities in various media and an accompanying overt and vigorous response from many quarters:

- anger is gathering in various communities about paedophile priests and religious brothers;
- more victims and victims' parents are coming forward to report these activities;
- public interest has accelerated as to whether past abuses were institutionally hidden and whether religious organizations, including senior leaders, were complicit in their suppression;
- some Catholic priests have now spoken out, as have members and leaders of other Christian denominations, police, lawyers, academics, social workers, child advocates, newspapers, television documentaries, legal inquiries and government-appointed commissions.

Evidence has been accumulating from various sources around the world that:

- by using their religious position and authority, perpetrators have managed to persuade victims to remain silent about the abuse;
- church leaders and administrators have been unwilling to report the perpetrators to legal authorities, commonly preferring to move them somewhere else where their reputation is not known;
- church leaders and administrators have been unwilling to accept and/or take seriously the reports of victims, preferring to doubt the truth of victims' claims or to make them feel responsible, as well as requiring them not to report to anyone what has happened;
- many or most victims have either voluntarily, or under pressure from the Church, maintained secrecy about the abuse, even considering they were to blame in some way; and
- for many decades after the offences occurred, victims have experienced devastating personal consequences, including misplaced guilt, shame, sexual dysfunction, alcohol and drug addiction, mental illness (often debilitating), serious relationship problems, criminal behaviour and suicide.

In religious institutions, particularly the Roman Catholic Church, this abuse has usually been of children and young people for whom the Church has had a duty of care. How could something so contrary to the Church's beliefs have occurred?

Regularities

For the purpose of this illustration, the research problem is expressed in the five regularities (see p. 43). They are assumed to be the conclusions drawn from the investigation of an initial 'what' research question:

Q. 1 *What* is the nature and extent of sexual abuse of children and young people in the Catholic Church? Before outlining possible findings from an investigation of this question, some comments are appropriate. It has to be answered before any 'why' questions can be researched; we need to know 'what' has been going on before we can begin to explain 'why' it has happened. This is a very broad question and requires a decision about what should be the focus of the research. Given the topics covered by the four regularities below, it could focus on the characteristics of the abuse, the perpetrators and the victims. This would cover the first part of the question on the nature of the problem.

It is not possible to provide an accurate answer to the second part of the question, on the extent of the problem, as evidence for this is only gradually being revealed and much of it may never be known. Even if the time frame for the research is limited to the last fifty years, many perpetrators, victims, church leaders and administrators will have died. Also, some perpetrators may never be exposed and some victims may prefer to remain silent. However, while accurate answers to this part of the question are not essential, there is now sufficient evidence available in many countries to establish that this is a very serious problem worthy of investigation.

Then why has this second part been included? Simply to illustrate that, while formulating research questions can be challenging, once a set of questions has been established, a decision has to be made as to whether they *can* be answered. Are data available, are data sufficiently complete and can access be obtained? Eventually, this has to be addressed in the design of the research. If the answer is 'no', then the design might have to be modified or the project abandoned. In this case, sufficient evidence from secondary sources can be obtained to justify proceeding with the other research questions.

We need to also note that this question can be answered without having to choose one of the three research paradigms as an explanation is not sought. However, the question can be answered using *inductive* logic and, possibly, also *abductive* logic. Answers will be

An illustration of paradigms in action 43

produced by collecting data from a variety of sources, using a variety of methods. Initially, secondary sources can be used and it may also be necessary to collect primary data from, say, victims, perpetrators, and church leaders and administrators.[2] To draw conclusions from all these data involves the use of *inductive* logic to produce generalizations that summarize the data. The following five regularities are examples of such generalizations.

1 Some priests and religious brothers have engaged in activities that are inconsistent with their formal religious beliefs, as well as broader humanitarian principles, and that run counter to the duty of care they are supposed to have for these children and young people.
2 In spite of evidence for the devastating consequences of this abuse for the victims, most victims have remained silent for decades, many for most or all of their lives.
3 Church leaders and administrators have maintained secrecy about the sexual abuse of children and young people and, in the process, have usually failed to take appropriate legal and humanitarian action to deal with the perpetrators and to respond to the harm caused to the victims in morally and religiously appropriate ways.
4 Once secrecy is breached through media investigations and reporting, as well as formal (e.g. government) inquiries, the Church has been forced to deal with offenders and victims but has done so in ways that are designed to limit the potential reputational and financial impacts on the institution.
5 For many decades after the abuse occurred, the consequences for victims have been devastating.

Further research questions

These regularities – descriptions of the nature and extent of the research problem – need to be explained. The following questions seek answers to various aspects of the research problem.

The reason for all these questions is that the research problem is multi-faceted. However, only the first four of these questions will be used, Question 3 in this illustration and Questions 2, 4 and 5 in one of the illustrations of multi-paradigm research in chapter 9. Questions 6 and 7 move the investigation in the direction of the victims and, in particular, the consequences of the abuse for them. They are included here as examples of other aspects of the research problem that could be pursued. We invite you to think about how these two questions could be answered.

Q. 2 *Why* have the perpetrators of child sexual abuse engaged in these activities?
Q. 3 *Why* has the Church maintained silence for so long?
Q. 4 *Why* have victims generally remained silent for so long?
Q. 5 *Why* have church leaders and administrators not dealt with perpetrators in appropriate legal and responsible humanitarian ways?
Q. 6 *Why* have church leaders and administrators not dealt with victims in appropriate morally and religiously responsible ways?
Q. 7 *What* have been the consequences of this abuse for victims?

Choice of research paradigms

Once the research questions are settled, it is necessary to decide which paradigm, or paradigms, would be most appropriate to answer them. This illustration will concentrate on a part of one of the regularities concerned with the lack of appropriate pastoral care of victims.

> Church leaders and administrators have maintained secrecy about the sexual abuse of children and, in the process, have usually failed to take appropriate legal and humanitarian action to deal with the perpetrators and to respond to the harm caused to the victims in morally and religiously appropriate ways.

Hence, only one question will be investigated.

Q. 3 *Why* has the Church maintained silence for so long? The question will be answered using all three research paradigms, each of which will attempt to answer it in its own characteristic way. Hence, we are not making a choice of any one research paradigm here; we are demonstrating that some if not many research questions can be answered using more than one research paradigm. The use of the three paradigms is sketched out and, in the process, hints are given about the consequences of choosing a particular one. Whether the paradigms come to the same or different answers is an open question and will depend to a considerable extent on the decisions a researcher makes about how each paradigm is used to produce an answer. More detailed discussions of these paradigms are to be found in chapters 4, 6 and 8.

Research paradigms in action

Neo-Positive paradigm A number of social actors are involved in the concealment of the sexual abuse of children and young people within the Church. While decisions of church leaders and administrators play a pivotal role, perpetrators, and the victims themselves, have to be complicit in it. Therefore, the question could be asked of each category of social actor, and a different type of explanation is likely to be required for each one.

Victims have usually been threatened with serious consequences if they were to reveal this deviant behaviour and have often been made to believe it was their fault, that it is they who have sinned. The perpetrators must have been aware that what they did was wrong in the eyes of both the Church and society. However, they may have managed to rationalize their behaviour (e.g. that when a homosexual relationship is involved, it does not contravene the vow of celibacy) and, if they have been prepared to reveal their activities to a priest, have had any guilt relieved through confession, penance and absolution. Church leaders and administrators may simply have given higher priority to protecting the reputation and survival of the Church over the sins of a few perpetrators and the welfare of victims.

These statements could be viewed as tentative hypotheses. However, the initial challenge for the researcher is to incorporate them into one or more theories that will explain the regularity, and then proceed to test the theory or theories in a particular social situation. The theory/theories could draw on more abstract ideas in theories from other fields, such as deviance, power and social control, and even from theology (e.g. the cycle of sin, confession, penance and absolution mediated by a priest). The new theory needs to form a *deductive* argument consisting of statements of plausible associations between concepts. It is the researcher's invention; it is not arrived at by negotiation and it does not require supporting evidence. The testing process will determine its status; if the associations in the collected data are consistent with the hypothesis derived from the theory, as well as propositions in the theory, it will be corroborated; if not, it will need to be revised and subjected to further testing, or it will have to be rejected and replaced by another theory. This process does not lead to certainty, just to the best available explanation, which may be replaced later by a better one. The task of deductively developing a suitable theory for this illustration will not be attempted but is left to the reader to consider. Examples of such theories will be given in chapter 4.

Interpretive paradigm In this paradigm, the researcher does not set out to test any theory, isolated hypotheses or even hunches. The initial stage is to try to discover how the social actors concerned conceptualize the phenomenon (their everyday typifications) and to discover the meanings (interpretations), motives (reasons) and justifications (rationalizations) they give for their actions and those of others in the situation.

Once the researcher has described these, the task is to use the logic of abduction to produce more abstract social scientific typifications. Everyday typifications are what social actors use in their everyday lives; social scientific typifications are the researcher-constructed ingredients to be used in the generation of a theory to answer a 'why' research question. Hence, the final stage – using iterative processes and confirmations ('member checking') as is used to construct social scientific typifications – is to generate a theory. The confirmation of this theory is built into the processes by which it is generated.

In this paradigm, at least initially, the researcher has to adopt the role of open-minded learner rather than expert, and has to be taught by the social actors about them and their social world. Unlike in the Neo-Positive paradigm, the researcher has little if any idea of how the research process will evolve or where it will end up. This process will be illustrated in chapter 6.

Critical Realist paradigm In this paradigm, the regularity will be conceptualized (modelled) as occurring in a particular social context, maybe geographical location and time frame, within particular social structures and cultures. The next task is to produce a hypothetical model of a mechanism or mechanisms that might causally explain the regularity. It sounds simple when put like this, but it usually requires a great deal of familiarity with the social phenomenon and potential theoretical ideas. These theoretical ideas are not expressed as a *deductive* argument, as occurs in the Neo-Positive paradigm.

On one side of the explanatory coin are the *reasons* social actors have for their actions, and on the other side are the *resources* available to them to carry out these actions. It would seem that church leaders and administrators have acted to preserve the reputation and resources of the Church (e.g. people and financial assets), and protect their career paths within it; these are all *reasons* for maintaining secrecy. Perpetrators and victims will have been concerned about the religious guilt and social shame that would be exacerbated if their actions and encounters were to be revealed, and victims have lacked knowledge, power and opportunities to expose what has happened to them; both have good *reasons* for keeping quiet. On the other side of the explanatory coin, church leaders and administrators have had the resources to keep victims quiet (e.g. powerful positions, institutional traditions, financial resources, legal and procedural protections and arrangements, blaming the victim, threats of religious sanctions) and the authority to sanction perpetrators and move them around. Victims have been subject to the weight of beliefs about sin and guilt.

In this research paradigm, we end up with sets of hypothetical reasons and resources that apply to each category of social actor. There are some overlaps but also distinct differences. The researcher's task is to gather evidence for their existence, and this involves actively seeking out both confirming and disconfirming evidence. Just as model construction is actively creative, so too is the search for disconfirming evidence. Examples of such explanatory models are given in chapter 8.

Comment

It is important to recognize that the phenomenon of institutional sexual abuse is not peculiar to religious institutions; the same thing has occurred, for example, in educational institutions more generally, in military organizations and in major first-world national and multi-national businesses, although in these latter situations children are not usually involved; it is more likely to be the sexual abuse of women by men. There is, therefore, a general phenomenon here, but whether the same or similar types of explanation apply is an open question.

Conclusion

The purpose of the discussion in the first part of this chapter has been to lay out the range of elements that need to be considered, and choices to be made, in any social research design. In the process, comparisons have been made between the three research paradigms in terms of how they deal with each element. This was summarised in Table 2.1 and is elaborated in Table 2.2 in order to highlight what is required in using a particular research paradigm as well as how the three research paradigms could be used to answer the same research question. The aim was to introduce the reader to what will follow in much more detail in the later chapters.

Table 2.2 Differences and similarities between the three research paradigms in the investigation of institutional sexual abuse of children and young people

Part A: Initial decisions and actions

Paradigm	Neo-Positive	Interpretive	Critical Realist
Starting point	The responses of church leaders and administrators to victims of sexual abuse have usually been morally and religiously inappropriate.	The responses of church leaders and administrators to victims of sexual abuse have usually been morally and religiously inappropriate.	The responses of church leaders and administrators to victims of sexual abuse have usually been morally and religiously inappropriate.
Purpose	To find or produce a deductive theory that will explain the regularity.	To understand, from everyday accounts, what has occurred and why.	To model the regularity and explain it in terms of underlying structures and mechanisms.
Assumptions	Instances of sexual abuse, and actions of moral and religious irresponsibility, are technically definable events or actions that exist independently of everyday constructions and meanings. These concepts can be defined and measured according to their nature and frequency.	The meaning of sexual abuse and lack of appropriate care are social constructions that may or may not be shared by participants. These typifications, and their variations, need to be derived from a range of everyday accounts of the experiences of victims and church leaders.	The observed regularity needs to be located in a specific social context and it can be explained by discovering an 'underlying' real mechanism. The nature and behaviour of the mechanism needs to be hypothesized and evidence for its existence sought.

Conclusion

Part B: Logic, concepts, theory and hypotheses

	Using extant literature	*Researcher's stance*
	1. To help formulate the research problem and questions. 2. To find or produce a deductive theory by gathering reports of investigations about cases of sexual abuse in religious and other institutions. 3. To help make decisions about which data collection methods to use.	Because of the nature of the topic and the characteristics of this paradigm, and its accompanying top-down 'outsider' stance (*detached observer*), the researcher will have to be content with: a) limitations of available secondary evidence; and b) how people are willing to respond to data collection methods such as questionnaires and structured interviews.
	1. To help formulate the research problem and questions. 2. A source of possible sensitizing concepts in research and theoretical literature on all types of sexual deviance and abuse, and organizational secrecy. Later in the research process, different literature to help organize emerging ideas. 3. To help make decisions about which data generating methods to use.	While the 'insider' role is ideal in this paradigm, the nature of the topic will require some modifications to it. *Empathetic observer* of victims willing to break secrecy agreements. For priests, brothers and nuns, and church leaders and administrators, a *faithful reporter* to discover their world not just as they present it but as they themselves understand it and how they behave in it.
	1. To help formulate the research problem and questions. 2. To help construct a model of the regularity and also a model of hypothesized explanatory structures and mechanisms. 3. To help make decisions about which data generating or collection methods to use.	Because of the nature of the topic and the characteristics of this paradigm, the researcher's role will need to be a combination of both *detached observer* and *faithful reporter*. For constructing models of the regularity and the hypothesized explanatory model, the emphasis will be more as a *detached observer*. Later in the search for evidence of the existence of the hypothesized explanatory structures and mechanisms: the emphasis will be more as a *faithful reporter*.

Table 2.2 (*cont.*)

Part B: Logic, concepts, theory and hypotheses

Paradigm	Neo-Positive	Interpretive	Critical Realist
Logics of inquiry	*Deductive* theoretical argument from which hypotheses can be drawn and tested.	*Abductive* to generate social scientific typifications from everyday typifications.	*Retroductive* to identify a possible causal mechanism for which evidence is sought.
Role of concepts	Concepts in the theory to be tested need to be formally defined and operationalized. These might include: social deviance, sexual deviance, sexual abuse, goal priorities, rationalization, unequal power relationships and forgiveness.	Sensitizing concepts need to be selected. e.g. sexual deviance, organizational secrecy, silence, harm (to victims, families, organizations), justice, morality, deviant subcultures. These concepts will give way to the discovery of everyday concepts in use, the researcher's accounts of these, the generation of more abstract types that will provide an understanding of the phenomenon, and the formulation of an explanation that will answer the research question.	Concepts are required in the construction and description of the elements of the model of the regularity and in the context and explanatory mechanism. Given the long life of religious institutions, a possible hypothetical mechanism for this study are the actions that preserve institutional identity, reputation, power and continuity.
Role of theory and hypotheses	See Part B in Table 2.1	See Part B in Table 2.1.	See Part B in Table 2.1

Conclusion

Part C: Data generation/collection and analysis

Main types and forms of data. *Main data sources*	Secondary and tertiary data from institutional records (e.g. courts, police, Church, media reports). Primary quantifiable data from structured interviews with perpetrators, church leaders and administrators, and victims.	Primary qualitative data from in-depth interviews with perpetrators, church leaders and administrators, victims and, where relevant, lawyers, counsellors and social workers. Textual analysis of secondary documents.	Primary, secondary (e.g. reports by investigative journalists) and tertiary data (e.g. related studies) as inputs for modelling the regularity, and as sources of evidence for the existence of the explanatory mechanisms.
Main types of data selection	Populations defined and probability samples selected up front.	Populations defined (and possibly redefined in the course of the research) and non-probability samples from each selected at various stages of the research. Redefinition may arise as insights emerge and gaps become evident.	A combination of defined populations and probability samples and non-probability samples, depending on the stage of the research. Evidence for the existence of mechanisms will be obtained in a variety of ways.

Further reading

Blaikie, N. (2007). *Approaches to Social Inquiry*. Cambridge: Polity. Ch. 1. Provides a briefer review of the decision points but a detailed discussion of ontological and epistemological assumptions.

Blaikie, N. (2010). *Designing Social Research*. Cambridge: Polity. Chs 1 and 2, and especially p. 33. Reviews in detail most of the elements and decision points discussed here.

3
Principles of Neo-Positive Research

Chapter summary

- The first part of the chapter reviews the principles of the Neo-Positive research paradigm:
  - the origins of the early forms of positivism are reviewed;
  - the main characteristics of the standard view that emerged from these developments are identified;
  - weaknesses of the standard view are discussed;
  - an alternative, Neo-Positivism, is proposed;
  - its main characteristics are outlined; and
  - its major deficiencies are identified.
- The second part of the chapter sets out the characteristic steps involved in using this paradigm.

Introduction

Positivism is a philosophy of science that rejects metaphysical speculation in favour of systematic observation using the human senses. It is also a general worldview that places scientific knowledge above any other source of knowledge, e.g. Greek philosophy and theology. In fact, in its most extreme form, positivism rejects all knowledge claims that are not based on evidence produced by observation.[1] It represents a common, layperson's view of 'the scientific method'.

For the purposes of the social sciences, it is the later development –

Neo-Positivism and a *deductive* logic of inquiry – that we focus on here and illustrate in chapter 4.

Origins

The positivist view of science can be traced back to Bacon (1620) and was later elaborated by Mill (1947 [1843]). Challenges to their views came from Whewell (1847), Hume (1888) and, more recently, Popper (1959 [1934]). Positivist ideas were introduced into sociology by Comte (1970 [1830]) and Durkheim (1964 [1895]).

Three broad versions of positivism have been identified: *positive philosophy*, *logical positivism* and the standard view (Outhwaite 1987). Positive philosophy, propounded by Comte, regarded all sciences as producing knowledge based on observation. Logical positivism originated in the 1920s with the Vienna Circle philosophers. Their catch-cry was that any concept or proposition that does not correspond to some state of affairs, i.e. that cannot be verified by experience, is regarded as meaningless. Social reality was regarded as a one-layer world comprised of experiences and impressions about objects, events and facts as they occur in the world – with knowledge of the world represented and exchanged using the universal and disciplined language rules of the natural and physical sciences.

The standard view, derived from logical positivism, dominated the English-speaking world in the post-Second World War period and up to the end of the twentieth century. It adopted the view that scientific language is 'theory neutral', in that it simply describes what is there, and the 'correspondence theory of truth', in which a statement is regarded as being true if it corresponds to 'the facts'. In other words, if concepts in a statement correspond to what has been observed, then the statement will be true. All sciences, including the social sciences, were seen to be concerned with developing explanations in the form of generalizations that can become universal laws. Any phenomenon can be explained by demonstrating that it is a specific case of a universal law. In spite of the differences in subject matter, it was argued that people and society can be studied using the same logic of inquiry that is used in the natural and physical sciences. This logic is *induction*, in which explanations are derived from facts obtained by observation.

Bhaskar has summarized the standard view as follows:

> At its most general, positivism is a theory of the nature, omnicompetence and unity of science. In its most radical shape it stipulates

An alternative: Neo-Positivism

that the only valid kind of (non-analytical) knowledge is scientific, that such knowledge consists in the description of invariant patterns, the coexistence in space and succession over time, of observable phenomena .... Its naturalistic insistence on the unity of science and its disavowal of any knowledge apart from science induce its aversion to metaphysics, insistence upon a strict value/fact dichotomy and tendency to historicist confidence in the inevitability of scientifically mediated progress. (Bhaskar 1986: 226)

Numerous attempts have been made to identify the central tenets of the standard view of positivism (e.g. Abbagano 1967; von Wright 1971; Kolakowski 1972 [1966]; Giedymin 1975; Keat and Urry 1982; Hacking 1983; Stockman 1983; Bryant 1985). See Blaikie (2007: 110–11) for a review.

The standard view has been subjected to severe criticism. In particular, it stands or falls on the status of generalizations. The following questions need to be considered. Are objective methods possible? Can universal generalizations be established? Is explanation achieved with just universal generalizations? If the answer to the first question is 'no' then this version of positivism fails. If it is 'yes', and the answer to the second question is 'no', the outcome is the same. And even if the first two answers are 'yes', we may end up with incomplete explanations.

In the last four decades, another form of positivism – Neo-Positivism – emerged to replace both logical positivism and the standard view. The logic of inquiry used by the logical positivists tended to be *deductive* rather than *inductive*, in which theory is applied to concrete cases to generate new knowledge. As we shall see, it is *deductive* logic that characterizes the form of positivism that we discuss in this book.

An alternative: Neo-Positivism

According to Popper, there are two fundamental problems with the standard view: its reliance on pure, 'objective' observation; and its use of the logic of *induction*. First, observations do not provide a secure foundation for scientific knowledge because objective observation is impossible. To imagine that we can start research without some kind of theory in mind is absurd; the act of observing itself involves interpretation; as human beings we cannot do otherwise. All observations are selective and occur within some frame of reference, perhaps a theory, but certainly a set of assumptions and expectations, possibly implicit, about the nature of the reality being observed and how it should be observed. How we perceive the world around us is influenced by many things, e.g. limitations of language, past experiences, the kind of socialization and education we have received, the discipline from which we come, etc. For researchers, we need to add to this the ontological and epistemological assumptions that are adopted. Second, it is not possible to conclusively claim universal status for a scientific law. How many observations of a regularity do you have to make? It is possible that at some time in the future observations will be made that do not fit with it. Hence, according to Popper, establishing the kind of universal laws that the standard view of positivism aimed at is just not possible.

Popper advocated the use of a different logic of inquiry, *deductive* logic, commonly known as the method of hypothesis. While he accepted that the aim of science is to establish truths about the world, he also claimed that we can never know if our theories are in fact true. All we can hope to do is to eliminate false ones, those that do not fit with our observations. Rather than science beginning with observations, Popper preferred to begin with a theory, a guess at why something has happened. This theory can then be tested by making some observations and by collecting data. What we end up with are theories that, for the present, have survived this critical testing process.

Hence, Popper's view of the status of scientific knowledge is that it is always tentative; that we cannot establish absolute truths about the world. The testing of *deductive* theories leads to three main outcomes: the theory is totally refuted; it can be modified and re-tested; or it is 'corroborated'. Popper used the notion of corroboration, meaning tentative support, to avoid being accused of resorting to the use of induction, such as, claiming that the more tests a theory survives the closer it will be to the truth. Popper was vehemently opposed to the use of *inductive* logic, which involves accumulating evidence to establish the 'truth' of an explanation. The problem is: How much evidence do you need? When do you stop looking for support? What happens if contrary evidence is found?

Popper was not alone in offering criticisms of the standard view of positivism and offering an alternative. For example, Hempel (1966) presented a view of science very similar to Popper's, and Homans (1964) and Merton (1957a) both showed how it could be applied by reconstructing Durkheim's (1970 [1897]) theory of egoistic suicide using *deductive* rather than *inductive* logic (see Box 3.1).

Box 3.1 An early Neo-Positive study: Durkheim's theory of suicide

Emile Durkheim is recognized as one of the early advocates and users of the standard view of positivism in sociology. He not only set out rules for the use of this paradigm (Durkheim 1938 [1895]), but he also claimed to have demonstrated its use in his study of suicide (Durkheim 1970 [1897]).

His primary aim was to establish the discipline of sociology as a science. He argued that social phenomena are things and should be treated as things, as external realities that are independent of people's perceptions. Individuals are dominated by a moral reality that is greater than them, a collective reality or consciousness that is capable of having a coercive influence on them. In other words, group consciousness exerts an influence on the consciousness of group members. In spite of being immaterial, he argued that these influences are nevertheless real. Hence, the subject matter of this new science is to be these 'social facts', these externalized social products.

His rules of sociological method clearly include key positivist features:

- all preconceptions must be eradicated;
- the subject matter should be defined in advance by its common external characteristics; and
- social facts should be considered independently from their individual manifestations (1938 [1895]: 31–46).

In addition, he argued that social facts should be established first and then theory will follow from them. For him, science should proceed from things to ideas, not from ideas to things. In other words, he advocated the logic of *induction* not *deduction*. However, it appears that he did not follow this rule.

In his research on suicide, he began with a definition of suicide as 'all cases of death resulting directly or indirectly from a positive or negative act of the victim himself [*sic*], which he knows will produce the result' (1970 [1897]: 44). He collected data over a 32-year period (1841–1872) from France, England, Denmark and states that are now part of Germany: Prussia, Saxony and Bavaria. All countries showed a steady increase in suicide numbers over this period, but there were marked differences between them in the changes and the numbers. He explored a range of possible physical and non-social causes for these changes and differences but concluded that they offered no explanations.

Durkheim divided suicide into three types: *egoistic* (weakened commitment to group norms and goals); *altruistic* (deep commitment to norms and goals that include suicide as a duty in certain circumstances); and *anomic* (when periods of crisis or rapid change undermine group norms and appropriate behaviour is uncertain). Somewhat out of character with his other rules, Durkheim argued that such classifications should be stimulated by possible causes. At the same time, he claimed that explanations for these types of suicide would come from social facts themselves.

The theory he developed for egoistic suicide was supposed to have come from his classification of the data by religion, Protestant and Catholic. What he found was that Protestant countries had higher rates of egoistic suicide than Catholic countries, and that within countries of mixed religious composition, the rates were moderate but there were still differences between Protestants and Catholics. The essence of his theory was that, while both religious traditions condemned suicide, Catholicism, as a unified religion in which activities are constant and regular, created solidarity and a sense of belonging. However, Protestantism encouraged people to think for themselves rather than subscribe to doctrine without question; a 'spirit of free enquiry' encourages controversy and schisms. It is worth noting that the rates in England, a predominantly non-Catholic country, were moderate, perhaps due to the Church of England having kept some of the Catholic emphasis on priesthood and sacraments (Thompson 1982: 111).

Just how a theory based on social solidarity could emerge from these 'social facts' is not clear. There is evidence to suggest (Douglas 1967) that many of the ideas Durkheim used were already in circulation. It seems highly likely that the types of suicide and the data analysis were influenced by existing theoretical ideas. Therefore, while claiming to be a classical positivist who used *inductive* logic, Durkheim seems to have been a closet Neo-Positivist who used *deductive* logic. He must have been entertaining tentative hypotheses throughout the study.

This has encouraged a number of sociologists (e.g. Merton 1957a: 97; Homans 1964: 951) to present reconstructions of Durkheim's theory of egoistic suicide in a deductive form. Homans's version contains three main statements and uses three concepts:

'suicide rate' (number of suicides per thousand of population); 'individualism' (the tendency of people to think for themselves and act independently, rather than conform to the beliefs and norms of the group); and 'Protestantism' (a collection of Christian groups formed as the result of the Reformation in Europe).

1 In any social grouping, the suicide rate varies directly with the degree of individualism.
2 The degree of individualism varies directly with the incidence of Protestantism.
3 Therefore, the suicide rate varies with the incidence of Protestantism.

Merton's version focuses on social cohesion rather than individualism, the other side of the coin, and includes stress and anxiety that individuals experience.

1 Social cohesion provides psychic support to group members subjected to acute stresses and anxieties.
2 Suicide rates are functions of *unrelieved* anxieties and stresses to which persons are subjected.
3 Catholics have greater cohesion than Protestants.
4 Therefore, lower suicide rates should be anticipated among Catholics than among Protestants.

To be fair to Durkheim, *deductive* theorizing post-dates his writings. He believed he was following the best scientific practices of his day. However, how he presented his rules and practice illustrates the impossibility of using the standard view of positivism and the necessity of having some ideas in mind, even a theory, to suggest a possible explanation that can be tested by collecting appropriate data. Our argument is that this process should be spelt out clearly and the candidate theory presented as a *deductive* argument.

Main characteristics

The main features of Neo-Positivism were summarized in chapter 2 (including Table 2.1) and will be illustrated in chapter 4. This section focuses on the ontological and epistemological assumptions adopted in this research paradigm, and the logic of inquiry used to generate new knowledge, in particular, the way in which 'why' research questions are answered.

Assumptions

Neo-Positivism works with the following ontological and epistemological assumptions. It accepts some of the ontological assumptions of the standard view of positivism but rejects its epistemology.

Ontological assumptions: cautious realist

1 Reality has an existence independent of human minds.
2 However, direct access to this reality is not possible.

Epistemological assumptions: falsificationism

1 Knowledge is produced by a process of trial and error in which theories are proposed and tested against empirical evidence.
2 Because of imperfections in human senses, and the fact that the act of observing is an interpretive process, tests of theories must be directed towards trying to falsify rather than confirm them.
3 As it is not possible to establish whether knowledge is true, it must be regarded as tentative and open to revision; a cautious and critical attitude must be adopted.

A different logic of inquiry: from pattern explanations to deductive theories

In its search for general laws, for constant conjunctions between events, the standard view of positivism adopted what has come to be known as the pattern model of explanation. Explanation is achieved by discovering relationships or interconnections. When such relations are shown to be common it is possible to arrive at a generalization about the connections. As we have seen, in this view of science, the search is for universal patterns that are regarded as scientific laws, which, once established, can be used to explain newly discovered specific instances.

For example, if a relationship between juvenile delinquency and family background has been well established, then an observation that John Smith has been convicted of a juvenile crime can be

A different logic of inquiry 61

explained[2] as being part of a general pattern. Q: Why is he a juvenile delinquent? A: He has a particular family background. An established pattern will provide an answer to such a specific 'why' question. We don't know why this pattern exists but, if it does, we may feel we have an answer to our question.

The major problem with the pattern model of explanation is that the logic of *induction* cannot establish the universality of such patterns. However, these difficulties do not detract from the fact that, as human beings, we are always generalizing; in fact, we need to do this in order to negotiate our way through life. And, as social researchers, we also generalize in order to be able to grasp what we want to study. Establishing patterns or regularities (and their boundaries) in what we observe is the starting point of research. We have to be able to describe the phenomenon under investigation before we can try to explain it. And so the first task is to establish patterns or regularities, not as the basis for an explanation but what it is that requires an explanation.

Such patterns or regularities are never universal; they are always subject to space and time limitations and, by working with different assumptions, different generalizations may be produced in the same social context. This is why it is important for researchers to be aware of their assumptions and to make them explicit.

The Neo-Positivists rejected the pattern model of explanation and offered an alternative, the deductive model of explanation. This view aims to put up an explanatory idea as a logical argument consisting of a series of associations between concepts, and then to see if it can be knocked down. Yes, it sounds strange, but it is meant to overcome the deficiencies of *inductive* logic. However, there is an important point to note here. If you examine the kind of deductive arguments that meet these requirements, they consist of a set of statements about relations between concepts.[3] Each statement does not look very different from the universal generalizations of the pattern model. Nevertheless, they have a different status as they start out just as ideas; it is the argument that they form that does the explaining, and they are open to challenge and revision by a trial and error testing process. Of course, once such a deductive theory has withstood testing, it can be used to both explain and make predictions about other phenomena, at least until something better comes along.

Researchers using the pattern model look for confirming evidence for a generalization. Researchers using the deductive model look for disconfirming evidence, or at least they should! In the latter, the name of the game is not 'proving' your hypothesis; it is trying to disprove it. And if you can't, it may be worth entertaining as a possible explanation. (See Popper 1976: 88–90, for his review of his position, or Blaikie 2007: 114–15.)

Is there an alternative to Popper's view that all scientific knowledge is tentative rather than absolute? Not if you accept Popper's arguments. So why include this paradigm if its outcomes are so uncertain? We share Popper's view about the tentative nature of all forms of knowledge generation. In this regard, Neo-Positivism is no different from the other research paradigms. What is necessary is to choose the research paradigm that is judged to provide the best explanatory possibility, given the kinds of assumptions that are regarded as being appropriate in the circumstances.

For a more detailed discussion of *inductive* and *deductive* logics, see Blaikie (2007: 59–82) and of positivism and Neo-Positivism (referred to there as 'critical rationalism') and their limitations, see Blaikie (2007: 109–17, 183–7).

Limitations of the Neo-Positive paradigm

Research paradigms have their limitations and Neo-Positivism is no exception. As we have seen, Popper's major case against the method of knowledge production and justification offered by the standard view of positivism was that pure, objective data is unattainable. This is because our observations are both facilitated by and filtered through the everyday and scientific language (concepts) we use to relate to the world around us. As observers we impose *our* concepts on the world and interpret what we 'see' in terms of the personal baggage we bring to our research; e.g. our past experiences, knowledge and expectations.

However, Popper appeared not to be fully aware that these limitations also apply to attempts to refute a theory. If all observation is interpretation, then refutation is itself tentative; testing cannot show a theory to be conclusively *not* true. Theories that fail the testing process are not 'disproved'; rather, belief in them declines and, like old soldiers, they may just fade away. We must also accept that any regularity, a generalization based on evidence, is produced from some point of view and is, therefore, always tentative and subject to revision.

Thomas Kuhn (1970a, 1970b) took this criticism even further. As a scientist and a historian and philosopher of science, Kuhn came to the conclusion that the views of science presented by philosophers did not reflect the historical evidence. He argued for a psychological and sociological view of science rather than a logical one (see Blaikie 1993b: 104–10; 2007: 186–7). For Kuhn, scientific knowledge is not advanced by a process of trial and error testing of tentative theories but by fundamental changes, or revolutions, in both the way a scientific community views the world and in the way scientific puzzles are defined and tackled. As a result of the natural sciences going through a series of paradigmatic revolutions, the way a discipline's subject matter is viewed will change, as will the 'truths' that it claims. Such a view of science challenges simplistic notions of objectivity and truth.

Whereas Popper separated science and non-science on the basis of the testability of theories, Kuhn argued that sciences have puzzles that they try to solve while non-sciences do not. Whereas Popper believed that science is the pursuit of absolute truths about the world, even though we can never tell when we have arrived at them, Kuhn was more inclined to regard truth as being relative, i.e. that it depends on the paradigm's assumptions (axiomatic foundations) you set out with, as well as the problem's importance (being interesting and potentially exemplary) and the inquiry's clarity (being rigorous and incisive). Hence, paradigms cannot be judged in terms of whether or not they produce truths about the world but, rather, in terms of how good they are at solving the puzzles that the paradigm defines, using its criteria for judging success. Truth becomes a matter of community consensus. Of course, members of a scientific community may believe they can achieve absolute truths, but Kuhn wanted to relativize such claims.

Kuhn was not without his critics. Lakatos and Musgrave (1970) contains a series of articles by Popper, Kuhn, Lakatos, Feyerabend and others, in which Popper's and Kuhn's ideas are put through the wringer, with a defence by Kuhn (1970c). It includes an interesting debate between Popper and Kuhn. The core criticism is that, in presenting his ideas on scientific revolutions, Kuhn's move from Popper's 'logic of discovery' to his 'socio-psychological' view of research undermined the status of all scientific knowledge. Lakatos (1970) wanted to pull back from that implication and Feyerabend (1970; especially 1978) wanted to go even further by arguing that 'anything goes'.

Kuhn's ideas were developed in the context of the natural sciences. However, the social sciences appear to have a different history. While a particular natural science paradigm may be dominant for a period, and while some competitors may fade away as a result of these battles, perhaps to be replaced by others, the situation in the social sciences has been characterized by the coexistence of paradigms (for an example of paradigm rivalry in sociology, see Blaikie 1977, 1978).

The wars between paradigms in the social sciences are akin to the wars between religions or sects within a religion. Adherents believe in the rightness of their position and are inclined to go into battle for it. If each generation of sociologists is socialized within only one tradition, they can act like ardent religious believers.

See Blaikie (2007: 183–7) and Lakatos (1970), Hindess (1977) and Stockman (1983) for critiques of Popper's approach. For other general reviews, critiques of and/or alternatives to positivism, see Adorno et al. (1976 [1969]), Giddens (1974), Keat and Urry (1982), Mulkay (1979), Bhaskar (1979), Halfpenny (1982), Alexander (1982), Chalmers (1982) and Bryant (1985).

Review

In the final decades of the twentieth century, criticisms of the central tenets of the standard view of positivism meant that it began to lose its position as the main philosophy of the social sciences. It was replaced by a modified positivism – Neo-Positivism – that was suited to a narrow class of contexts, research questions, purposes and social problems rather than the grand aim of producing universal knowledge. Over time, Neo-Positivism has become one of a number of possible research paradigms.

This chapter has focused on the origins of the Neo-Positive research paradigm and the key feature that distinguishes it from the standard view of positivism, in particular, its use of *deductive* rather than *inductive* logic. The major implication of this difference in logic is the starting point of any research project. In the standard view, the starting point is with data collection, followed by a search for general and, hopefully, universal regularities. These regularities are then used as the basis for a certain kind of explanation, i.e. the pattern model.

On the other hand, having established a regularity for which an explanation is sought, Neo-Positivism begins by either borrowing an existing theory or constructing a new one, the conclusion of which is the regularity to be explained. Hence, the real starting point of Neo-Positive-based research is theorizing (as a compelling yet tentative explanation for a problem's regularity) rather than data collection. The latter follows in order to test the theory by attempting to disconfirm hypotheses deduced from it.

These two forms of positivism have some ontological assumptions in common but differ in their epistemological assumptions. It is the difference in the logic used to produce explanations that distinguish their epistemologies, i.e. how we gain knowledge of the social world. This difference has nothing to do with the types of methods that are used to collect or generate and analyse data. While quantitative methods may be predominantly used in both versions of positivism, this preference is not exclusive. Hence, focusing on differences in methods ignores the more fundamental differences in the way knowledge is produced. While this is evident between these two versions of positivism, the differences are more pronounced between the Neo-Positive research paradigm and the Interpretive and Critical Realist paradigms, where both ontological and epistemological differences are present. Time will tell whether another version of positivism will arise to deal with the deficiencies of Neo-Positivism or whether further paradigms will be added.

In the following chapter, two illustrations are provided of the Neo-Positivist paradigm in action. However, before we get to them, the remainder of this chapter outlines practical steps used in Neo-Positive research.

Characteristic steps of the paradigm

Eight steps

Research framed within the Neo-Positive research paradigm can be considered in terms of eight steps.

1 *Outline some particular phenomenon* in social space-time and *identify an important problem*: this may be an intellectual problem involving a lack of knowledge of the phenomenon; or a practical problem about a situation, event or process that someone considers needs to be changed. Indicate why the problem is important.
2 *Critically review literature* that relates to the problem. Note seminal articles as well as patterns, themes and debates evident from previous research, reports and observations. Summarize evidence, ideas, factors and links that characterize the problem and its possible solutions. Literature helps to characterize the landscape in which a piece of research can be located. One research report contributes a small dot on this knowledge landscape and reviewing the literature helps to locate the dot we want to add or where mining/drilling could be fruitful.
3 *Provide a description of what is going on* in this social situation, or in this event or process, in order to start to make the problem

researchable. Characterizing the phenomenon and/or problem of interest usually involves scanning literature as well as answering initial and subsequent (i.e. drill-down) 'what' questions about the phenomenon and the associated problem. One or more 'what' questions may be proposed about the extent, quantum and form of the phenomenon; its nature, scale, social relevance and boundaries. Tentative answers may be evident from incidental observations, but these would need to be confirmed by previous or new research. No paradigm choice is required at this stage but ontological and epistemological assumptions will inevitably be made and need to be stated.

4 *Identify a regularity*[4] from the answers to one or more 'what' questions. A regularity is a description of some state of affairs, an association between concepts or a sequence of events, for which an explanation is sought.

5 *Ask one or more 'why' questions* and *construct or borrow a tentative theory* that will answer it, that is, produce a deductive argument from which the regularity follows. The ideas that go into the argument are typically drawn from established associations, attributes, patterns, themes, concepts and existing theories. Associations may be in the form of 'this goes with that' or 'if–then' type statements – neither of which suggests causation but rather some sort of regularity or sequence of events. This set of logically related statements constitutes a theory.

6 *Define and operationalize key concepts in the theory.* Firstly, formally define the concepts in terms of their meaning within the theory. Secondly, identify proxy variables for each concept. Thirdly, check that the regularity still follows deductively from the operationalized concepts and that data for the proxy variables can be obtained.

7 *Test the theory* by collecting data on propositions in the theory and/or, if a stronger test is desired, making new and counter-intuitive predictions and testing them. From the findings about relationships between the proxy variables, it is possible to conclude that the posited theory is *tentatively confirmed or disconfirmed.* Conclusions are generally tentative not only because operationalized variables are 'approximate' by nature but also because it is not logically possible to establish absolute proof or disproof. When taken together, a lack of strong *disconfirming evidence*, and the presence of strong *confirming evidence* that is consistent with the theory, strongly corroborates the theory but never absolutely verifies it.

8 *Critically review* the approach taken and offer suggestions for further study. Suggestions may relate to the research problem,

the regularity or its characteristics, research questions and their context, paradigm choice, population definition and sampling, deductive theorizing, operationalizing the posited theory, and data sourcing, collection, analysis and interpretation.

Constructing a theory

A theory that is constructed in order to provide an explanation for the identified regularity is derived from three sources: direct field observations by the researcher or others; existing theory; academic research; and published reports (e.g. by government, NGOs or industry/business). These sources offer definitions, findings, patterns, themes and ideas that can stimulate and contribute to the process of constructing a tentative theory. This theoretical argument must be able to explain the regularity and be testable.

This tentative theory is developed in two steps.

1 Compiling statements of association between concepts or sequences of events.
2 Sequencing these statements in such a way that the regularity becomes the conclusion to the argument.

The process of constructing a theory is a process of discovery. It involves a theoretical and pragmatic imagination and careful gap filling. It is an occasionally linear step-by-step process but is predominantly iterative – involving a mental trial-and-error process. It is also reflexive because the researcher must remain constantly alert to the ontological and epistemological consequence of definitions, meanings and practicalities that are introduced with every conceptual, logical and operational refinement or correction that is part of constructing a deductive argument.

A deductive argument is simply a stack of plausible[5] paired associations between clearly definable concepts that will eventually form the pathway between the theory's starting and ending concepts. Adjacent members in the stack appear in the form of 'A↔B, B↔C, C↔D, etc.' statements, thus producing a 'daisy chain' of paired statements. The propositions in Homans's reconstruction of Durkheim's theory of egoistic suicide are of this form; there are two related 'theoretical' associations and a conclusion (see Box 3.1). Merton's version also has two related 'theoretical' associations, but then adds a factual third statement to arrive at the conclusion, which is what needs to be explained.

Concepts in these statements may start out as being rather broad and not clearly defined. However, once they form part of the argument, they will need to be formally defined. Formal concepts will usually relate to specific meanings used in the literature and, while constraining the scope of the intended theory, will link to the current state of knowledge, which, in turn, may usefully inform theory building and its later operationalization and testing.

Testing a theory

Before a theory can be tested, the key concepts must be operationalized (measures devised for them). Once a suitably compact theory has been constructed, the researcher must define proxy variables for these formally defined concepts so that the 'theoretical' relationships between concepts can be measured and analysed.

There are two settings in which a deductive theory can be tested.

1 In the context in which the regularity to be explained was established.
2 In a different context in which a prediction is made and tested.

The first setting enables a limited testing of the theory, but this would be much stronger if all or most of the theoretical associations were tested. The second setting enables a strong test and, at the same time, can provide some evidence for the generality of the theory. Both approaches can either help to corroborate or challenge the theory.

Returning to Homans's version of Durkheim's theory, the first two propositions could be individually tested by measuring 'suicide rate', 'individualism' and 'incidence of Protestantism'. Alternatively, a prediction could be made from the theory in a context that is different from that in which the regularity was established. For example, two further statements could be added to the three statements in Box 3.1.

4 The incidence of Protestantism in Spain is low.
5 Therefore, the suicide rate in Spain is low.

Statement 4 is factual and evidence for it could be obtained. If supported, the prediction, statement 5, will follow logically. If the evidence supports it, the theory would be corroborated; if not, a modification may be necessary or the theory abandoned. However, the former would be more likely if evidence had already been obtained that supported either or both of the first two statements in the theory.

As individual associations between pairs of concepts may be derived from existing theories, they may have already been tested in other contexts. Hence, theories that include such statements will already have some corroboration. If an existing theory is borrowed in its entirety, the testing will be concerned with its applicability in the selected context.

Because the results of tests of individual associations may not be clear-cut, when constructing and subsequently testing a theory, a balance must be drawn between the number of pairs of associated concepts, the plausibility and clarity of each association, the use or adaptation of established formal concepts and the practicality of operationalizing concepts and collecting and analysing their proxy data.

While theories may be stated in very general terms, they are only useful in research if they can be related to a particular social context, which usually means a particular population. Being clear about this relationship, and the character of the population, serves to anchor concepts' meanings as well as practicalities that must be considered in order to test the theory. If data for the entire population cannot be obtained, then an appropriate criteria-based probability sample, which reflects the aims and constraints of the research, must be established in order to gather and process necessary and sufficient data.

Once a population and its characteristics have been defined, the sample that is chosen must suit the needs of the research questions. Characteristics of the sample will define its informative and representative value. Bases for choosing a sample may include: the motivation and aim of the study; the importance of the research problem and questions; access to data sources and the commensurate or comparative value of the data; the desired level of generality of the findings; and practicalities such as funding or even legal and reputational pressures on the study's design and conduct or oversight. Whatever the rationale and choice of population and sample, the character of the sample, and the concepts' proxy variables, must be accounted for when interpreting the products of data analysis and the subsequent answers to the research questions.

For these reasons, and because not every pair of associations in an argument may be readily testable or data practically obtainable or processable, constructing a theory to explain a regularity may involve constructing and comparing several candidate theories. The chosen argument is often a compromise about *elegance* (i.e. compact simple yet comprehensive), *practicalities* (i.e. readily operationalized with ready access to good samples and data that are readily analysable) and *generalizability* (i.e. concepts, associations and their meanings that are readily applied in contexts and across populations beyond that for which the theory is first developed).

A researcher may also consider the possible value that a theoretical contribution may have, such as: (1) affirming an existing theory in a way that deepens knowledge of the theory's implications or expands its practical and general use; (2) challenging an established theory in a way that defines previously unknown constraints on it or replaces it with a more detailed, nuanced, stable and general explanation of the phenomenon or problem of interest; and (3) opening new possibilities for theory development or testing.

Review questions

The Appendix has a set of review questions for each of the research paradigms. We invite you to use them to not only test your knowledge of the paradigms but to help stimulate the process of designing and conducting your own research.

Further reading

Barnes, B. (1982). *T. S. Kuhn and Social Science*. London: Macmillan. Useful review and evaluation of Kuhn and his relevance to the social sciences.

Blaikie, N. (2007). *Approaches to Social Inquiry*, 2nd edn. Cambridge: Polity. Chapters 4, 5 and 6 provide reviews and critiques of positivism, Popper's Neo-Positivism and other major research paradigms.

Bryant, C. G. A. (1985). *Positivism in Social Theory and Research*. London: Macmillan. Provides detailed reviews of the major positivist traditions.

Chalmers, A. F. (1982). *What is This Thing Called Science?* St Lucia: University of Queensland Press. Both advocates and critiques Popper's views, with special reference to the logics of induction and deduction. Also reviews Kuhn's alternative position.

Johnson, P. and Duberley, J. (2000). *Understanding Management Research*. London: Sage. Chapters 2 and 4 offer a detailed philosophical discussion of the origins and deficiencies of positivism.

Keat, R. and Urry, J. (1982). *Social Theory as Science*. London: Routledge & Kegan Paul. Chapters 1 and 4 offer a useful discussion of positivism in general and its use in sociology in particular. They argue for the use of a realist paradigm.

Outhwaite, W. (1987). *New Philosophies of Social Science: Realism, Hermeneutics and Critical Theory*. London: Macmillan. Chapter 1 briefly reviews the major varieties of positivism and early alternatives.

Popper, K. R. (1961). *The Poverty of Historicism*. London: Routledge & Kegan Paul. Is a general critique of the standard view of positivism and makes a case for the use of Neo-Positivism in the social sciences.

4
The Neo-Positive Research Paradigm in Action

Chapter summary

- The first part of the chapter presents an illustration of a Neo-Positive study into the relationship between age and environmentalism.
- The second part of the chapter presents necessary background on a research programme concerned with leadership in natural disaster crises. This is used in:
  - this chapter's Neo-Positive study of crisis leadership; and
  - in the illustrations of the other paradigms in chapters 6, 8 and 9.
- The third part of this chapter presents an illustration of a Neo-Positive-based inquiry into crisis leadership in a bushfire.

1 Age and Environmentalism[1]

Introduction

This illustration of the Neo-Positive research paradigm describes and offers an explanation for an association between age and environmentalism, i.e. between age and attitudes and behaviour related to environmental problems and their solutions.

While concern for the environment goes back many decades, there was a wave of public and political awareness in the late 1960s and the 1970s, followed by another wave in the late 1980s and early 1990s. The basis for this illustration is studies conducted in Melbourne,

Australia, in 1989 (Blaikie 1992; Blaikie and Ward 1992). At this time, concern was with global problems – such as the greenhouse effect (which has morphed into global warming and now climate change) and the depletion of the ozone layer in the South Polar Region – and local issues – such as the logging of native forests and mining in national parks.

The illustration begins with a statement of the problem, presents three research questions to address this problem, provides a brief review of some relevant literature, identifies a regularity in the 1989 studies that requires an explanation, presents a possible explanation for this in the form of a deductive theory, defines the concepts in the theory and suggests ways of testing it.

The problem

Research over many decades in the United States has shown that there is a consistently stronger association between age and environmental attitudes and concern than with any other socio-demographic variable; younger people have more positive attitudes and greater concern than older people (Van Liere and Dunlap 1980; Blaikie and Ward 1992). However, the findings of the 1989 studies – samples of university students and residents in Melbourne – did not show a linear association. It was curvilinear (Blaikie 1992): the level of environmentalism was about average for youth, rose to a peak around the age of 40 and then declined in older age. The research problem, then, is to establish why the form of this association is different to that found in the United States a decade or so earlier.

Research questions

To address this research problem, it is necessary to first *describe* the form of the relationship between age and environmentalism, and second, to *explain* this by developing and testing a theory. This is done by posing three research questions.

Q. 1   To *what* extent is age related to environmentalism?
Q. 2   If there is a relationship, *what* is its form?
Q. 3   *Why* does this relationship exist?

The first two questions set the scene and have already been answered in the 1989 studies. The challenge is to answer question 3.

Review of extant literature

In the Australian studies, a measure of environmentalism was constructed using mainly components from a scale developed in the United States by Catton and Dunlap and their associates (Catton and Dunlap 1978a, 1978b, 1980; Dunlap 1980; Dunlap and van Liere 1978, 1984; see Blaikie 1992 for details of the origin, construction, content and use of this scale). With scores for each of the 24 items in the scale ranging from 1 to 5, Blaikie found that the highest overall mean scores (most favourable attitudes towards the environment) were for the 25–44 age categories, the lowest mean scores were for the 65+ category and that the mean score for the 18–24 category was the same as the mean for all ages. This pattern was more pronounced for two sub-scales: the need to make 'sacrifices for the environment'[2]; and level of 'confidence in science and technology'[3] to solve environmental problems. In both instances, the most favourable scores were for ages around 40.[4]

It is this non-linear form of the relationship between age and environmentalism that constitutes the regularity that needs to be explained: *that the middle-aged cohort in the late 1980s had the highest level of environmentalism and the oldest age cohort had the lowest level.*

There have been some attempts in the literature to understand the nature of the association between age and environmentalism; three hypotheses have been proposed. One suggests that it is due to the socio-biological ageing process (the 'ageing' hypothesis). The second suggests that important historical events have a differential influence on birth cohorts (the 'cohort' hypothesis). The third claims that there are period effects due to changes in social, cultural and economic conditions (the 'period' hypothesis) (see Buttel 1979; Lowe, Pinhey and Grimes 1980; Honnold 1981, 1984; Lowe and Pinhey 1982; Mohai and Twight 1987; Arcury and Christianson 1990).

The 'ageing' hypothesis is based on the view that young people have a lower level of commitment to dominant social values and institutions, the 'cohort' hypothesis relates to Mannheim's (1952) theory of generations, or to C. Wright Mills's (1959) notion of the intersection of biography and history, while the 'period' hypothesis requires that both the ageing and cohort explanations can be overridden by influences from changing circumstances.

The ageing hypothesis might be relevant if the relationship is linear and negative: that level of environmentalism decreases with age. However, if the form of the relationship is not linear, one of the other hypotheses might be more appropriate. There has been some support

Age and Environmentalism

for the 'cohort' hypothesis (Mohai and Twight 1987; Samdahl and Robertson 1989) and the 'period' hypothesis (Honnold 1984). The advocates of the 'cohort' hypothesis pointed to events in the late 1960s and early 1970s in American society.

A possible explanation for the regularity

It is possible that a particular age cohort has been differentially influenced by an earlier wave of public interest in environmental issues, i.e. they were youth during this earlier wave and have now experienced a second wave. They may be passing through history as a ripple of a high level of environmentalism as their biography has intersected with history over a particular time period (Mills 1959: 5–8).

In the late 1960s and early 1970s, young people in various parts of the world were influenced by a period of student radicalism and a concern for environmental issues followed. These experiences could have had a lasting impact on this age cohort, even though the intensity may have subsided somewhat. In the late 1980s and early 1990s, there was another wave of environmentalism. Other 'period' changes, such as economic cycles, are assumed to have influenced all contemporary generations more or less equally. The youth cohort of the late 1960s and the 1970s, who were middle-aged in the late 1980s and early 1990s, were possibly the most receptive age cohort during this second wave of environmental concern. Therefore, because this middle-aged cohort experienced two waves of environmental concern, they have the highest level of environmentalism.

These ideas can be presented in the form of a testable theory whose strength as a tentative explanation for the regularity can be partially corroborated by testing individual propositions in the theory, or by testing one or more deduced hypotheses, either in the same context or in different contexts. Such a theory needs to be expressed as a deductive argument that consists of at least some propositions that hypothesize relationships between pairs of concepts. Other propositions in the argument may be descriptive statements that can be verified. The conclusion to the argument is the regularity that needs to be explained. Note that the concept of 'environmental concern' refers to the public discourse about environmental issues, and the concept of 'environmentalism' refers to the level of individual concern for the environment.

1 The late 1960s and 1970s was a period of a high level of environmental concern.

2 At this time, level of environmentalism varied inversely with age; high amongst youth and low amongst the aged.
3 The youth-aged cohort in 1970 became the middle-aged cohort in 1989.
4 Level of environmental concern in 1989 was high.
5 The middle-aged cohort in 1989 had their previous high level of environmentalism reinforced by a second period of environmental concern.
6 Therefore, in 1989, the level of environmentalism of the middle-aged cohort was higher than the youth-aged cohort and much higher than the older-aged cohort.

Propositions 1 and 4 are statements of fact that can be verified; proposition 3 is true by definition, and propositions 2 and 5 can be tested individually. Proposition 6 is the regularity that is to be explained. The critical explanatory proposition here is 5.

Concepts

In order to test this theory, it is necessary to first identify key concepts that can be operationalized to create variables. The concepts are mainly derived from the literature reviewed earlier.

These concepts are defined as follows.

Environmental concern: the expression of concern for environmental issues and problems in public discourse.
Environmentalism: (a) attitudes towards issues such as the preservation of wilderness environments and natural flora and fauna, the conservation of natural resources, environmental degradation, environmental impacts of economic growth, and the use of science and technology to solve environmental problems; (b) individual actions that help preserve nature and conserve resources; and (c) involvement in communal actions that confront environmental problems and seek solutions.
Age: number of years since birth.

To make these concepts researchable, they need to be operationalized, i.e. measures of them need to be developed.

Level of environmental concern: by content analysis of major forms of media.
Level of environmentalism: measured in two ways:

Age and Environmentalism

1 *Environmental attitudes*: by means of responses to a set of attitude items concerned with the range of environmental issues. Five Likert-type response categories were used: 'strongly agree', 'agree', 'neither agree nor disagree', 'disagree' and 'strongly disagree'. These categories were assigned values from 1 to 5 in the direction that gives the highest value to responses that are pro-environment. The scale was pre-tested and subjected to item analysis to establish the degree to which responses to each item are consistent with the total score. It was also post-tested using factor analysis to establish its degree of unidimensionality and the possible presence of sub-scales.
2 *Environmental behaviour*: by two measures. First, the degree to which the use of environmentally dangerous products is avoided. Respondents were asked how frequently they avoided such products ('regularly', 'occasionally' and 'never'), and then to list them. Second, support given to environmental groups. This was measured by two questions: the degree of support ('regularly', 'occasionally' and 'never'); and an open-ended question on the forms of this support (responses were coded for analysis).

Age: by asking respondents how old they are in years.

It is now possible to express the theory in terms of variables rather than concepts. For readers who do not suffer from symbol paralysis, the propositions in the theory can be expressed by using the following symbols.

Level of environmental concern in 1970 (EC70)
Level of environmentalism in 1970 (E70)
Level of environmental concern in 1989 (EC89)
Level of environmentalism in 1989 (E89)
Age in 1970 (A70)
Age in 1989 (A89)
Youth-aged cohort in 1970 (YC70)
Youth-aged cohort in 1989 (YC89)
Middle-aged cohort in 1989 (MC89)
Older-aged cohort in 1970 (OC70)
Older-aged cohort in 1989 (OC89)

The theory then becomes:

1 EC70 is high.
2 E70 varied inversely with A70; high for YC70 and low for OC70.
3 YC70 becomes MC89.

4 EC89 is high.
5 High E70 of YC70 is reinforced only for MC89.
6 Therefore, MC89 has the highest E89 and OC89 the lowest EC89.

Testing the theory

The task now is to test this theory rigorously within the Neo-Positive paradigm. As noted earlier, individual propositions in a theory can be tested. However, in this case, we are restricted by the absence of data from the 1970s. It would have been possible to ask participants in the 1989 study to recall their level of environmentalism in the 1960s and 1970s, but it would not have been possible to obtain data on this equivalent to that in the 1989 study. Such retrospective data have limitations in terms of both their quantifiability and reliability.

However, there is another way to test this theory, i.e. by making predictions from it, perhaps about other time periods. Given that there has been another wave of public concern, starting in the late 2000s and continuing into the 2010s, particularly about climate change, it would now be possible to assess the level of environmentalism in a similar population and location and look to see if the earlier waves of environmental concern have produced ripples in the levels of environmentalism in today's age cohorts. Some members of today's population will be in either their second or their third waves of environmental concern; the possible effects of this could be examined.

This is what the theory would predict and this becomes a general hypothesis to test.

> The linear and inverse association between age and level of environmentalism is tempered by age cohorts who, having been influenced in their youth by particular waves of environmental concern, and who maintain a relatively higher level throughout their lives, at any point in time cause ripples in the form of the relationship between age and environmentalism. Hence, the form of this relationship will change depending on the position of previously influenced age cohorts in their life trajectories.

The important theoretical assumption here is that, during any wave of environmental concern, it is youths who are likely to be most influenced by it. In other words, the 'ageing' hypothesis underlies this one. However, it adds the idea that, if people were influenced in their youth, they would be likely to respond positively to successive waves of environmental concern, perhaps more than other age cohorts. Clearly, this hypothesis is rather complex and would need to be broken down into testable propositions.

It is important to note that the theory does not attempt to explain the 'ageing' hypothesis, i.e. why young people are most likely to be influenced by successive waves of environmental concern, and, if they are, why those who have been through an influential period in their youth have their level of environmentalism reinforced by successive waves. Other theories would have to be developed to explain these. A network of theories is needed to deal with the complexity of this apparently simple phenomenon.

Summary

This illustration has been used to elaborate many of the features of the Neo-Positive paradigm. Although an association between age and environmentalism may seem to be a relatively simple proposition to explain, it should be clear that it is not. It is complicated by the passage of time and the way individual biographies intersect with social changes and waves of environmentalism.

It should also be clear that the 'middle-range' theory that has been presented here applies to the phenomenon in specific social contexts and during a specific time period. It also leaves some aspects of the phenomenon unexplained. Ideally, such theories should be tested in a variety of social contexts, and at different times, to both strengthen their relevance and establish their level of generality.

In conclusion, it is worth noting that it would also be possible to conduct a different kind of study to investigate individual biographies on questions concerning the influences of previous waves of environmental concern, responses to these, levels of commitment to a pro-environmental position and involvement in individual or group activities designed to deal with environmental issues. By getting research participants to recall their history of environmental concern and action, it would be possible to investigate a number of the propositions in the theory. Such a study might best be conducted within a different research paradigm, preferably the Interpretive. Therefore, a research programme on environmentalism could use more than one research paradigm to investigate the many research questions that need to be answered, thus making it a multi-paradigm study. We will return to this idea in chapter 9.

2 The Impact of Leaders' Experience on the Effectiveness of First-Responder Actions: Background to Crisis Leadership Illustrations in Chapters 4, 6 and 8

This Neo-Positive illustration is the first of three related and adapted illustrations, each of which uses a different research paradigm (see chapters 6 and 8) to investigate problems about 'leadership in natural disaster crises' in the case of one of the catastrophic Black Saturday fires of February 2009 in Australia's south-eastern state of Victoria. These fires received attention worldwide for their scope, impact and leadership consequences.

To set the scene for these three illustrations that have been adapted for this book, and to provide some context, we note:

- the extensiveness of natural disasters worldwide;
- the special case of rural and remote bushfires in Australia;
- the need for understanding the 'what' and 'why' of effective crisis leadership;
- Australia's catastrophic Black Saturday fires;
- the particular case of the Kilmore East fire, which was one of the worst of the Black Saturday fires;
- emergency services arrangements at the time of the Black Saturday fires; and
- some aspects of experience when leading responses to such events.

The Neo-Positive illustration that follows is about the impact of leaders' experience on the effectiveness of first-responder actions. It starts by noting a problem and an associated regularity. The problem is then characterized, research questions introduced and a deductive theory (the 'maverick theory of leadership') constructed to answer the research questions. The theory is tested in the context of the Kilmore East fire. The test strategy highlights sample selection, sources of data, hypotheses, concepts' formal and operational definitions and notes about treatment of data.

Leadership in natural disaster crises

The wide span of natural disasters

Earthquakes, tsunamis, volcanic eruptions, cyclones, bushfires, floods and epidemics are all examples of the types of natural disaster that have impacted humans for millennia. However, from early last century there has been, worldwide, a trend increase in the frequency, ferocity and resulting devastation from such disasters. This trend is set to continue through the current century – a prospect attributed largely to climate change and the growth and distribution of the human population and its activities.

Natural disasters often arise very quickly and, typically, with insufficient warning. The consequence can be catastrophic. Human responses to natural disasters aim to limit loss and disruption and enable speedy recovery.

Critical[5] natural disasters are 'wicked' (Rittel and Webber 1973; Conklin 2006) challenges for leaders of first-responder organizations and are notoriously resistant to treatments by predefined procedures. Their impacts can persist for years.

The effectiveness of first-responder efforts in an emergency is partly reflected in stakeholders' cumulative perceptions of emergency agencies' responses. When the speed and scope of the unfolding emergency is within the competencies, capabilities and capacities of the first-responder organizations,[6] responses can be well managed. However, when the speed and unfolding scope of a disaster increasingly overwhelm the abilities of such organizations, the disaster becomes a critical emergency or crisis.

A special case: rural and remote bushfires in Australia

In this illustration about crisis leadership, and the ones that follow in chapters 6 and 8, we restrict ourselves to aspects of leadership associated with forest fires. To further narrow the focus, we will consider forest fires in Australia – colloquially referred to as bushfires – because, per head of national population, they are typically the most frequent and destructive of life and property. This illustrative focus covers the research interests of one of the authors which span the three ideal-typical paradigms discussed at length in this book.

To further limit the scope of this illustration, and those in chapters 6 and 8, we focus on identity,[7] sense making and decision making that are aspects of the reasoning of emergency-management leaders who shape the actions, impacts and perceived effectiveness of first-responder agencies and groups. This focus is pertinent because perceived ineffective leadership is associated with billions of dollars of adverse economic impact as well as perceived avoidable social dislocation and economic disruption.

Understanding the 'what' and 'why' of effective crisis leadership

A problem associated with crisis leadership as a part of managing critical emergency responses (www.InfoServ.com.au) is that, in Australia at least, currently accepted know-how about leaders' formal sense making and decision making is not sufficient to ensure acceptable critical emergency responses.

Because the proportion of bushfires that outstrip the competence, capability or capacity of first-responder agencies is predicted to increase over coming decades, it is clearly important to better understand how responses to such events can be well handled, even if response capacity is less than required. This can help to increase the effectiveness of future responses, as well as inform research and practice.

Catastrophic Black Saturday fires of February 2009

In Australia, the bushfire season is the three-month summer season that runs from December to February. In the state of Victoria (population nearly six million and covering about 240,000 square kilometres), the 2009 summer season was one of the driest and hottest since records began in the 1800s. The 2008–9 fire season followed several years of below-average rainfall and above-average temperatures. Heatwave conditions over the state peaked on Saturday, 7 February 2009, with temperatures in many parts of the state exceeding 45°C.

The Black Saturday bushfires of February 2009 were the worst in Australia since records began in the late 1700s, comprised more than 300 separate bush and grass fires and were estimated to have released energy equivalent to more than 3,500 Hiroshima atomic bombs. The estimated value of direct losses attributed to these catastrophic bushfires was A$4.5 billion (approximately €3 billion, or US$ 3.5 billion or CNY 20 billion). Fifteen of these bushfires were the largest and accounted for more than 90 per cent of the total losses and damage. The causes, response-management and losses associated with these fifteen bushfires were the focus of a Royal Commission.[8]

The Kilmore East fire

The Kilmore East fire (Cruz et al. 2012; Teague, McLeod and Pascoe 2010a, 2010b) was the most destructive of the Black Saturday fires and was the single most destructive bushfire to occur in Australia since the first European settlement was established well over two centuries ago. In its first twelve hours, 119 people died, 1,242 houses and other structures were destroyed and 125,000 hectares of forest and farmland were burned.

The Kilmore East fire was ferocious and tragically fatal. The speed, intensity, accessibility, emergency agency response capability and capacity, as well as its social, infrastructure and economic impacts, combined to present crisis leadership with 'once in a lifetime' challenges. The leadership challenges spanned the executive levels of all emergency agencies' and emergency incident management teams' incident controllers, regional and brigade leaders, as well as appointed and emergent leaders of community organizations and volunteer groups (Endsley 1995; Smith and Hancock 1995; Grunwald and Bearman 2011; Hayes and Omodei 2011).

Emergency services arrangements at the time of the Black Saturday fires

At the time of the Black Saturday bushfires, the overall leadership and management of the state's fire response was under the control of relevant fire agencies. Leading responses to the bushfire emergencies were typically handled by a lead agency's chief officer who declared bushfire incidents and coordinated assessments and responses to each incident by delegating to each one a critical incident controller[9] (IC) with a supporting incident management team (IMT). Each IC+IMT group worked as a shift, with membership and hierarchy reflecting the assessed severity of the incident and progress being made. The role identities, reasoning (Weick, Sutcliffe and Obstfeld 2005) and actions of an emergency agency's chief officer and critical IMT leaders strongly influenced assessments, decisions and response actions.

As well as the extremely adverse weather conditions that existed during these bushfires, and in the days and weeks leading up to them, a critical context factor that strongly influenced fire-response management and leadership was the then new and yet to be proven state-wide information and communications facility to support coordination between fire response agencies.

Aspects of experience when leading responses to emergencies

In crises, rehearsals and experience with low-level agency responses cannot always meet the leadership challenge of constantly reinterpreting and reassessing the unfolding situation, and the consequences of previous decisions, in order to decide on new actions. In overwhelming crises, the only additional experience and know-how that a leader can call on, apart from agency-based experience, is other (external) life experience derived from coping in unanticipated challenging situations that are unusually demanding and personally confronting.

Also relevant in these situations is a leader's self-permission to use her or his other experience and know-how, even when it challenges or confronts agency orthodoxy or community traditions. Such permission rests, in part, on a leader's combined sense of personal, agency, professional and community identity and the ability of the leader to establish and maintain identity clarity[10] in a conflicted[11] situation.

Summary

Leading effective responses to increasingly frequent and more damaging natural disasters is challenging. Societies and communities expect much in situations that are hard to anticipate and that often overwhelm emergency agencies. Sometimes a leader's personal resources are all that remain unused and that can still be called on. Better understanding of how leaders can respond to these challenges raises important questions for researchers, as well as opportunities for practitioners.

3 Crisis Leadership in Australia's 2009 East Kilmore Fire

Problem and regularity

As noted earlier, the frequency and severity of Australian bushfire emergencies is predicted to increase over coming decades, and a growing proportion of these are expected to overwhelm first-responder agencies. This trend presents a problem for emergency-response agencies as they try to recruit and develop leaders whose effectiveness will increasingly depend on more than traditional training and agency resources.

Research over recent decades has pointed to an apparent regularity that links perceived effectiveness of leaders' response actions in natural disaster emergencies and crises with leaders' experiences beyond formal organization decision making. It appears that:

> In emergencies for which agency capability and capacity is rapidly overwhelmed, leaders' challenging lived experiences, beyond formal agency

sense making and decision making, are increasingly associated with first-responder actions and outcomes that appear to gain greater public approval than those that are linked with agency-approved sense making and decision making alone.

This problem and regularity suggests the need to better understand the part that experience plays in sense making and decision making and its consequences.

In the case of Australia's 2009 Black Saturday fires, the Victorian Bushfires Royal Commission's (VBRC's) findings reinforced this regularity. For instance, the VBRC directly criticized the inability of the chief officers to step beyond their formal institutional roles and adopt a leadership and management orientation that better matched the nature of the unfolding disaster and the known inadequacies being faced at incident-management level (Teague, McLeod and Pascoe 2010a). It is notable that the two chief officers were career officers with extensive operational fire-management experience, and throughout the Black Saturday fires they persistently maintained strong agency identities – relying heavily on established and predetermined agency policies and practices. Interestingly, no verifiable pattern of data was identified that highlighted extensive internalized know-how from lived experience of crises beyond fire and organization events. However, verifiable data did point to increasing non-institutional incident management experience further down the reporting line. The VBRC specifically noted in its final report that the informal, creative, local-area and community-centred problem-solving roles from IMT level, and especially further down the line, helped to limit further loss of life and property. The VBRC concluded that senior agency leaderships' commitment to institutionalized situation assessment and reasoning resulted in '[s]ome poor decisions [being] made by people in positions of responsibility and by individuals seeking to protect their own safety' (Teague, McLeod and Pascoe 2010a: 4). IMT members and their ICs, who did manage to step beyond the orthodox orientation of their fire agencies and use informal local knowledge and decision-making criteria that favoured community safety actions, were later judged to have facilitated community safety outcomes that were better than hoped for, considering the catastrophic conditions being faced. Qualified public approval of the efforts of these IMTs and their ICs, as well as supporting lower-level leaders, increased as public awareness of the difficulties they faced and the initiatives they took – beyond their formal roles – became more widely known and verified.

Characteristics of the problem

Characteristics that need to be considered when trying to construct a tentative theory that accounts for the regularity are as follows.

- Natural disaster crises are 'wicked' problems and, by definition, are unanticipated and unprepared for.
- Each of a leader's personal identity, professional identity, organization identity and social identity are influences on the identity that a leader adopts when making sense of and decisions about emergency responses, and especially when the pace and scope of the emergency extends beyond an agency's capacity.
- Practised scenarios mostly reflect hybrids of past cases rather than unimagined future realities beyond an organization's identity, mission, resourcing and normal practised and anticipated operations.
- A leader's formally developed agency experiences and know-how do not fully equip the leader for responding effectively to crises beyond the agency's capacity.
- The expectation for a leader to function in a manner consistent with organization identity increases with increasing seniority of the leader.
- A leader's extra-normal sense making and decision making reflects experience and know-how established and verified within and outside the employing agency. In particular, dealing with extra-challenging situations is especially valuable for the purpose of developing competence in sense making and decision making (Endsley 1995; Smith and Hancock 1995; Pye 2005; Weick Sutcliffe and Obstfeld 2005).

Research questions

Research questions often arise from preliminary exploration and previous research into aspects of a problem. Such work produces informative descriptions of the problem's context, one or more regularities and their associated questions. From this work, a researcher selects a particular regularity and frames related 'what' and 'why' questions – having regard for importance, interest, anticipated outcome value and likely effort.

For the purpose of this illustration, the 'what' and 'why' questions are:

Q. 1 To *what* extent is a leader's external experiences associated with response-effectiveness in critical emergencies?
Q. 2 If leaders' external experiences are increasingly associated with response-effectiveness in critical emergencies, then *why* is this so?

The 'maverick theory' about leading in a crisis

In this section, the theory that is constructed in order to answer the 'why' question about the regularity is derived from: (1) primary sources – those of one of the authors' direct operational and 'off work' observations and discussions with participants, as well as that author's practice research into crisis leadership (in commercial organizations and in emergency-management settings); and (2) secondary sources – mainly research literature about emergency management, sense making, identity and decision making, as well as industry and government reports such as Royal Commissions.

Developing the theory – the argument The regularity indicates that, when faced with an emergency, the formally well-prepared leaders who also have situation-relevant informal experience, and a clear sense of identity for the actual emergency situation, are most able to take on and execute an inevitably maverick position when involved in sense making and decision making.

For the purpose of this illustration, the 'maverick theory' of effective crisis leadership can be stated as follows.

1 An emergency agency is faced with a natural disaster *crisis* when its preparations and resources are inadequate for the task of responding effectively to the natural disaster.
2 In order to deal with an unfolding crisis, a leader must constantly interpret and anticipate unfolding events while accounting for perceived interests, needs, resources and the impact of leader-initiated actions on the unfolding crisis.
3 In such situations, the leader's formal organization preparations and commitments are unlikely to equip the leader to deal effectively with such challenges; the leader is left with his/her broader experience and reasoning as the basis for assuming an identity that he/she considers appropriate in all the circumstances.
4 A leader's identity may strongly reflect a conventional agency leadership role but, depending on the situation and the leader's

broader experience, the adopted identity may much more strongly reflect a community or idiosyncratic orientation.
5 In any event, the identity that the leader takes on will shape the way the leader then recognizes and prioritizes interests and needs to be served.
6 This involves sense making and decision making about actions to take, and these actions or commissions (and inactions or omissions) mediate perceptions of the unfolding crisis situation.
7 Once the crisis has passed, stakeholders assess the effectiveness of the leader (and the leader's agency) by attributing and weighing up perceived intentional and unavoidable outcomes as a result of the leader's and the agency's role and conduct.

Theory simplified

This theoretical argument links leadership experience to 'response outcomes' in 'escalating emergencies'. It can be reduced to a succession of four statements, each of which asserts a strong association between two concepts, thus forming a deductive argument. The concepts that the theory refers to are about leaders' EXPERIENCE, IDENTITY, REASONING (i.e. situational sense making and decision making), ACTIONS and the OUTCOMES for the associated emergency. The conclusion to the argument reflects the regularity and answers the 'why' question. It can be expressed symbolically, where '$\leftrightarrow$' means 'varies directly with'.

EXPERIENCE	$\leftrightarrow$	IDENTITY
IDENTITY	$\leftrightarrow$	REASONING
REASONING	$\leftrightarrow$	ACTIONS
ACTIONS	$\leftrightarrow$	OUTCOMES

Therefore

EXPERIENCE $\leftrightarrow$ OUTCOMES

The meanings of these five concepts are as follows.

- EXPERIENCE – the variety and extent of a leader's lived experiences that have resulted in relied-on lessons incorporated into the leader's practice repertoire.

- IDENTITY – the combination of the leader's construction of their decision making and directing role, and the construction of the leader's decision making and directing role by peers and others with a direct stake in the consequences of the leader's directives; in this arrangement, the meaning of role is about expectations and attributions of authority, conduct and performance of decision making and directing.
- REASONING – the rationale and processes used to notice, frame, bound, select, classify, link, associate, interpret and judge during the course of sense making and decision making.
- ACTIONS – the types of activities and associated resources that are deployed or suspended solely as a direct consequence of a leader's reasoning about a situation or issue.
- OUTCOMES – stakeholders' progressive post-emergency assessments of the effectiveness of response actions (where responses are the impacts of the actions taken).

So far, the meanings of the maverick theory's five concepts have only briefly been noted. However, testing the theory requires a technically clear meaning for each concept and then an operational definition for each one. This is done in the following section that sets out to illustrate how the maverick theory may be tested in the case of the Kilmore East fire.

Context, data and concepts to test the theory

According to this maverick theory, in a crisis such as the Kilmore East fire, leaders would need to draw on significant-challenge life skills and experiences, as well as local knowledge, rather than solely relying on emergency agency training, position descriptions and associated assumptions.

In the context of this fire (Cruz et al. 2012; Teague, McLeod and Pascoe 2010a), and according to the maverick theory of crisis leadership, if emergency response leaders had strictly adhered to agency training and role identities that were normally expected of them by their respective emergency agencies, then the outcome of the total emergency agency response to the Kilmore East fire would have largely failed to satisfy public stakeholders' expectations.

Unfortunately, this predicted outcome was the actual outcome. The emergency response leaders whose efforts and impact was most appreciated by public stakeholders were the lower-level response leaders who did go beyond agency-expected training and rehearsal to deal with the actual problems in imaginative ways, often informed by previous externally-based life experience.

This maverick theory assertion is consistent with the position of the executive of Volunteer Fire Brigades Victoria (VFBV) and with the findings of the subsequent VBRC. The VFBV executive identified the desirability that, for key roles within IMTs, and especially for Level-3 ICs, the valuable life skills of volunteers be harnessed in order to strengthen the standard and experience of future fire managers beyond that which is available through formal and scenario-based training (VFBV 2010). Subsequently, in the VBRC final report (Teague McLeod and Pascoe 2010a), recommendations 1, 8, 14, 18 and 22 incorporate references to the need for leadership reasoning and action, when facing a crisis-level bushfire, to take account of local knowledge, inter-operational systems and experience beyond normal agency preparations.

Sources of data to test the theory: population and sampling

For the reasons noted on page 69, more than one population may be defined for the purpose of constructing and testing a theory. As the meanings of concepts and proxy variables are not independent of the population to which they apply, the task in defining these elements is a reflexive one.

For illustrative purposes, the chosen population for testing the maverick theory comprises all leaders of emergency and associated agencies (governments, NGOs, mandated business and community organizations) who have responded to escalating rural and remote bushfires in Australia since 1990 (but not other types of natural disaster emergencies). A leader is a person with a formally acknowledged role as leader, or a person who voluntarily takes on a leadership role that is accepted by others who act as the leader's followers or adopters.

The chosen sample comprises leaders who are ICs and IMT members (typically: operations, planning and logistics), division and sector coordinators as well as brigade leaders, together with senior managers and government leaders (e.g. chief officers, commissioners, department secretaries, functional specialists and ministers) who are more senior than the ICs. Finally, we would include community volunteer leaders of first-responder efforts (as nominated by the community, local government or local agency unit coordinators).

The sample is an accessible group, supported by extensive and accessible incident data records, which also covers extreme incidents and, therefore, allows for better juxtaposing and 'testing' the merits and failings of traditional wisdom about leadership practice, compared to the maverick theory's arguments for more broadly based leadership reasoning and action as being a precondition for more acceptable response outcomes. It also represents leadership roles played by other agencies (e.g. police), essential infrastructure providers (e.g. meteorology, communications, transport, energy and water) and by informal leaders (e.g. particular community members), all of whom also played a part in the response and its outcomes.

Testing the theory

There are several ways to test the theory. It may be partially tested by collecting data relevant to propositions within the theory. It is also possible to derive and test hypotheses that follow logically from the theory. Another way is to apply the theory to a context beyond that from which the theory was developed and make predictions about the relationships between the theory's concepts in this other context. The following hypotheses and predictions illustrate the point.

Hypotheses to test in the chosen population The following hypotheses could be tested using the selected sample.

(a) When leaders enjoy greater congruence between the IDENTITY they operate with and the situation they have to deal with, their OUTCOMES are more effective as their REASONING increasingly incorporates *other* EXPERIENCE beyond *agency* EXPERIENCE.
(b) Given commensurate *agency* EXPERIENCEs of two leaders, each with high IDENTITY-situation congruence,[12] the leader with greater relevant external experience will be associated with more effective OUTCOMES from *actions* associated with unexpected situations.
(c) When comparing two cohorts of leaders with comparable EXPERIENCE mix, the cohort with higher IDENTITY-situation congruence will initiate actions with more effective OUTCOMES.
(d) Compared to leaders with limited challenging lived EXPERIENCE, leaders with more diverse and challenging other experience will initiate more effective ACTIONS associated with

a greater variety of challenging issues or situations in an escalating emergency.

Hypotheses to test in different populations The following hypotheses could also be tested on samples from populations associated either with natural disaster response agencies in Australia that deal with other than rural and remote bushfire or flood, or with natural disaster response agencies elsewhere in the world. If the hypotheses are not refuted, then the theory is further corroborated.

(e) Recruiting for more diverse and challenging *other* EXPERIENCE will increase the likelihood of developing leaders who later initiate more effective responses to escalating emergencies compared to leaders with less diverse *other* EXPERIENCE.
(f) In Australia, when needing to lead agency responses to industrial-ecological disasters, leaders with similar *agency* EXPERIENCE but greater *other* EXPERIENCE will generate actions that stakeholders assess as more effective in the long run.
(g) If emergency agency leaders with similar Australian agency EXPERIENCES were sent to another country to take on an emergency response leadership role, then the leaders with more *other* EXPERIENCE will initiate more effective and acceptable response actions to the emergencies than will their less experienced colleagues.

Concepts and their formal and operational definitions

The five concepts in the theory, as well as in hypothesis (a), need to be formally defined and operational or proxy variables created.

Formal and operational definitions of the concept of EXPERIENCE A leader's lived experiences cover not only agency type work but all non-agency activities, i.e. all other aspects of the leader's life. Agency-related employment experiences range across current and previous similar work. Other experiences range across distinctly different employment as well as community, family and personal activities.

Each experience, and therefore a collection of experiences, may be considered as a mixture comprising *routine, demanding, developmental, challenging* and even *confronting* experiences. Depending on the nature of the experience it may markedly contribute to or mediate one's identity and the reasoning one employs when dealing with situations. The following are the formal definitions of the five types of experience:

- *Routine* experience is about everyday common experience that involves know-how, emotions and effort that is readily dealt with and sustained.
- *Demanding* experience is about intense everyday common activity but the load (e.g. concurrent routine experiences) is notably and persistently more intense and the mental or physical effort is usually tiring or even exhausting.
- *Developmental* experience involves considerable albeit orderly or paced new learning or adaptation that requires persistent reflection, practice, rehearsal and adjustment before mastery can be attained and retained. For this category, a sense of mostly being in control and being able to cope persists.
- *Challenging* experience invokes and sustains the prospect of a lack of competence or capacity and/or loss of control. This may be as a result of a perceived disorderly and/or overly fast pace, or as a result of the inability to verify or achieve mastery, despite expectations of mastery.
- *Confronting* experience involves a mixture of intense or persistent demands, uncertainty, complexity, conflict and ambiguity such that coping with the experience is extremely taxing or even overwhelming.

To help judge the extent to which an experience comprises elements that correspond to one of the five categories, it is necessary to consider the experience's setting, novelty and difficulty, where each of these three facets may be graded high, medium or low.

The two aspects of the concept of experience that are raised in the theory, and in hypothesis (a) to be tested, are about: (1) the experience as an *agency*-related experience or an *other*-related experience; and (2) the experience mix, i.e. the proportion of the experience across the five categories of experience. Therefore, the variables to be considered are:

TYPEe The experience as either *agency* experience or *other* experience. This is a categorical variable with one of two possible values.

MIXe The proportion of the five categories of experience: *routine, demanding, developmental, challenging* and *confronting*. (These could be expressed as percentages, e.g. 45 per cent *routine*, 25 per cent *demanding*, 15 per cent *developmental*, 10 per cent *challenging* and 5 per cent *confronting*, or simply as a series of ratios, e.g. 9:5:3:2:1.)

With these definitions, a researcher may prepare an experience profile of a leader by inquiring about the experiences that the leader nominates as 'formative' to their own identities and situational reasoning.

Formal and operational definitions of the concept of IDENTITY In a particular situation, a leader's identities combine views constructed and articulated by the leader, by those relying on the leader and by the leader's peers. The range of current and past identities comprises the leader's repertoire and these derive from the leader's agency or other experiences.

In the maverick theory, an identity for a leader is conceptualized as the set of standpoints about the *values, authority, performance* and *accountability* that typify the leader's orientation and conduct when undertaking an organizational or situational role. The identity-in-use may markedly contribute to or mediate the leader's reasoning when dealing with situations.

- *Values* – the moral, ethical and cultural beliefs on which the identity's *authority, performance* and *accountability* are articulated and assessed.
- *Authority* – the span of decision making responsibility and the scope of directive responsibility that a leader and others assume is permitted and, when routinely acted on, is not challenged.
- *Performance* – the standards against which the leader's reasoning and personal or directed actions are assessed.
- *Accountability* – the organization and other stakeholders whose interests and needs are to be satisfied notwithstanding the conflicting demands that may arise or persist.

Hypothesis (a) refers to two aspects of the concept of identity: (1) the identity that the leader takes on when in an organization or situational role; and (2) the identity that stakeholders perceive as most appropriate for the organization or situational role. The result of these two views of role identity is that the actual identity that the leader assumes may be one of three states: *unsurprising, challenged* or *conflicted*. An *unsurprising* identity is consistent between all standpoints from which the identity is constructed or evaluated. A *challenged* identity is marked by dysfunctional standpoint differences that need to be negotiated in order to be accepted in use. A *conflicted* identity is marked by episodic or chronic incongruence between the leader's and others' attributed expectations about values, authority, performance or accountability.

To test hypothesis (a), the variable that serves as a proxy for the concept of identity is a categorical variable called *status*, which takes on three possible values – *unsurprising, challenged* or *conflicted*.

If later hypotheses involving degree of identity congruence were to be developed and tested, then proxy variables could be constructed as vectors whose components represented each of *values, authority, performance* and *accountability*.

Formal and operational definitions of the concept of REASONING A leader's REASONING reflects the know-how used to assess and deal with a situation. Such know-how combines awareness and competencies that are derived from a leader's agency experience and other experiences. Reasoning comprises cognitive, emotional and social processes that are used to notice, frame, select, classify, link, associate, interpret and draw conclusions in order to make sense of, and decisions about, an issue or situation.

Hypothesis (a) is concerned with the source of reasoning rather than the process of reasoning. Source is defined as a mix of *agency* experience and *other* experience that is mediated by the identity that is assumed by the leader. The proportion of the mix is the variable MIXr whose values range between 0 and 1. A value of the variable is determined by a leader judging the proportion of their *agency* experience compared to their *other* experience that informed the scope and process of the sense making and decision making and that led to a deliberate (in)action or set of (in)actions.

As the leader determines many actions during the unfolding emergency, successive values for the variable need to be recorded according to each of the actions that collectively determine the overall impact of the leader's identity-based reasoning.

Formal and operational definitions of the concept of ACTION Actions are about the resources and activities that are directly initiated as a result of the leader's reasoning. An action's residual impact is confounded by the continually evolving situation; it is the combined legacy result that is eventually assessed by stakeholders. The status of an action may be considered in terms of the actual-to-expected impact of the action (much greater, greater, similar, less, much less); with independent assessments of actual-to-expected impact being made by the responsible leader, the leader's peers and the dependent leaders immediately above and below the responsible leader.

To test the maverick theory by using hypothesis (a) and its reference to a leader's actions, ACTION can be considered in terms of its type and impact.

- TYPE of action is comprised of two attributes: STATUS which takes on one of three nominal values *unsurprising, challenged* or *conflicted*; and reasoning MIXr (from 0 to 1), being the proportion of *agency* experience compared to *other* experience associated with the reasoning that led to the action.
- IMPACT of the action reflects the immediate intervention effect on the inertial direction of that part of the emergency issue or situation that the action was intended to influence. It is an ordinal variable (5 = *highly productive*, 4 = *somewhat productive*, 3 = *unproductive*, 2 = *somewhat counterproductive*, 1 = *highly counterproductive*).

Formal and operational definitions of the concept of OUTCOME The outcome of an agency's response to an escalating emergency is reflected in stakeholders' progressive post-emergency assessments of the effectiveness of leaders' response actions. A stakeholder's assessment of outcomes involves their assessments of inertial, expected and actual outcomes. A stakeholder's assessment of the inertial outcome of a crisis reflects what the stakeholder believed would have been the impact of the crisis had there been no response from emergency agencies. The expected response is the stakeholder's assessment and subsequent judgement of what would have been the impact of the crisis if the emergency response agencies had performed as the stakeholder believed they should have been able to do. Each stakeholder's assessment is recorded according to one of five ordinal categories: (5 = *very good*, 4 = *good*, 3 = *modest*, 2 = *weak*, 1 = *very weak*).

Impact assessments span quantitative as well as qualitative views. Examples of quantitative assessments include number of:

- and value of assets destroyed or damaged;
- deaths;
- hospital admittances of more than one-day duration;
- emergency agency personnel hours deployed in the field;
- residents and visitors housed in temporary accommodation for more than 48 hours;
- hospital admissions of agency personnel lasting more than 24 hours;
- civilian hospital admissions of more than 48-hours duration; and

- hours of unsolicited phone calls dealt with until the disaster response has been declared as having ended.

Examples of qualitative assessments include:

- assessments about aspects of satisfaction, relief, acceptability and confidence in agency and volunteer efforts and outcomes; and
- communities' dominant 'post-event' view of a particular emergency agency's response effort.

Designing, testing, issuing, collecting and analysing assessment instruments needs to account for a wide variety of considerations that are reflected in the following questions:

What is to be assessed and why?
Who should make an assessment?
When, where and how should the assessment be introduced, facilitated and collected?
How is assessment response quality to be gauged?
What is an acceptable sample response, and how is this to be gauged?

Once sufficient quality assessments have been collected, aggregation and analysis of quantitative and qualitative responses is undertaken in order to identify themes and patterns in the data and to draw lessons and recommendations from the assessment studies. The temporal and spatial scope, as well as the substantive foci of assessments, are all matters of judgement that reflect experience and, typically, also political, social, economic, technological, environmental and legal purposes.

More about testing the theory

Once concepts of the theory have been operationalized as proxy variables, applicable to a defined sample of the population selected, the theory can be tested by assembling and analysing data about the behaviour of the concepts' proxy variables according to hypotheses and/or predictions deduced from the theory. The corroborating or disconfirming nature of the evidence so obtained is not definitive because interpretation of analysed data rests on several assumptions including: (1) uncertain representativeness of the proxy variables; (2) suitability of the sample and sample response from what is often a changing population; and (3) difficulty in assembling, comparing and analysing the data.

Therefore, as chains of evidence reflect many assumptions – practical and theoretical – even findings from one well designed and executed Neo-Positive study can at best reassure the researcher about the value of further investigations of the regularity by undertaking further tests of the same theory, or by testing refinements of the theory that are argued to better explain the regularity that may still only be one aspect of the problem of interest.

The tentative maverick theory could also be retrospectively tested by studying a recent bushfire, such as the 2013 Forcett fire in the state of Tasmania (Hyde 2013; Marsden-Smedley 2013), subject to access to relevant agencies, their leaders and associated community and other corporate responders. Alternatively, proxy data about future natural disasters and responses – both within and outside agencies' prepared-for scope – could be collected and analysed in order to assess associations between leaders' *agency* experience or *other* experience compared to stakeholders' retrospective assessments of response effectiveness.

5
Principles of Interpretive Research

Chapter summary

- The first part of the chapter reviews the principles of the Interpretive research paradigm:
  - its origins are reviewed, particularly in the work of Max Weber;
  - the main characteristics are summarized;
  - its particular philosophical assumptions are identified;
  - the central theme – of how to move from description to explanation by developing ideal types and generating theory from them – is elaborated in the work of Weber, Becker, Schütz, Rex and Giddens; and
  - the paradigm's limitations are identified.
- The second part of the chapter sets out the characteristic steps involved in using this practice.

Introduction

Interpretivism is a well-established tradition in the social sciences, with a number of antecedents and a variety of manifestations. While it is sometimes seen as a reaction against positivism, many of the principles on which it is based can be traced back to the end of the eighteenth century when the discipline of hermeneutics expanded from the interpretation of ancient religious texts to questions about the nature and objectives of social knowledge in general (Bauman 1978: 8). More recent contributions have come from the traditions of phenomenology, symbolic interactionism, ethnomethodology and ordinary language philosophy.

The major feature that distinguishes Interpretivism from any type of positivism is the claim that there is a fundamental difference between the subject matters of the natural and social sciences. As a consequence, it is argued that natural scientists have to invent their concepts and theories and impose them on the universe of nature; they have to study nature from the 'outside'. By contrast, social reality is not a pre-given universe of objects; it is produced and reproduced by its members (Giddens 1976: 160). Because social worlds are already interpreted before the social scientist arrives on the scene, it is possible to study social life from the 'inside'.

In order for social life to exist, people have to continually interpret their own actions, other people's actions, social situations, the natural world and humanly created objects. The aim of Interpretive social science is to describe, understand and hopefully explain any area of social life by first getting inside that world and learning how the inhabitants conceptualize and understand it.

In spite of the differences in the subject matters of the natural and social sciences, some social scientists have argued that the methods, or more specifically, the logic of inquiry used to explain natural phenomena (e.g. *deductive*) can also be used in the social sciences; hence, the use of the Neo-Positive paradigm. However, other scholars have argued that a different logic of inquiry is required. It is to this tradition that we now turn.

Before doing so, it is important to note that arguments for a different logic of inquiry should not be seen as Interpretivism wanting to reject science. As we shall see, a common theme amongst the contributors to this research paradigm is the desire to create a science of society, an objective science of subjective meaning structures (Schütz 1963a: 246).

Origins

The intellectual roots of the version of Interpretivism we present here can be traced back mainly to a German intellectual tradition, to scholars such as Schleiermacher, Dilthey, Husserl, Heidegger and Gadamer. However, it is not necessary to discuss their ideas here. (For reviews and critiques of hermeneutics and Interpretivism, see Blaikie 1993b: 28–49, 63–77; 2007: 117–31, 151–7, 187–8, 195.)

It is only necessary to focus on later contributors to this version of Interpretivism: Weber, Schütz and Giddens.

As the most important contribution over the past hundred years has come from Max Weber (1864–1920), we will give considerable attention to his work. Throughout his writings, Weber was concerned with the subjective meaning social actors attach to their actions, and with the sociologist's interpretive understanding of that action. This is clearly evident in his definition of the discipline of sociology.

> Sociology . . . is a science which attempts the interpretive understanding of social action in order thereby to arrive at a causal explanation of its course and effects. In 'action' is included all human behaviour when and in so far as the acting individual attaches a subjective meaning to it. . . . Action is social [when] . . . it takes account of the behaviour of others and is thereby oriented in its course. (Weber 1947: 88)

Weber also defined a third concept that takes us from individual actions, through social action to social relationships. 'The term "social relationship" will be used to denote the behaviour of a plurality of actors in so far as, in its meaningful content, the action of each takes account of that of the others and is oriented in these terms' (Weber 1947: 118). Weber saw sociology as a *science* that is concerned with *explaining* social action. He saw the three key concepts – 'action', 'social action' and 'social relationships' – as the building blocks of such explanations.

Based on this definition as a foundation, Weber then went on to elaborate 'meaning', 'action' and 'understanding'. He suggested that there are two kinds of 'meaning' of relevance to the social scientist, but these can be seen as three: *actual meaning* used by a specific actor; *average meaning* used by a number of actors; and *hypothetical meaning* used by hypothetical actors. 'In no case does it refer to an objectively "correct" meaning or one which is "true" in some metaphysical sense' (Weber 1947: 89). There is an important difference between actual or average meaning on the one hand and hypothetical meaning on the other hand; the former two are descriptive and the latter moves towards explanation. We shall come back to this difference later.

Weber then distinguished two kinds of 'action': *rational* and *emotional*, or artistic. The former is understood as being oriented towards some goal; means are selected that are considered to produce the desired goal. The latter is understood through empathetic participation in a social situation to grasp the emotional context in which the action takes place. However, Weber argued that in those cases where action is reactive, and has no subjective meaning attached, understanding is not possible (1947: 91–3).[1]

For Weber, 'understanding' is of two kinds: *direct observational* understanding of the subjective meaning of a given act, including verbal utterances; and *explanatory* understanding in terms of the motive(s) a social actor has for the action. 'A motive is a complex of subjective meaning which seems to the actor himself or to the observer an adequate ground for the conduct in question' (Weber 1947: 98–9). Hence, the subjective interpretation of a coherent course of action is adequate at the level of meaning when its component parts constitute a 'typical' complex of meaning. As we shall see, typicality is what Weber's notion of ideal types is about.

> A correct causal interpretation of a course of action is arrived at when the overt action and the motives have both been correctly apprehended and at the same time their relation has become meaningfully comprehensible.... If adequacy in respect to meaning is lacking, then no matter how high the degree of uniformity and how precisely its probability can be empirically determined, it is still an incomprehensible statistical probability. (Weber 1947: 99)

Embedded in this statement, that explanation needs to be based on subjective meaning, is another kind of causal explanation based on statistical uniformities. What Weber meant by this is that a sequence of events will be causally adequate if there is a strong probability that it will always occur in the same way (Weber 1947: 99). Here he resorted to what we have referred to as the 'pattern model of explanation', which is based on inductively produced generalizations. It is not clear why he did this, but he did go on to say that such generalizations can only be *understood* if the meaning of the action is known. 'Statistical uniformities constitute understandable types of action ..., and thus constitute "sociological generalizations," only when they can be regarded as manifestations of the understandable subjective meaning of a course of social action' (Weber 1947: 100). To cast this statement in the best possible light, and to link it to a major theme in this book, what Weber might have intended is that, until a statistical uniformity has been established (we refer to it as a regularity), there is nothing to explain. Then explanation is achieved by discerning the subjective meaning that lies behind it.

Weber, like others, saw this latter kind of explanation as not being possible in the natural sciences, which he saw as having to use the pattern model on its own. 'The natural sciences ... [are] limited to the formulation of causal uniformities in objects and events and the explanation of individual facts by applying them' (Weber 1947: 103).[2]

A number of writers have developed, modified or supplemented Weber's approach to social scientific explanation and the nature and use of ideal types. We will encounter some of them in the later sections of this chapter where we discuss the use of ideal types.

Main characteristics

The main characteristics or principles of the version of Interpretivism being presented here can be summarized as follows.

- Social reality is socially constructed; it is a skilled accomplishment of active human beings; it is the product of its inhabitants who reproduce and maintain it as a necessary part of their everyday activities together.
- As social reality is already interpreted before researchers arrive on the scene, social researchers need to grasp these interpretations if they want to understand and explain social life.
- Language is seen as the medium of social interaction, and everyday concepts as structuring social reality.
- Interpretivism aims to establish an objective science of the subjective; producing verifiable knowledge of the meanings that constitute the social world.
- Social researchers need to focus on meaningful social action, which is used to understand patterns or regularities in social life.
- These regularities can be understood, perhaps explained, in terms of typical meanings used by typical social actors engaged in typical courses of action in typical social situations.

Assumptions

Interpretivism adopts the following ontological and epistemological assumptions.

Ontological assumptions: idealist

1 Social reality is made up of shared interpretations that social actors produce and reproduce as they go about their everyday lives.
2 Idealist ontologies differ in the extent to which the existence of an independent external world is acknowledged and, if so, whether or not it constrains or facilitates individual and social activity.

3 Mainstream Interpretivism focuses more on the degree to which social actors agree or disagree about the nature of their social reality, rather than on whether it has an independent existence.[3]

Epistemological assumptions: constructionism

1 As access to any social world has to be through the language of the participants, social reality has to be discovered from the 'inside' rather than being filtered through or distorted by an expert's concepts and theory.
2 Social scientific knowledge is the outcome of social scientists' mediation between everyday social language and technical social scientific language.

Description and beyond: the use of typologies

Contributors to Interpretivism have argued that it must be based on the accounts that social actors can give of their activities. However, a genuine science of social life needs to go beyond these accounts and be concerned with explanation and possibly prediction (Becker 1940, 1950; Schütz 1963a; Garfinkel 1967). The question is: how is this done? The Interpretive answer was and should still be: use typologies.[4]

The early use of typologies was largely confined either to providing generalized conceptualizations of types of civilizations, societies or institutions, or to identifying stages in evolutionary theories of society, for example from 'simple' to 'complex' (e.g. Comte, Spencer, Tonnies and Durkheim). The initial stimulus came from the desire to go beyond an ideographic approach to a nomothetic science (Becker 1940) and to transform the comparative method into a more precise procedure (Martindale 1959).

The founders of sociology were faced with a more fundamental problem: how to measure social phenomena. Weber argued for the use of ideal types[5] as measuring instruments. In his efforts to distinguish between different types of legal or legitimate authority, he proposed the pure type of 'rational' bureaucratic administration and contrasted this with 'traditional' and 'charismatic' authority (Weber 1964: 328–36). In his pure type of bureaucracy, he accentuated certain features that focus on the considered choice of the best means to achieve a goal, this being his idea of rationality. He recognized that this description was not derived from any particular bureaucracy and may not even exist in reality. However, the pure or ideal type can act as a yardstick that can be 'placed against' any existing bureaucracy and deviations noted, thus facilitating comparisons between bureaucracies (see Rex 1974: 64–5). Weber was at pains to point out that such abstract descriptions were not meant to suggest what a perfect bureaucracy should be like, but a close examination of his description of this ideal type suggests that he preferred bureaucracies that embody these 'rational' characteristics.

This is clearly a very crude form of measurement. However, the idea of using abstract descriptions, to reduce social complexity to graspable summaries of social characteristics or processes, has persisted and is unavoidable.

A great deal of attention was given to ideal types in the 1940s and 1950s (e.g. Becker 1940, 1950; Loomis 1950; Rose 1950; Lazarsfeld and Barton 1951; Hempel 1952; Watkins 1953; McKinney 1957; Winch 1958; Martindale 1959), and by the 1960s a number of writers had suggested ways of developing them (e.g. Schütz 1963a, 1963b; McKinney 1966; Fallding 1968). However, in spite of the enthusiasm for their use during this period, little if any advances have since been made in how they might be constructed and used.

There are various reasons for this: some social scientists judged them as being inadequate; there have been disputes about their purpose (see e.g. McKinney 1957; Martindale 1959); and it has been argued that they are only necessary in the early stages of the development of a science and then need to be superseded by more sophisticated techniques (Hempel 1952; Martindale 1959).

With the growing sophistication and use of quantitative methods, particularly in the last sixty years or so, ideal types as Weber defined them have played a minor role in social theories and research. In addition, sociologists who have engaged in qualitative research have often been content with offering descriptive accounts and have not seen the need for, or even the legitimacy of, developing theory. However, with orthodox approaches in social science having come under attack from various quarters (e.g. feminism and post-modernism), the way has opened up for a re-examination of both the role of typologies and the methods by which they are constructed.

The revival of interest in the use of qualitative methods in recent years, and the apparent subsidence in the paradigm wars of the 1960s and 1970s, has created a climate in which a theme that was present in the work of Weber and Schütz, i.e. how to produce verifiable theory from subjective meaning structures, can be revisited. Their ideas, as well as those of fellow travellers (Becker, Rex and Giddens), are now examined.

Weber – ideal types

As we have seen, Weber's solution to the problem of producing an objective science of social phenomena was to use ideal or pure types. However, he offered little help with the question of what elements should be included, i.e. what should be accentuated. While, for him, ideal types are not derived from systematically gathered data (this would have been either very difficult or impossible in the research problems he chose to investigate), what any social scientist includes will no doubt be influenced by knowledge of the phenomenon and judgements about what is considered to be important or useful. This was Weber's position[6] (see Box 5.1).

Box 5.1 An early Interpretive study: Weber's Protestant ethic thesis

Weber's aim in *The Protestant Ethic and the Spirit of Capitalism* (1958), originally published in German (1904–5), and in his other books on major world religions, was to explain why capitalism emerged in Europe and not elsewhere. The capitalistic adventurer has existed everywhere, but their behaviour is irrational and may even involve the use of force to achieve their aims. He argued that unlimited greed for gain is not capitalism or its spirit. Capitalistic acquisition is rationally pursued and rational industrial organization was peculiar to western capitalism. It requires the separation of business from household, rational book-keeping, law and administration and the rational organization of labour. '[C]apitalism is identical with the pursuit of profit, and forever *renewed* profit, by means of continuous, rational, capitalistic enterprise' (1958: 17).

As an integral part of this project, Weber wished to explain a particular European regularity – the relationship between religion and occupation. He expressed this as the 'greater relative participation of Protestants in the ownership of capital, in management, and the upper ranks of labour in great modern industrial and commercial enterprises' (1958: 35).

To do this, he typified the spirit of capitalism as the expectation of profit through the utilization of opportunities for economic exchange and the rational organization of free labour. It involves the impulse to accumulate through continual investment and reinvestment, is associated with a lack of interest in worldly pleasures

> and is accompanied by a frugal lifestyle in which wealth is accumulated for its own sake and not for material rewards.
>
> Weber then typified the meaning given to work by the early Calvinists as the 'Protestant work ethic'. He used this to explain why Protestants, but more particularly Calvinists, were at the forefront of the rise of capitalism in the West. This typification included the concept of work as a calling, as a moral obligation to serve God in everyday mundane activities. It is associated with the doctrine of predestination, the consequence of which is the need to be able to attain some assurance that you have been chosen by God to go to heaven. The ability to lead a sober and industrious life and to be successful in business were regarded as such signs. These doctrines forced the Calvinists to see the everyday world as the sphere in which to practise their religion and serve God.
>
> Hence, Weber regarded the meaning that Calvinists gave to work as the explanation not only for the relationship between religion and occupation but also for the rise of capitalism in Europe. It was the presence of this particular meaning of work amongst Protestants, and its absence amongst Catholics, that was offered as an explanation for this relationship in Europe, certainly until about a hundred years ago. The Protestant work ethic provided the appropriate work attitudes and motivation. Further, it was the presence of this-worldly asceticism in Protestantism, and its absence, or the presence of other-worldly beliefs in other major world religions, which was offered as an explanation for the rise of modern capitalism in Europe. In short, Weber concluded that the spirit of modern capitalism is derived from the rational ethics of ascetic Protestantism.[7]

Weber recognized that there are some fundamental problems in discovering the meanings that social actors use. His solution was to construct theory using typical meanings of typical social actors involved in typical social processes and in typical social contexts. In other words, theories are not about actual people but about abstractions that are produced by social scientists based on the knowledge they can gain of such actions, processes and situations.

> The theoretical concepts of sociology are ideal types not only from the objective point of view, but also in their application to subjective processes. In the great majority of cases actual action goes on in a state of

inarticulate half-consciousness or actual unconsciousness of its subjective meaning. The actor is more likely to 'be aware' of it in a vague sense than he [*sic*] is to 'know' what he is doing or be explicitly self-conscious about it. In most cases his action is governed by impulse or habit. Only occasionally and, in the uniform action of large numbers often only in the case of a few individuals, is the subjective meaning of the action, whether rational or irrational, brought clearly into consciousness. The ideal type of meaningful action where the meaning is fully conscious and explicit is a marginal case. Every sociological or historical investigation, in applying its analysis to the empirical facts, must take this fact into account. But the difficulty need not prevent the sociologist from systematizing his concepts by the classification of possible types of subjective meaning. That is, he may reason as if action actually proceeded on the basis of clearly self-conscious meaning. (Weber 1947: 111–12)

When it is possible for the social scientist to have some direct involvement in, or observation of, social phenomena, a different approach can be adopted from that advocated by Weber. As we shall see, Schütz took up this challenge and clarified what is required. However, before turning to him, we need to make a deviation to Howard Becker's views on ideal types.

Becker – constructive typologies

Even after more than seventy years, it is impossible not to be impressed with the depth of Becker's understanding of how social scientists theorize using abstractions in the form of typologies. According to Becker, practitioners in the humanities and social sciences can be divided into two groups: those concerned with unique individuals, events and social processes, and those concerned with generalizing from such unique individuals, events and processes. Most historians, and some social scientists, fall into the first category. For those who see themselves in the second category, the task is threefold: describe what is typical across individuals, situations and processes; compare different forms of typicality; and then establish the extent of these similarities and differences. Here we have the crux of the matter.

Because of the undeniable uniqueness of people, social situations and social activities, some means of transcending the unique is required in order to be able to theorize. As Becker put it:

> The modern sociologist can say, with the ideographic historian, that each human being is unique; that the social situations in which he [*sic*]

has developed are unique; and that history never repeats itself in any ultimate or final sense; but he is also correct in saying that *for certain purposes*, which are not those of the ideographic historian, it may be entirely legitimate to say that certain phenomena can be treated as identical with certain other phenomena. (Becker 1940: 43)

The key difference between ideographic and nomothetic sciences is that they have different purposes: describing the unique compared with describing and explaining the general. However, according to Becker, to deal with the general we have to construct the general from the unique.

Becker suggested that even the ideographic historian has to work with constructed types, but these are dated and localized. In contrast, the sociologist uses undated and non-localized types. However, these are not completely timeless or non-spatial. The aim is not universal propositions about the social world, but general ones. However, particularity and generality are matters of degree. 'If everything is *absolutely* different, there can be no analysis; if everything is *absolutely* identical, there can be no analysis. Sociological types are *relatively* general, but the exact point at which the *relatively general* becomes *relatively particular* can be determined only in the light of the *purpose* in hand' (Becker 1950: 114).

Constructive types are tools created by the investigator. For Becker, they are constructs that are influenced by numerous observations, but do not correspond exactly to observed phenomena. If they did, they would have no comparative value. He described the process of constructing types very briefly. It 'begins with a vaguely defined problem, the framing of a hypothesis, selective observation . . . with reference to it, and eventual construction of a type, or a battery of them, that aids further research' (Becker 1940: 46–7). It sounds quite simple!

For Becker, the process of verification is essentially pragmatic – if it works, it is verified. Putting types to the test, i.e. making predictions and checking outcomes, is part of the process of their construction. While they do not describe reality, they are nevertheless constrained by it. '[I]t should be clear that the constructed type is not itself a hypothesis and that it is not self-validating. Facts are stubborn things. Constructed types must be drawn from them and continually thrown back upon them if empty speculation is not to replace sound generalization' (1940: 50). In other words, the construction and validation of types is an iterative process.

Becker reviewed some criticisms of constructed types and countered them.

- *Exceptions can be found.* Exceptions must be found. If there were no exceptions we would be bogged down in the morass of the particular.
- *Predictions based on constructed types are always conditional.* They must be because they relate to conditions that may vary.
- *Constructed types are assumed to be equally general.* But they are not; it depends on the context and purpose. The more general a type is, the less detailed can be the predictions based on it.

Constructed types are neither true descriptions nor statistical averages. They are working fictions, but not just any fictions. 'The constructed type is a conscious, planned selection and combination of the "empirically given", relatively free from value-judgment' (1940: 55). They are a 'systematic statement of the probability of the potential or actual recurrence of phenomena which, for the purpose at hand, are regarded as identical'.

Becker argued that 'the ultimate goal of scientific generalization in sociology is the prediction of the recurrence of social phenomena' (1940: 43), that certain types of social conduct recur *if and when* certain conditions are given. According to Becker, constructed types make prediction possible. If some of the characteristics designated by the type can be identified in a particular situation, then, under certain conditions, other characteristics can be expected to occur or be identified.

Once established, Becker argued that constructed types might be altered or revised should the purpose for which they were originally devised be changed (1950: 123). It follows from this that the appropriateness of the types must be tested in every new application, and modified if necessary. Constructed types are not intended to be true (1940: 54); they are tools devised for particular purposes, tools that must be reshaped if the purpose or the situation changes.

There are many attractive features in Becker's constructed types:

- they address the ultimate goal of science – prediction (in the Popperian sense);
- they establish a satisfactory relationship with, as well as a distance from, 'empirical reality';
- they are not simply untested speculations;
- they remain tentative in the sense of always being linked to some purpose and context, and therefore are not reified; and
- a procedure for developing them is offered.

However, Becker's approach to the development of constructed types is not entirely satisfactory. We need to turn to Schütz for help with this.

Schütz – improving Weber

In pursuing the task of improving Weber's interpretive sociology, Schütz (1899–1959) not only elaborated the concept of action (1976) but he also offered a method for developing ideal types (1963a, 1963b, 1970). He argued that, in assuming that the concept of the meaningful act is the basic and irreducible component of social phenomena, Weber failed, amongst other things, to distinguish between (a) the meaning the social actor *works with* while action is taking place, (b) the meaning the social actor *attributes* to a completed act or to some future act and (c) the meaning the sociologist *attributes* to a completed act. In (a), the meaning worked with during the act itself, and the context in which it occurs, is usually taken for granted; in (b), the meaning attributed will be in terms of the social actor's motives; and (c), the context of meaning will be that of the observer not the social actor. Weber appeared to assume that (c) is an adequate basis for arriving at (a) and that there will be no disputes between actors, or between actors and observers, about what is the appropriate meaning of a completed or future act.

Schütz has provided the foundation for a methodological bridge between the meaning that social actors attribute and the meaning that the social scientists must attribute in order to produce an adequate theory. According to Schütz, social life is possible, in both face-to-face and more anonymous situations, to the extent that social actors use typifications – everyday types of both persons and courses of action – and these are socially constructed, transmitted and refined by a trial-and-error process. The particular typifications used by social actors will be related to their biographically and situationally determined system of interests and relevances (Schütz 1963a: 243).

As we have seen, Schütz was not just concerned with developing a more adequate account of everyday life; he, like Weber, was also concerned with the problem of how to arrive at a science of the subjective (Schütz 1963a: 246). He accepted Weber's view that this can be achieved by the use of ideal types but adopted a different conception of their nature and origin.[8] Whereas Weber was prepared to allow the sociologist to attribute typical meaning to an ideal type, Schütz insisted that the sociologist's typifications must be derived from everyday typifications. He labelled the latter as *first-order constructs*, and the sociologist's typifications as *second-order constructs*.

> The thought objects constructed by the social scientist, in order to grasp this social reality, have to be founded upon the thought objects constructed by the common-sense thinking of men [sic], living their daily life within their social world. Thus, the constructs of the social sciences are, so to speak, constructs of the second degree, that is, constructs of the constructs made by the actors on the social scene, whose behaviour the social scientist has to observe and to explain in accordance with the procedural rules of his science. (Schütz 1963a: 242)
>
> The scientific constructs formed on the second level ... are objective ideal typical constructs and, as such, of a different kind from those developed on the first level of common-sense thinking which they have to supersede. They are theoretical systems embodying testable general hypotheses. (Schütz 1963a: 246)

According to Schütz, the critical difference between first-order and second-order constructs is that they are constructed with a different purpose in mind and within different contexts of meaning. First-order constructs take a particular social stock of everyday knowledge for granted and are designed to deal with an everyday (social) problem – to make social interaction possible and understandable to the participants. Second-order constructs are designed to deal with a scientific (sociological) problem – to explain some social phenomena – and have to relate to a sometimes taken-for-granted scientific (sociological) stock of knowledge (Schütz 1963b: 337–9).

> [A]lthough the social sciences start out from, and take for granted, the same social world in which we live from day to day, yet their methods of gathering knowledge are quite different from those of everyday life. For the social scientist organises and classifies his [sic] data into quite different contexts of meaning and works them up in quite different ways. (Schütz 1976: 220)

Schütz offered very little help to the practising social scientist on how second-order constructs might be constructed. However, it is possible to glean his main ideas from two sources (1963a: 247–8; 1963b: 339–43). What he did stress is that the process is much like that used by social actors to test their first-order constructs; ideal types can be verified by predicting 'how a puppet or system of puppets might behave under certain conditions' (1963a: 248) and in this way build up propositions that state relations between sets of variables.

Rex – refining Weber

Rex (1974) was a keen exponent of Weber's interpretive sociology and his method of ideal types, but he offered some modifications to overcome what he regarded as its weaknesses. He followed this path because he lamented the attempt to replace sociology with social statistics, with variable analysis, and he also rejected Weber's causal explanations based on statistical uniformities.

At the same time, Rex had an aversion to phenomenology and, in particular, to Schütz's phenomenology of everyday life, which he regarded as anti-structural and anti-macrosocial (Rex 1974: 50; see also Lassman 1974). He argued for the use of a Weberian structural sociology with its interest in actual historical structures (1974: 50).

However, in spite of his rejection of phenomenology, Rex supported the idea that social actors' constructs and theories play some part in the process by which sociologists construct ideal types, but argued that the sociologist's ideal types are, and need to be, distinct from actors' theories (1974: 49). He argues that without this, the sociologist cannot give an account that may be different from that derived from social actors. In this regard, he was critical of Schütz's postulate of adequacy because he believed that it can place constraints on the sociologist's analysis.

> The particular problem which the phenomenologists and ethnomethodologists have difficulty in dealing with is that of 'false consciousness'. It may well be, of course, that for certain purposes some sociologists may wish to establish the actual facts of the actor's own consciousness in an uncritical and descriptive way. But surely for most purposes we may wish to enquire whether the actual meaning of the actor's action is not different from his [sic] own account of it? . . . [And] surely, the sociologist can claim that he can give a different and competing account of the actor's actions from the actor's own. (Rex 1974: 47)

There is a solution to the problem Rex has raised. The researcher does not need to stop when 'verified' typologies have been produced and theories based on them have been generated. The researcher is free to use a different paradigm, and to offer a structural critique of how social actors understand their world.

Giddens – new rules

Drawing on the work of Schütz, Winch and Garfinkel, Giddens (1976) offered a positive critique of interpretive sociologies in which he both reviewed and explicated a methodology for relating sociological constructs and theories to the 'frames of meaning' produced and used by actors in social life. Like Schütz, Giddens argued that the social scientist has to penetrate these frames of meaning, using the same sorts of skills as those whose conduct he/she seeks to understand (1976: 79, 155). This is a hermeneutic task requiring immersion in the 'form of life' being investigated to the extent that it is possible 'to find one's way about in it, to be able to participate in it as an ensemble of practices' (Giddens 1976: 161). The task is to mediate these frames of meaning – to generate 'descriptions of them that are potentially available to those who have not directly participated in them' (1976: 145). The social scientist is then in a position to reinterpret those frames of meaning within his/her own theoretical schemes.[9]

Giddens was critical of Schütz's view of the relationship between first-order constructs and second-order constructs, and the role of the 'postulate of adequacy' in this relationship, which he suggested Schütz had got the wrong way around (Giddens 1976: 158). However, on closer inspection, they seem to be in agreement. Where they differ is in their views of how many 'foreign' concepts and theoretical ideas can be imported into the sociologist's account before it ceases to be authentic and useful.

Giddens has summarized his position as follows.

> The schools of 'interpretive sociology' ... have made some essential contributions to the clarification of the logic and method of the social sciences. In summary form, these are the following: the social world, unlike the natural world of nature, has to be grasped as a skilled accomplishment of active human subjects; the constitution of this world as 'meaningful', 'accountable' or 'intelligible' depends upon language, regarded however not simply as a system of signs and symbols but as a medium of practical activity; the social scientist of necessity draws upon the same sorts of skills as those whose conduct he [*sic*] seeks to analyse in order to describe it; generating descriptions of social conduct depends upon the hermeneutic task of penetrating the frames of meaning which lay actors themselves draw upon in constituting and reconstituting the social world. (Giddens 1976: 155)

Limitations of the Interpretive paradigm

The most obvious strength and limitation of the Interpretive research paradigm is its foundation in social actors' conceptualization and

Limitations of the Interpretive paradigm 115

understanding of their everyday life. However, the key dilemma is how close to these views a researcher should remain in developing understanding and explanations. The limitation that critics usually focus on is the consequent lack of recognition of social structures, particularly those of which social actors may not be aware.

As we have seen, Rex and Giddens have both made significant contributions to the view of Interpretivism presented here, but they have also raised some concerns. Rex's concerns are best summed up in the following extract.

> Unfortunately phenomenological sociologists [e.g. Schütz] and ethnomethodologists [e.g. Garfinkel] have too often sought to dissociate their work from all structural sociology, representing all that is not cast in terms of members' meanings or the actor's definition of the situation, as though it must either be positivist, in the sense of quantitative sociology which takes no account of meaning, or structural-functionalist, and as such separated from an interest in the meaning of social action. We believe that there is a kind of structural sociology of a Weberian kind which is based upon a dialogue of languages and which leads to a systematic sociological typology. It is in fact the closest of all sociologies to the work of the latter-day phenomenologists. But unlike these, it still continues to interest itself in actual historical structures as they appear to the sociologist and not merely the structures which actors believe to exist, or believe that they make, in the process of thinking them to exist.
> (Rex 1974: 50)

Giddens addressed this issue with his concepts of *duality of structure* and *structuration* (1979, 1984). For him, social structures are both the conditions and consequences of social interaction but are not external to social actors either in the sense of them having no part in their production, or as being purely conceptualized by an external observer.

In his theory of structuration (1984), Giddens defined 'structure' as the properties of groups that enable and constrain agency. Structures have only a virtual existence; they are the rules and resources that social actors draw on as they engage each other in social interaction (see Blaikie 2010: 115 for a diagrammatic representation of structuration theory.)

This difference in the way Rex and Giddens think about the nature of social structures (actual vs virtual) indicates the importance of ontological assumptions and the need to articulate them. It also demonstrates that variations within the Interpretivist tradition are possible.

Characteristic steps of the paradigm

The iterative and evolutionary character of Interpretive inquiry is in stark contrast to the predominantly linear processes used in Neo-Positive research. This section of the chapter discusses the overall process and tasks that are characteristic of Interpretive research. Our purpose here is to alert the reader to some of the particularly challenging aspects that are characteristic of the paradigm.

Because of the quite abstract nature of this discussion, the reader may wish to first scan this section of the chapter, not be too concerned about grasping all the details, and then come back to it after reading the illustrations in chapter 6. However, it will be easier to follow the illustrations with an understanding of this section. This process is analogous to the hermeneutic circle that underpins this research paradigm.

The overall process

In an Interpretive study, the inquiry process plays out as a series of reflexive cycles. Each cycle involves the six important interwoven activities of *sensitizing, questioning, exploring, analysing, theorizing* and *checking*. These activities commonly produce issues for the researcher to further explore, cross-check, qualify, elaborate and/or better illustrate or define when next engaging with participants. In this way, participants and researcher act as co-producers of data and meaning.

1 *Sensitizing* for the researcher is a twofold process that initially draws on methodological and substantive literature that relates to the study's context and questions, and then helps to alert the researcher to matters to be aware of, or aspects that could be investigated, as part of engagement with participants, other researchers involved in the study or, where relevant, even research sponsors.
2 *Questioning* is about identifying aspects in the literature or participants' accounts that call for exploration, elaboration, wider cross-checking or critical review.
3 *Exploring* is about eliciting rich accounts from participants by asking them open starting questions, followed by drill-down questioning, or presenting items for clarification (e.g. gaps, apparent contradictions, points of confusion, paradoxes or dilemmas) that the researcher has identified within or between participants'

accounts or between them and other sources of data. It also involves asking participants to clarify (e.g. elaborate, redefine, explain, illustrate) so that the researcher is better able to apprehend what they or other sources are referring to or operating with.

4 *Analysing* involves transforming all units of data into successively more abstract and compact descriptions that still account for their meanings. A unit of data may range from coarse grained (e.g. a particular case) to quite fine grained (e.g. a participant's response to a researcher's question) or it may be, for instance, each 'idea' or 'concept' that arises in a participant's account or in another source of data. Such a transformation involves the researcher in a layered process of first recognizing everyday typifications and grouping them according to shared 'subtext' to form first-order abstracted categories. These are then further abstracted into types. Types of the same concept (e.g. types of people, types of processes, types of resources, types of structure) constitute a typology.

5 *Theorizing* is the iterative process that builds on the theoretical potential of a typology or typologies in order to construct an understanding or an explanation of participants' reported life-worlds. This step is needed because a typology does not describe the dynamics and relationships that are the stuff of the life-world being studied. To answer a 'why' question using this research paradigm is to take this step of analytically and imaginatively generating discriminating insights about associations or relationships between one or more typologies or subtypes. It may also be necessary to refer to specific elements of the study's research questions, or even elements of the regularity, in order to expose a sense of the dynamics or the ecology of participants 'in action'. Only after the researcher has generated one or more confirmed discriminating typologies[10] and their inter-relationships,[11] which account for the regularity, can the researcher claim production of a theory that provides understanding of a life-world and answers a 'why' question.

6 *Checking* is the iterative process by which the researcher, using the language and context of participants' accounts, checks with them the degree to which they understand and concur with the researcher's account of the area of their social life under investigation.

In the early stages of investigation, each successive reflexive cycle is likely to expand the variety and richness of data and possible meanings. Eventually, however, each cycle is increasingly likely to reduce the variety of abstracted categories being generated and, at the same time, expand the richness of a few constructs that increasingly account for most, if not all, of the data that have been generated through all cycles.

These iterative cycles also respond well to a mixture of familiarity and distance, with the researcher concurrently functioning in both states. Building familiarity with data sources, data generation and data analysis intensifies a working knowledge of the phenomenon at a fine level of detail. Maintaining cognitive, sensitizing and psychological distance from the detail helps to suspend premature judgement and see afresh categorical and abstract analysis and theorizing. This state of distance is an important element in imaginative yet disciplined abstraction that is essential to discerning a simple typology.

These iterative cycles (www.InfoServ.com.au) help to engage participants, and so help the researcher to get inside individuals' stories, in order to construct a compact and confirmed scheme of concepts, meanings and interplay that enables understanding of the stories of participants' life-worlds. Depending on the sample scope, each cycle may run over many weeks or months, and successive cycles may be separated by enough time and cognitive space to allow for effective reflection and detailed analysis.

Populations and samples

In an Interpretive study, the importance of characterizing a population usually incorporates at least three aims: first, to apprehend the patterned and idiosyncratic nature of social actors and the contexts in which they operate; secondly, to apprehend the politics, the practicalities and the processes that can be expected, initially at least, to shape the way the research may be structured, described, explained and permitted to proceed; thirdly, to prepare the researcher for the critical task of sampling, engaging, re-sampling and also verifying the substantive inputs and products of what can often be an evolving research design that must respond to emerging data and analyses. As a consequence, sampling is usually an evolving process. This is in stark contrast to the emphasis on unbiased 'representativeness' that is common when sampling in, for instance, the Neo-Positive paradigm.

Generating data

In Interpretive research, data are generated progressively. This starts with the original sample, and the central research questions, but evolves in response to emerging themes, gaps, dilemmas and apparent contradictions in the growing body of data and emergent analyses. It

Characteristic steps in the paradigm 119

is commonly the case that a variety of data sources, and the scope and depth of data needed, requires purposeful selection of data sources.

The processes of generating data remain largely the same as the body of data evolves. The only adjustments to the processes are refinements and subtleties that distinguish earlier and later ways of raising, exploring, drilling down, cross-checking and concluding data generation.

Common ways to assemble various classes of data include:

- primary open[12] interviews with participants and/or focus groups, and with those who have long and/or close relationships with, or knowledge of, a principal informant;
- primary documents, like activity or event logs, communication logs, personal diaries that participants keep, as well as the researcher's record of interaction with participants during their everyday lives and observations of participant activities, both systematic and opportunistic;
- secondary sources comprising reports from other than participants; and
- tertiary sources such as others' research reports.

These secondary and tertiary sources help to sensitize the researcher to substantive matters that can help stimulate, but not lead, participant disclosure and elaboration.

Analysing data: categorizing data from everyday typifications

Regardless of where the researcher is in the iterative cycles of data generation and analysis, the analytic task involves the same kind of activities: *producing everyday typifications* from data; *deriving abstracted categories* of everyday typifications; *developing abstracted types* that together enable a depth understanding of all or most data in terms of a few technically described caricatures; and *assessing conditional associations* between elements of different typologies in order to develop tentative theory to explain the regularity.

Analysis of data usually evolves with data generation and involves the following steps.

1 *Analytically formulate first-order abstract categories from everyday typifications.*
   The analytic task of constructing abstracted categories that still account for all units of data is a practical task of inductively

identifying and testing categories – each of which is defined in the language of the data – that are intended to represent a recognizable theme that is common to some everyday typifications.

2 *Analytically construct second-order abstracted types from the set of first-order abstract categories.*
When an interesting and comprehensive set of abstracted categories has been generated, the analytic task continues by abductively constructing types. This process involves de-constructing the first-order abstracted categories and their meanings to form a larger set of thematic elements. From this enlarged set, a more compact set of second-order types and their meanings is abductively generated.

3 *Analytically and imaginatively generate a theory to provide the understanding needed to answer a 'why' question.*
This process focuses on investigating associations and relationships between types, purposeful sub-samples, elements of the foundation regularity, as well as elements of the prime 'why' question(s).

It is useful to maintain groups of everyday typifications, which are in participants' language, and plausible corresponding first-order abstracted categories, which the researcher develops. These facilitate progressive verification and also illustrate the level of language that operates in this early part of analysis. This helps to anchor what is often a process that may continue for months. It should also be noted that regardless of where the researcher is in the cycles of data generation and analysis, the proximity of the researcher's language to participants' everyday language remains much the same. Only meanings may change as the researcher generates and becomes familiar with the meanings of the growing body of data.

Analysing data:
deconstructing meanings of categories and their typifications

A researcher will, from time to time, judge that a set of abstracted categories and their everyday typifications span a sufficiently large proportion of all data, and also appear to offer prospects for higher level abstraction, to enable the formation of overarching types.

The task of transforming a set of categories and component typifications into more abstract types involves further analysis followed by synthesis. The analysis involves deconstructing the meanings of categories and their constituent typifications into atomistic components of meanings. The synthetic task abductively recombines atomistic components of meanings in order to progressively reconstruct a more compact set of concepts.

Deconstructing participants' data is not about disclosing an underlying or privileged truth. Rather, it is about offering an alternative social construction (the researcher's) of reality that may, but not necessarily, lead to alternative meanings that participants and researcher find enable a more perceptive and nuanced understanding of the participants' social world than the meanings they commonly work with and initially or superficially convey. This process of higher-level abstraction is episodic. It combines craft and technical skills in the two main steps of analytic-deconstruction and abductive-reconstruction.

The products of a researcher's deconstruction may be checked with participants by exploring with them the extent to which the set of deconstructed component words for an abstracted category and its everyday typifications trigger recall or recognition of particular important aspects of commonplace, important and unusual phenomena or experiences in their social world. Increasingly, wide recall or recognition, followed by subtle elaboration, indicates stronger confirmation.

Synthesizing types: reconstructing types from components of meaning

The process of constructing types works mainly with the list of deconstructed meaning elements produced from analysis of first-order abstracted categories and their everyday typifications. However, the reconstructive process does not necessarily limit itself to component meanings associated only with one abstracted category at a time. While the researcher is free to group component meanings from across the list, in order to propose and test new concepts and their technical definitions, the aim is always to progressively construct more abstract yet also more compact meaning structures that collectively account for most if not all everyday meanings. The dominant logic of this principally creative process is abduction, although induction plays a part in testing the scope (i.e. breadth) of a constructed concept and its technical meaning, and deduction plays a part in testing the mapping of a technical meaning to a variety of related everyday meanings.

This step starts with the list of deconstructed meaning components from earlier analysis. By abductively linking subsets of components, according to plausible themes that may be inferred from the question or analytic hypothesis the researcher progressively produces, a more compact set of concepts and associated technical meanings can be produced which still account for participants' everyday, aggregate, intentional meanings and meanings in use.

The deconstruction and reconstruction processes (www.InfoServ.com.au) can be summarized as follows:

- types are produced by analytic deconstruction of everyday typifications and abstracted categories and then synthetic *abductive* reconstruction of the meaning components is used to form types;
- types are concepts with technical (i.e. social scientific) meanings that succinctly yet comprehensively describe features and roles within some important aspect of a social world;
- a typology is a collection of types – a taxonomic scheme – of one particular feature of the social world; and
- several typologies may be developed – each for a different yet possibly related feature of the social world.

From generating types to elaborating types to generating theory

In an Interpretive study, well-constructed typologies have three important attributes:

- they are compact;
- they provide clear technically based meanings; and
- they succinctly describe characteristics of a large class of data.

For these reasons, typologies not only provide descriptions but also enable a clear exchange of deeper understanding about the meanings with which social actors work. Hence, typologies answer 'what' questions but not 'why' questions. However, they can have theoretical potency, i.e. explanatory potential. Therefore, once several typologies have been produced, a researcher is in a position to start generating theory to answer a 'why' question.

Theory development is about proposing and testing discriminating insights about associations between elements that are typically subtypes of the typolog(y/ies) *vis-à-vis* elements of the regularity and the primary 'why' question. Because a theory should at least hold across the sample, the testing must be applied to each unit of an astutely selected sample to reduce the influence of likely confounding factors.

Typologies provide a ready starting point for examining the prevalence or absence of various combinations of types. Inquiring about patterns within and between typologies supports theorizing.

Characteristic steps in the paradigm

One way to do this is to develop and analyse collocation statistics such as *co-frequencies* and *co-occurrences* (Deese 1965; Smadja 1993; Bartsch 2004). Co-frequencies measure the prevalence of a language element (e.g. a type) in purposefully chosen sub-samples and co-occurrences measure the prevalence of combinations of language elements (e.g. types) across purposefully selected samples or their subsets.

This analytic process involves cycles of questioning, hypothesizing and testing as the researcher looks for strong or weak associations and surprising independence within and between types and purposeful sub-samples. The process benefits from deep familiarity with the growing body of details in participants' accounts. This familiarity, together with good working relationships with participants, and the worlds in which they operate, may tend to render this form of analysis a partly collaborative undertaking as pre-theoretical possibilities are explored and tested.

Summary of principles to help answer 'what' and 'why' questions in an Interpretive study

Interpretive analysis typically occurs in repeated cycles, each of which combines questioning, hypothesizing, testing, reconstructing – all under the guidance of the study's regularity of interest and the research questions. These cycles move through data, everyday typifications, abstracted categories, typologies and conditional associations between typologies. The results are increasingly compact descriptions of participants' static worlds. Interpretive theorizing is also an iterative process, but it concentrates on typologies, conditional associations between typologies and theory as narrative understanding and aims to establish a compact description of participants' dynamic worlds.

To answer a 'what' question, it is necessary to:

- identify everyday typifications and construct first-order abstracted categories that clump typifications according to common ideas;
- deconstruct each first-order abstracted category to expose its component meanings;
- look for an underlying purpose or focus that is common to as many deconstructed components as possible;
- abductively reconstruct a second-order social scientific-technical construct of these components, called a type; and
- group types that deal with a common idea to form a typology.

More than one typology may be constructed from all the categorized data, and these typologies provide answers to 'what' questions.

To answer a 'why' question, the researcher can start by focusing on an aspect of interest across the typologies. An examination of associations between types, and how they vary across the sample, or other purposeful samples or sub-samples, is undertaken. The aim is to identify strong and weak associations by using inferential theorizing to identify dynamics between typologies' objects of interests. When clear dynamics involving purposeful samples, and strong associations between types within these samples is confirmed, then the theory is confirmed.

And what about grounded theory?

Readers familiar with grounded theory (Glaser and Strauss 1967) will be aware of its techniques of 'open' and 'axial' coding (Strauss and Corbin 1998; Corbin and Strauss 2008) that are analogous to the use of deconstruction and reconstruction advocated here. However, the early variants (Glaser 1978, 1992, 2001; Strauss 1987) embody classical positivist assumptions about an independent, external social reality, unproblematic 'objective' data and a dominant *inductive* logic, and this is reinforced by software packages that are now available.

Although the more recent variant (Seale 1999; Charmaz 2000, 2005, 2006, 2007; Charmaz and Mitchell 2001; Clarke 2005; Bryant 2002) assumes a socially constructed reality, with data constructed or generated by researchers from social actors' accounts and their feedback, the dominant logic and techniques appear not to be consistent with these assumptions. For example, when textual data are coded into the researcher's categories, the techniques are top-down rather than genuinely bottom-up.

This raises the question of whether grounded theory is anything more than a collection of techniques that can be used with different ontological assumptions. It is certainly not a research paradigm in its own right, and the earlier versions do not sit easily in either our Neo-Positivist or Interpretive paradigms (see Blaikie 2010: 140–4 for a review and critique, and Ong 2012 for a comparison of grounded theory and our use of abductive logic in the Interpretive paradigm).

Summary

The principles of the Interpretive research paradigm provide a distinct contrast to those of the Neo-Positive paradigm. Interpretive research works with very different assumptions and logics of inquiry, with the result that the processes used to answer 'what' and 'why' research questions are totally different.

An important distinguishing characteristic of our version of the Interpretive paradigm is the focus on the nature, roles and generation of typologies as the core devices not only for analysing data but also for presenting the findings. The process of moving from everyday typifications to social scientific typifications (typologies) has been neglected in the literature. While some techniques developed in grounded theory can be used, the use of typologies requires more sophisticated and demanding methods.

In this chapter, we have attempted to systematize this process as a series of iterative cycles and their reflexive steps. It should be clear that particular attributes and skills are needed for this task. In the next chapter, we illustrate how this has been done in two research projects.

Review questions

We invite you to use the review questions in the Appendix not only to test your knowledge of the paradigms but to help stimulate the process of designing and conducting your own research.

Further reading

Becker, H. (1940). *American Sociological Review* 5(1): 40–66. Constructive typology in the social sciences. In spite of its relatively early publication date, his discussion of the differences between descriptive and explanatory social sciences, and the need for abstraction in the latter, is still very relevant. Becker presents a different view to Weber of the way typologies are developed.

Blaikie, N. (1993). *Approaches to Social Enquiry.* Cambridge: Polity. Chapters 2–4 provide a review and critique of Interpretivism, its antecedents and competitors.

Blaikie, N. (2007). *Approaches to Social Enquiry,* 2nd edn. Cambridge: Polity. Chapters 4–6 are later versions of the 1993 chapters above.

Giddens, A. (1976). *New Rules of Sociological Method.* London: Hutchinson.

Chapter 1 reviews Schütz's existential phenomenology and the related work of Garfinkel and Winch, as well as key contributors to hermeneutics and critical theory. The Conclusion sets out nine rules that express Giddens's ontological and epistemological assumptions.

Rex, J. (1974). *Sociology and the Demystification of the Modern World.* London: Routledge & Kegan Paul. Chapters 1–4. He follows Weber rather than Schütz, whose work he regarded as only a prolegomenon to sociology.

Schütz, A. (1970). Interpretive sociology, in H. R. Wagner (ed.), *Alfred Schütz on Phenomenology and Social Relations.* Chicago: University of Chicago Press. A useful overview based on extracts from a range of his writings. See also Schütz 1963a and 1963b, or 1964.

Weber, M. (1947). *The Theory of Social and Economic Organization.* New York: Free Press. Pp. 87–120 set out the key concepts in his interpretive sociology.

6
The Interpretive Research Paradigm in Action

Chapter summary

- The first part of the chapter presents a high-level illustration of Interpretive research into technology management practice.
- The second part presents a more in-depth illustration of an Interpretive study about leadership in natural disaster crises. This illustration focuses on:
  - questions raised by the chapter 4 Neo-Positive illustration of crisis leadership;
  - nuances of data generation and analysis in line with the Interpretive paradigm;
  - generating typologies to answer 'what' questions; and
  - typologies and forms of reasoning to generate theory to answer 'why' questions.

1 Technology Management

Introduction

The following illustration of the use of the Interpretive research paradigm is adapted from Priest (2000). It briefly illustrates one way to answer a 'what' question.

128 Interpretive Research Paradigm in Action

Road map for this illustration

The illustration is highlighted under the following sections:

- the phenomenon, problem and regularity;
- literature and questions;
- research design;
- population and sampling;
- generating and analysing the data;
- findings – a typology to help to answer a 'what' question; and
- conclusion.

The phenomenon, problem and regularity

Since the 1950s, the power-to-cost of computing and communications devices that enable business information systems (IS) has increased by a factor over one trillion (Nordhaus 2007).

This is reflected in the now ubiquitous nature of IS. Today, the annual level of investment worldwide by business and governments in new IS amounts to several trillion US dollars. This is on top of worldwide annual expenditures of trillions of dollars for support of already installed IS.

Paralleling this worldwide growth has been an approach to managing investments in such information systems (MIS) using knowledge and practice guided largely by methods that are positivist in nature. Managing the effectiveness of these financial outlays is clearly important for governments and businesses, as well as for those they represent or serve.

In 2000, Priest reported that, for the past fifty years, the annual effectiveness rate of investments in new and existing IS was stable at around 10:55:35 (10 per cent succeeded, 55 per cent were marginal and 35 per cent failed). Despite this poor investment performance, no model of management practice had been identified that was unique to successful investment performance or unique to failed investments.

This regularity, which was prima facie evidence for a gap in knowledge about effective management know-how, was the basis of this author's research.

Literature

Four classes of literature were reviewed as part of the study's preparation and throughout the study.

1 Emerging types of IS, their enabling technologies, their expected uses, risks and value and their associated management challenges.
2 MIS (including methodologies, practices, training, skills, recruiting and promotion criteria).
3 Extant MIS research – questions, paradigms, populations/samples, methodologies and methods and patterns of findings.
4 Research paradigms, methodologies, methods and practices used in management and organization research but not apparent in MIS research.

The aim of the literature reviews was to identify themes that were relevant to the regularity and primary research question, as well as identify opportunities and strategies for investigating and answering the research question.

The eventual design and conduct of the study was informed by the following themes that were identified from the various literatures.

1 In the early decades of commercial IS, managers were continually in 'catch-up' mode and were generally ill-prepared to deal with the challenges of new forms of business information systems.
2 In more recent decades, most management challenges associated with investments in established types of IS and their enabling technologies arose in relation to organization and business issues rather than technical matters.
3 An increasing trend over five decades was that the majority of MIS management challenges arose in relation to uncoordinated technical, business and management issues, with technical matters being the easiest to resolve.
4 Whether managing investment in new IS, or expenditure on existing IS, managers have focused much more, or even exclusively, on budget and time as the overriding measures of success, rather than risk and value.
5 Methods used by managers to guide the steps needed to define, acquire and install an IS assumed that it could be well described and sufficiently well understood by everyone involved in acquiring it and using it.

130   Interpretive Research Paradigm in Action

6 It was slowly being recognized that MIS had somehow to better coordinate business, organization and technology capabilities in order to deliver improved value outcomes, as well as reduce risks.
7 IS managers were mainly recruited, developed and rewarded for technology and business nous appropriate to the IS investment and least for their organization and non-technical management know-how.
8 Between 1960 and 2000, more than 95 per cent of MIS research was positivist, with the result that it mainly reported patterns in collective practice without discriminating practices unique to success or to failure. Over this period, less than 1 per cent of MIS research was Interpretive and none of the previous three decades of this Interpretive MIS research examined management practices that were unique to either successful or failed IS investments. Finally, less than 0.5 per cent of MIS research was conducted within any type of critical paradigm and none developed causal theories for MIS success or failure.

The literature review reinforced two key messages. First, an examination of MIS practice must at least account for business (B), organization (O) and technology (T) aspects of what has to be managed, as well as management (M) know-how itself. Secondly, a useful contribution to knowledge would be research that illuminated the nature of MIS practice that was either unique to IS success or failure.

Research questions

The core research questions that arose from the literature were.

Q. 1 *What* management knowledge and practice in persistently effective IS investments is different from management knowledge and practice in persistently problematic IS investments?
Q. 2 If there is management knowledge that is unique to effective IS investments, *why* is this the case?

Answering the 'what' question was achieved by constructing discriminating typologies of management concepts and practices. In the following pages we briefly illustrate the approach that was taken.

Answering the 'why' question is not examined here because the second Interpretive illustration will lead the reader step by step through this important process. For now, it is sufficient to note that the 'why' question was answered by investigating the varying strengths of association between the typologies' types or subtypes across the sample and across different sub-samples. This was in response to questions that arose as part of inferential theorizing about possible dynamics involving the objects to which the typologies referred. The process and results that emerged were the basis of a theory that answered the 'why' question.

Research design

The research approach was an Interpretivist case-based examination of management practice with a focus on the tacit experience-based know-how that managers accessed to do their work. The scope of inquiry covered business, organization and technology, as well as management challenges and practices related to risks and value associated with IS investments.

A purposive sample comprised persistently successful and persistently problematic IS investments within companies that were comparatively 'technologically advanced' and companies that were 'technologically basic'. This sample design deliberately involved polar extremes (Markus 1997) to reduce the influence of confounding factors that the literature suggested may affect management practice.

The overarching logic of the study was to compare and contrast abductively constructed typologies of management practice in order to see if there were subtypes that were unique to long-run successful IS investments and others that were unique to long-run problematic IS investments.

The population

The population relevant to this study comprised managers in major SMEs (small-to-medium-sized enterprises) who directly and significantly impacted the purpose, conduct and outcome (i.e. success or failure) of major IS investments in their companies. These people typically included managers and supervisors from their companies' technology and business departments, as well as managers from prime contractors and major subcontractors. A relevant IS investment was one that a company regarded as being of strategic or major operational importance.

The sample

The sample was constructed using criteria that were commonly referred to when predicting the chance of success or failure of a major IS investment. First, two industries with very different levels of technology sophistication and MIS experience and skills were selected – these were financial services and food manufacturing. Within each industry, two companies with similar prospects of success were chosen. Then, within each company, one surprisingly persistently successful (SPS) investment case and one surprisingly persistently problematic (SPP) investment case was selected. In the SPP investment case, there were unexpectedly chronic management problems. In the SPS case, major management difficulties were expected but few arose and those that did were, mostly, effectively dealt with. The two sample companies were polar extremes with respect to their IS-maturity intensity, technology focus and their rates for refreshing management experience. Also, each company's SPP and SPS cases occurred in very similar business contexts yet, between the two companies, the business contexts for the investment cases were polar extremes.

Forty-two managers were interviewed in depth and the majority on several occasions. Twenty-five of the managers participated regularly in progressive verification of emerging and penultimate findings. All four IS investment cases were well represented in the interview and verification cohorts.

Data generation

The Interpretivist paradigm and *abductive* logic was used to generate data, and analyse and validate emergent sociological theory. Iterations of high-level and low-level analysis followed the generation of thick descriptions of each manager's context, together with in-depth accounts of each manager's assessments, choices, actions and reflections.

Data generation and analysis occurred together in a repeated cycle. Managers' accounts of management practices within an investment case were typically drawn from in-depth interviews with CEOs, sponsors, division or plant managers and project managers. They were approached as 'elites' (Hertz and Imber 1995) with special steps being taken to ensure the researcher had a good grasp of the interview topic in order to facilitate interviews as informed conversations (Kvale 1996: 101; Brinkmann and Kvale 2015). In-depth interviews were preceded by extensive background data gathering that spanned likely salient issues about each investment case.

In-depth interviews were open ended and semi-structured and were recorded electronically in order to create a faithful account of the spoken text. The typical interview structure incorporated elements of funnelling and storytelling with refinements around narrative interviewing. To help elicit extensive and richly nuanced descriptions of specific situations, interviewees were invited to more thoroughly describe or explain ambiguities, inconsistencies, ambivalences, contradictions, dilemmas and paradoxes.

A wide variety of company, contract, project and personal documents were collected in order to help stimulate or cross-check interview data and analysis.

Data analysis

Data analysis occurred in co-constructed cycles of data generation and analysis. After a round of generating and analysing data, gaps and apparent contradictions that arose typically required further data gathering and analysis. By co-constructing and co-validating abstracted descriptions that helped understand the typicalities of reported managerial practice in very different situations, knowledge about what 'made the difference' between effective and ineffective investment management practice was developed.

The analytic task involved producing everyday typifications from managers' in-depth accounts; deriving abstracted categories of everyday typifications; developing abstracted types that enabled deep understanding of all or most data in terms of a few technically described caricatures; and assessing conditional associations between elements of different typologies in order to develop tentative theory to explain the regularity. The descriptions of types were enhanced by investigating, for instance, the prevalence of types of influences between more effective managers and managers who were less effective. The processes used in this type of analytic work are described and exemplified in the illustration that follows (pp. 143–51).

Analysis generated six typologies of focal issues that turned out to be essential to effective managerial practice. These typologies were about the nature of investment, investment outcome, functional people, shared meaning, braided-work and progressive adaptation. Together they were found to uniquely differentiate accounts of MIS practice in the two successful (SPS) cases from MIS practice in the two problematic (SPP) cases.

134   Interpretive Research Paradigm in Action

Because the term *braiding* is used in this book's later illustrations, a cameo illustration of the kinds of analysis that helped to generate the typology called braided-work is now outlined.

Analysis that led to the braided-work type

Managers reported many forms of work when describing what occupied their minds and the kinds of activities they attended to. Typifying and categorizing these forms of work generated twelve types of work. The researcher's labels and meanings for these twelve types are:

1 *PRODUCING* (a systematic approach to constructing a new product or outcome);
2 *INVENTING* (new initiatives that are novel and arise through creative effort);
3 *PROJECT* work (systematically repeating change or development through to 'adoption');
4 *CHANGE* (negotiating and adapting identities, roles, capabilities and social relationships);
5 *REPETITION* (a standardized and controlled recital – more of the same);
6 *REVISION* (amending in a creative rather than routine way to improve future instances);
7 *TECHNICAL* work (a formal and structured way to perform, inform or instruct);
8 *SOCIAL* work (a typically open and culturally adaptive way to explore or test);
9 *DOCUMENT* work (formal ways to record or inform);
10 *STORIES* (genres of informal dialogue with the aim of engaging or eliciting);
11 *ACTION* (putting intention into practice); and
12 *REFLECTION* (analytic retrospection about intention or practice).

The early analytic process of typifying and categorizing also identified each of these types of work as exhibiting two unexpected but interesting characteristics. First, each type of work was either 'left brain' or 'right brain' in nature. The kind of analytic work that identified this is illustrated in the next section. Six 'left-brain' types of work (types 1, 3, 5, 7, 9 and 11 above) were classified this way because they each typically exhibited and focused on systematic performance, predominantly exhibited attention to normative structure and routine and reflected persistent attention to specific and well-defined procedure. Six 'right-brain' types of work (types 2, 4, 6, 8, 10 and 12 above) were so classified because each type characteristically exhibited a frequent focus on unusual and surprising links and associations, followed by improvised and spontaneous action. Also, their approaches were commonly informal, adaptive and even creative or inventive.

Secondly, the twelve types of work formed natural pairs that were 'opposite in character' – one of a pair being 'left brain' and the other 'right brain' – but both having the same purpose. Table 6.1 below highlights these two features.

Analytic work that identified 'left-brain' and 'right-brain' types of work

Managers' in-depth interview accounts were scanned and coded according to the process outlined in the 'Characteristic steps of the paradigm' section of chapter 5 (pp. 116–24). The scope and detailed steps in the analytic cycles are simplified here in order to reinforce a process principle rather than provide the reader with a comprehensive illustration.

Table 6.1 Opposite types of work combined for a common purpose

'Left-brain' types of work	'Right-brain' types of work	Common purpose of the combined 'left-brain' and 'right-brain' forms of work
PRODUCING	*INVENTING*	INNOVATING – devise something significantly new
PROJECT	*CHANGE*	DEVELOPING – sensitive orderly adoption and use
REPETITION	*REVISION*	MANUFACTURING – repeated quality delivery
TECHNICAL	*SOCIAL*	COORDINATING – orderly responsive collaboration
DOCUMENTS	*STORIES*	KNOWING – comprehensive engaged awareness
ACTION	*REFLECTION*	LEARNING – reflexive and considered practice

136   Interpretive Research Paradigm in Action

Table 6.2 shows coding, then analytic notes, followed by the researcher's comments about their implications. Many extracts and corresponding iterations of coding and note making are typically needed to form and test pattern inferences before types and typologies start to emerge.

Table 6.2 comprises a top section and a bottom section. The top section presents two italicized extracts from interviews. For the purpose of the illustration, each extract includes superscripts with underlined text to highlight analytic notes. The superscript (a) and underlined words show elements of text that are indicative of what

Table 6.2 Illustration of coding that identified 'left-brain' and 'right-brain' types of work

Interview extract ↓

1. *The documents[a] we use to monitor project work have been standard for some time[a], like variations, time spent[a], hours to go,[b] problem report codes[a] and that sort of thing.*

2. *Creativity was essential for systems' new ideas [b]. . . . I think you'll find the people who keep coming up with the ideas [b] usually see things differently[b], just different ways to look at stuff[b], like (. . .) a bizarre[b] sense of humour[b], you'd think, why didn't I think of that[b].*

Analytical (interpretive) notes ↓

(a) A focus on concrete well-defined procedures or structured and codified 'objective' data. Here the focus is on unequivocal and clear-cut meanings, purpose and process.

   Further investigate: *This appears to be indicative of 'left-brain' work, but is it? How widespread is it? Are there particular patterns of expression – such as sub-samples of challenges, firms, managers and investments?*

(b) Unusual perspectives, processes or content are referred to in statements like 'see things differently', 'different ways to look at stuff' and 'bizarre sense of humour'. This is typical of 'right-brain' thinking where the focus is on irony, surprise and the unusual or even unexplained perspective that is commonly associated with creativity.

   Further investigate: *It appears that there are commonly activities that typically exhibit unusual and creative elements – somewhat 'right brain' in character. How widespread is this? In what types of situations does this arise? Is it uniformly expressed or associated with particular types of challenges, contexts, managers or investments?*

later emerged as 'left-brain' features of work. The superscript (b) and underlined words emphasize elements of the text that are indicative of what later emerged as 'right-brain' characteristics of work. The bottom section of Table 6.2 illustrates analytic interpretive notes. In this section, the block of text labelled (a) comes from elements of the idea category (a) noted in the representative interview extracts 1 and 2 in the table's top section. These (a) elements are followed by the researcher's tentative query about the possibility that these elements represent 'left-brain' work. Similarly, (b)-associated elements from the two representative interview extracts are interpreted with a concluding label and note from the researcher suggesting that they may represent 'right-brain' work. In the (a) and (b) text of this bottom section, underlined elements highlight meanings that are part of a possible definition of the concepts of 'left brain' and 'right brain' – an important dimension of the typology of work that the full study eventually generated and validated.

Deriving sociological constructs from the analytic notes

'Left-brain' work is typically reproducible and uses well-defined procedures with clear and agreed meaning. Forms of work that are of this type typically and predominantly reflect a formalized normative approach, systematic performance and a well-defined and ordered or highly structured conceptualization that reinforces a uniform approach or routine.

'Right-brain' forms of work are typically irreproducible, being creative, unstructured and improvised. The meanings of such work are harder to exchange yet commonplace when managing IS-investments. Forms of work of a 'right brain' type typically reflect an informal approach to cope with the unusual. Performance often involves creativity, improvisation, surprising associations and unexpected outcomes. Conceptualization is abstract and loosely defined, informal or even completely unstructured and spontaneous.

The reader should note that the actual study and the eventual product 'BOTM*line*™' (www.InfoServ.com.au) on which this brief illustration is based confirmed that a large majority of all the managers' accounts referred to types of work that were either 'left brain' or 'right brain' by nature.

As these two types of work are opposite in character, a question arose: Do 'opposite' types of work co-operate in some way and, if yes, then under what conditions and in what way?

In summary, we note that the study on which this illustration is based found, through associative analysis of subtypes and sub-samples as outlined in chapter 5 (pp. 119–24), that a particular form of cooperation of the six 'opposite' pairs of work types was a significant technical concept that clearly distinguished SPS investments from SPP investments. The researcher coined the term *braiding* to refer to this distinctive mechanism.

Findings: a typology to help answer the 'what' question

Only in well-managed and effective IS investments does one find the six pairs of 'opposite' work types that constitute the typology of work the researcher has called braided-work. The pairs and their common purpose are:

- Innovating (Producing + Inventing);
- Developing (Projects + Change);
- Manufacturing (Repetition + Revision);
- Coordinating (Technical + Social);
- Knowing (Documents + Stories); and
- Learning (Action + Reflection).

Generating and verifying the types of work helped to construct an answer for this illustration's question: '*What* management knowledge and practice in persistently effective IS investments is different from management knowledge and practice in persistently problematic IS-Investments?'

Conclusion

A conclusion to such a study would reasonably be expected to comment on: its strengths and weaknesses; suggestions for further research; constraints under which the findings may be used; important questions arising from the study; and suggestions and reasons for particular paradigm-based approaches to tackling these questions.

As this illustration was adapted in order to emphasize important characteristic aspects of the Interpretive paradigm in action, rather than report an entire study, it is not appropriate to offer this type of conclusion here.

Leaders' Experiences and Agency Effectiveness 139

2 First-Responder Leaders' Experiences and Perceived Effectiveness of Agency Response Effort

The Neo-Positive illustration in chapter 4 indicated one way to answer the question '*What* is the kind of leadership experience that can make a difference?' and '*Why* does this kind of experience help to make a difference to the outcomes that follow management of responses to the crisis?'

The illustration showed how a tentative explanation could be developed for the regularity that: 'Perceived "greater" effectiveness of first-responder efforts in dealing with emergencies is regularly associated with broader experience of those leading the first-responder efforts'. A 'maverick theory of leadership' was constructed as a potential explanation for the regularity. The conclusion of the Neo-Positive illustration was that 'broader leader experience matters'.

The following illustrative Interpretive study is an adaptation of the author's research (Priest and Sarne 2006; Priest 2008, 2009) into aspects of emergency-management leadership. It is a counter to the Neo-Positive illustration outlined in chapter 4. The early part of chapter 4 (pp. 80–4) provided the necessary background about bushfire emergencies, first-responder agencies and leaders' readiness and experience for sense making and decision making.

The linear structure of written reports about Interpretive research does not model their iterative and threaded character. Therefore, each of the following sections is introduced and summarized with signpost remarks to remind the reader about three aspects of the section:

1 the distinctive character of the research process relevant to that section;
2 the reflexive relationship between it and other sections; and
3 the research content discussed in the section as it relates to the overall research problem and research questions.

Comments on the overall process, and how the steps were conducted (i.e. *sensitizing, questioning, exploring, analysing, theorizing* and *checking*), are covered in the second part of chapter 5.

Road map for this illustration

This illustration of the Interpretive paradigm in action (www.InfoServ.com.au) is about generating data, analysing data, describing findings as typologies that answer 'what' questions, developing tentative social theory that attempts to answer 'why' questions and, finally, noting conclusions as well as suggesting directions for further research. It is discussed in the following sections and subheadings.

Study's focus and scope

- The phenomenon of interest, the particular problem and the regularity to be studied.
- Relevant literature and the study's 'what' and 'why' questions.
- Population and samples.
- Generating data in the early stages of the research.

Analysis and types

- Low-level analysis – categorize data from everyday typifications.
- High-level analysis – deconstruct meanings of categories and their typifications.
- Abstract analysis – synthesize types from components of meaning.

Analysis and understanding

- Extending a typology's meanings.
- Answering the 'what' question with more than one typology.

Analysis and theorizing

- Beyond understanding enabled by typologies.
- Theorizing and investigating typologies and their associations.
- Theory – developing an argument from results of investigations.

Findings – typology based answers and theory based answers.
Conclusion – a critique of the study, practice implications and further research.

Study's focus and scope

The phenomenon, the problem and the regularity For this illustration, the starting regularity is:

> In bushfire emergencies and crises, leaders with challenging lived experiences beyond formal agency experience are linked to more acceptable first-responder actions and outcomes than is the case with other

leaders who have similar formal agency experience but less broader lived experience.

Literature and questions Relevant literature and background have been noted in chapter 4. Interesting questions arise from this apparent regularity, for instance:

Q. 1 Under *what* conditions does this regularity hold or fail? And *why*?
Q. 2 In *what* other types of emergency situations does this regularity hold? And *why*?
Q. 3 *What* types of formal and also broader leadership experience are more or less helpful for leaders' reasoning in a crisis?
Q. 4 *Why* do the types of more helpful experience help to increase perceived first-responder effectiveness?

The last two questions are the bases for this chapter's illustration.

Because this study can be expected to explore matters involving trauma as well as crisis, it is appropriate that the researcher is particularly well prepared and this would include reviewing literature spanning:

- reports of pre-season assessments of Australian bushfire risk as well as community and agency response readiness;
- post-event reports from first-responder and support agencies, bushfire research centres and commissions of inquiry (Teague McLeod and Pascoe 2010a, 2010b); and
- social research practice when exploring people's accounts of living through traumatic crises and their aftermath.

Population and sampling The population for this illustration is defined within Australia's 2009 Black Saturday fires. Hundreds of first-responder leaders were involved and spanned all levels from the most senior at state coordination headquarters (the iECC), through middle-level coordination teams, to unit leaders on the many separate fire grounds.

Two bushfire emergencies reported to have been 'well handled' in the circumstances and two reported to have been 'poorly handled' in the circumstances were selected from nearly fifty of these major fires (see chapter 4, p. 82).

The sample comprises all leaders in all shifts for the duration of each fire, a total number of around two hundred. Refinement of the sample was achieved by selecting two 'well handled', and two 'poorly handled' bushfires that differ from each other in terms of major risk factors, such as terrain, fuel profile, local resources available for community response and community fire-response readiness.

Generating data in the early stages In this study, the data were generated progressively – evolving in response to emerging themes, gaps, dilemmas and apparent contradictions in the growing body of data and emergent analyses.

What significantly evolved through the many iterations of contextualizing, generating and analysing the growing body of existing and new data were ways of seeing and reading the data afresh; this aspect was a characteristically critical part of working in the Interpretive paradigm.

Within the selected sample, the experiences of leaders at all levels were explored from the following sources:

- primary open interviews with leaders and, later, focus groups with leaders and familiar[1] associates;
- primary documents, such as agency communication logs and personal diaries that some leaders keep, the researcher's observations of overall work flows, the researcher's interaction with leaders during training, and the researcher's opportunistic observation of various levels of leaders' work in other fire events;
- secondary sources comprising reports, such as agency self-assessments and court proceedings (e.g. coronial inquests); and
- tertiary sources, such as others' research reports.

The secondary and tertiary sources helped to sensitize the researcher to substantive matters that stimulated, but did not lead, leaders' disclosure and elaboration of their experiences.

Two rounds of interviewing for each sampled leader were conducted. Typically, the first interviews took place 4–9 weeks after the relevant fire had been officially declared as no longer active, and the second was 2–4 months after the first. Leaders at all levels within first-responder emergency agencies and community groups provided biographical data about their formal and informal lived experiences that they considered relevant to the role(s) that they adopted during the fire response.

Regardless of where the researcher was in the iterative cycles of data generation and analysis, the analytic task involved the same kind of activities:

Leaders' Experiences and Agency Effectiveness 143

- producing everyday typifications from data;
- deriving abstracted categories from everyday typifications;
- developing abstracted types that together enable a depth understanding of all or most data in terms of a few technically described caricatures; and
- assessing conditional associations between elements of different typologies in order to develop tentative theory to explain regularities in the problem domain.

Analysis and types

Low-level analysis – categorize everyday typifications constructed from the data This section illustrates the results of, first, producing everyday typifications from data and, second, abstracting categories from these everyday typifications. What follows are groups of everyday typifications (in participants' language) and plausible corresponding first-order abstracted categories. These typifications and abstracted categories illustrate the level of language that operates at this early part of analysis.

Reasoning was about what was happening when choosing and articulating role identity, sense making and decision making. Each numbered item below (1–6) is an abstracted category arrived at after considering which everyday typifications share a broad meaning. Each lettered statement – items (a)–(r) – is an example of an everyday typification of the two separate excerpts that follow it.

1. Setting The social and organization background in which the experience occurred.

(a) *Formal*: organization arrangements that are well defined and where 'fitting in' requires conformity.

> 'It was really bureaucratic – rules, procedures, hierarchy and politics in spades.'
> 'Everyone here has a role and a place – you gotta know the rules and where things fit.'

(b) *Informal*: social scenes that allowed a person considerable freedom to find their way and fit in.

> 'The clubs around here have one thing in common – they're easy going, few rules.'

'It's just a bunch of well-intentioned people trying to get jobs done – they just work it out.'

2. Ownership Perceived share of key aspects of experiences owned by 'others' or by the 'leader'.

(c) *Public*: situations in which others were largely responsible for dealing with the situation or challenge.

'I had been trained for this. Knew what to do. But they had to own it and not rely on us.'

'There's amazing skills out there and you're a mug if you ignore that – you'll not win.'

(d) *Shared*: the leader and others each took some responsibility and helped to deal with the situation.

'We worked with the locals. We had the gear and they sure were willing and able.'

'If you ride roughshod you'll be up against it. We learned to work together real fast.'

(e) *Personal*: the leader weighed up the situation and had others doing what was needed to deal with it.

'They just relied on me. I was the only one with a chance of working out what next.'

'She was a great team leader – you knew if she said do X not Y, then you just did it.'

3. Interest The sort of impressions that an aspect of a leader's lived experiences had on the leader.

(f) *Novel*: aspects of an experience that a leader saw as new and possibly beneficial.

'She was a gem – organized this social media thing and pulled resources from all over.'

'We were sold this fancy equipment but there's a lot of work to fix inter-operability.'

(g) *Expected*: aspects of an experience that a leader was not surprised about and could even anticipate.

Leaders' Experiences and Agency Effectiveness 145

'You can read all the manuals you like but its havin' the foresight like we did that time.'

'The chief was very good at reading the signs and he'd just take it by the throat.'

(h) *Unsettling*: some aspects of an experience that disturbed or unsettled what the leader relied on.

'Police had an overall coordinating role but they only talked to the top echelon, the *fog*.'[2]

'The local coordination centre set-up was a disaster as their training was only basic.'

(i) *Affirming*: elements of the experience that reinforced or emphasized things the leader still relies on.

'Even in very stressful situations some things never change like "stop and think".'

'Every time we're up against it we say "get real, get focused, get going" and it works.'

4. Depth How the fundamental or ordinary were particular lessons that leaders drew from their experiences.

(j) *Fundamental*: things that are not normally questioned or even noticed and are just taken for granted.

'It made you think about why you're on the planet – like who else cares about you?'

'It's only when you're like a fish out of water that you get to realize you ain't got a clue.'

(k) *Everyday*: day-to-day functional capabilities that involved procedures, skills, rules of thumb and focus.

'There was training and procedures and the rest you just worked out as it all blew up.'

'It's like map reading – you have to learn to read the signs when the pressure's on.'

5. Use The levels of usefulness that leaders attributed to their take-outs from their lived experiences.

(l) *Adopt*: about having identified some aspect of an experience that needs to be borrowed and used later.

'Some of the lessons we've learned are tops and I want to push that in our unit.'

'I watched the way they coordinated their preparations – we have to learn from that.'

(m) *Park*: about aspects of an experience that may be useful but adopting it is challenging so it's on hold.

'Really interesting techniques were on show but we have to think how we'd do it here.'

'It's a great idea but to trial it back home is pricey so we still have homework to do.'

(n) *Reject*: aspects of an experience that were seen as never-to-be repeated or trivial, or even repugnant in the sense of being career limiting, ethically dubious, morally offensive and/or totally impractical.

'We just couldn't even agree to disagree. For me it was an immoral policy.'

'I said no. It was a great idea in theory but definitely a career-limiting move so it was "think again".'

6. Know-how The sorts of lessons leaders drew from their lived experiences.

(o) *Choice*: bases for choosing[3] or applying particular behaviours, knowledge or skills to suit a situation.

'For problems like this, Jay's checklist rules really helped sort the wheat from the chaff.'

'You just had to know when to let go and listen to the locals and their priorities.'

(p) *Behaviour*: expressing, relating, engaging, coping, ignoring, relaxing and practising.

'Each team member was under pressure and it was a real skill to keep them focused.'

'Meeting with angry people was challenging but he had the knack and it worked.'

Leaders' Experiences and Agency Effectiveness   147

(q) *Thinking*: aspects from an experience that highlight types of knowledge, heuristics and such like.

'When there's stuff coming from all sides I found the diamond idea helps you think.'
'She shared some great stories about judging just how far she could push up the line.'

(r) *Skills*: experiences that include performance abilities (competencies) in selecting, behaving and thinking.

'We spent a long time talking with him about what he did to make sense of all this data.'
'She had this ability to explain the politics and the people and how to work them.'

Higher-level analysis – deconstruct meanings of categories and their typifications The researcher eventually judges that a set of abstracted categories and their everyday typifications span a sufficiently large proportion of all data, and also appear to offer prospects for higher-level abstraction to form overarching 'categories' or types. The task of transforming a set of categories and component typifications into types involves further analysis followed by synthesis.

Table 6.3 shows a possible deconstruction of the abstracted categories outlined in the previous section. The reader will see that each row of the table comprises an everyday typification in the left-hand column and keywords in the right-hand column that reflect the interpreted meaning of the everyday typification and the abstracted category of which it is a part.

This step starts with the list of deconstructed meaning components and, by abductively linking subsets of components according to plausible themes, the researcher progressively produces a more compact set of concepts, and associated technical meanings, that still account for participants' everyday meanings.

Abstract analysis – synthesize types from components of meaning Table 6.4 shows a possible *abductive* reconstruction of tentative types. Short labels and meanings of the four constructed types appear in the left-hand column. The lower case words in the right-hand column correspond to meanings of component words in the right-hand column of Table 6.3. In this way, it is possible to trace the progress of the deconstructive and reconstructive task. The right-hand column

148   Interpretive Research Paradigm in Action

Table 6.3 Deconstruction of abstracted categories and their everyday typifications of experience-based influences on leaders' repertoire

Everyday typification	→	Deconstructed components of everyday typification
a) Formal setting	→	Politics; Authority; Structure; Compliance
b) Informal setting	→	Buy-in; Ownership; Acceptance
c) Public ownership	→	Needs; Ownership; Buy-in; Stakeholders
d) Shared ownership	→	Situational fit; Priorities; Buy-in; Stakeholders
e) Personal ownership	→	Needs; Competence; Permission
f) Novel interest	→	Value; Interests; Needs; Suitability
g) Expected interest	→	Verification; Situational relevance; Practised
h) Unsettling interest	→	Risk? Value? Needs? Competence?
i) Affirming interest	→	Verification; Reliability
j) Fundamental depth	→	Perspective; Insight; Time and place
k) Everyday depth	→	Wide use; Acceptable; Reliability
l) Adopt use	→	Reliability; Situational fit; Availability
m) Park use	→	Risk? Value? Defendable?
n) Reject use	→	Risk? Value? Defendable? Politics? Authority?
o) Choice know-how	→	Holistic; Context; Time and place; Justified; Defendable
p) Behaviour know-how	→	Context; Informing; Defendable; Politics
q) Thinking know-how	→	Context; Informing; Authority; Defendable
r) Skills know-how	→	Context; Informing; Competence

in Table 6.4 also shows some structuring by the researcher using labels in upper case; these are the researcher's choice and highlight an attempt to thematically regroup component words into new and more compact yet comprehensive meaning structures.

The short descriptions of the four types in the left-hand column of Table 6.4 are not sufficiently nuanced or qualified to permit an insightful understanding of the part that experiential influence plays within the regularity being studied. One step that is still

Table 6.4 Typology of experience-based influences on leaders' repertoire as a result of abductively constructing types from components of meaning

Reconstructed second-order TYPES of experiential influence ←	Reconstruction of second-order components that serve the following repertoire purposes: *PRIME FOCUS (source well – situations, stakeholders, needs, outcomes)* *CONTENT (maintain well – relevant resources at high competence)* *CHOICE (deploy well – perspectives, criteria, justification, suitability)* . . . plus . . . .
'POLITICAL' Influences on what a leader believes will be of relevance to organization units and key people who the leader works with. Included in this type are influences the leader sees as relevant to the leader's development or reputation.	PRIME FOCUS: Politics; ← authority; ownership; buy-in; acceptance. CONTENT FOCUS: Interests; needs; priorities; value; stakeholders. CHOICE FOCUS: Context; usefulness; reliability.
'SITUATIONAL' These are influences that a leader seeks out, examines, qualifies and chooses to attend to because of their impact on the leader's aim of broadening his/her repertoire or range of work.	PRIME FOCUS: Situation fit; ← needs; priorities; usability; time & place. CONTENT: Adds valuable resources; wide use; acceptable source. CHOICE: Valuable; serves needs & interests; on good authority.
'AFFIRMING' Influences that a leader sees as reinforcing existing content, attitudes, outlooks, behaviours, know-how and skills of the leader's repertoire.	PRIME FOCUS: Situational ← relevance; deployable; low risk. CONTENT: Insight; know-how; skill; authority; verification. CHOICE: Justified; reliable, contextually informed, competent.
'ADAPTIVE' Influences that shape a leader's particular choice of repertoire (i.e. reasoning about role identity, sense making, decision making, directing action) to better match a particular situation.	PRIME FOCUS: Place in ← perspective; right tools for the job; holistic. CONTENT: Practised; reliable; flexible; accessible; explainable. CHOICE: Suitable; dependable; available; defendable.

needed is to elaborate a technical description of each type. The four points below, while still brief, indicate that informative elaboration starts by including conditions and associations as well as clearer definitions.

1 POLITICAL influences on a leader's beliefs are about what will be relevant to the organizations, organization units and key people with whom the leader operates. Such influences may even be attended to because of the potential or actual benefit or risk to a leader's own values, career or reputation. These types of influences affect the relationships, networks and affiliations that a leader cultivates or overlooks and are often mediating factors on operational role identity, sense making and decision making.
2 SITUATIONAL influences on a leader affect what a leader seeks out, examines, qualifies and chooses to take on or modify with the aim of enhancing the leader's repertoire and so extending the leader's ability to effectively cope with a wider variety of everyday but also demanding situations. Such influences are sought out, recognized or responded to because of the contextual challenge or opportunity they represent to a leader. These types of influences on a leader are about what the leader sees as a need for opportunity for more variety or growth in repertoire and actual work.
3 AFFIRMING influences reinforce and clarify the bounds as well as content of a leader's attitudes, outlooks, ways of seeing situations, behaviour, know-how and skills that comprise the leader's repertoire. This type of *experiential influence* on a leader also underpins a leader's choice to withdraw or withhold. Hence, influences of this type may also operate to limit a leader's ability or potential to effectively deal with atypical or radically unfamiliar situations or, with what the leader notices when extending or limiting application of his/her repertoire.
4 ADAPTIVE influences are those influences that shape a leader's particular choice of repertoire for particular situations. This is about the range and forms of influence that a leader attends to when choosing or changing particular role identities, ways of sense making and decision making. These types of influences are very much about shaping the leader's view of reality and what the leader judges is best for the situation.

The POLITICAL and SITUATIONAL types of experiential influences share a focus on external realities in as much as the implications of predominant influences are interpreted and actioned in order to produce a result *beyond* the leader (e.g. for powerful others or for other situational needs). The AFFIRMING and ADAPTIVE types of experiential influences share a focus on internal realities where predominant influences are interpreted and actioned in order to produce a result *for* the leader (e.g. stay out of trouble; conduct oneself more effectively).

Analysis and understanding

Extending a typology's meanings The initial four-element typology outlined above goes some way to answering the study's 'what' question about a leader's experience and a leader's reasoning as it relates to their role identities, sense making, decision making and action directives in an emergency situation. However, as the above descriptions of the four types do not distinguish between influences and exhibited responses in 'well-handled' or 'poorly handled' agency responses, the descriptions invite further development.

An approach that may help here involves co-frequency or co-occurrence analysis of participants' accounts. In this form of analysis, the strength of associations between types and sample subsets are examined. Co-frequency analysis determines and interprets the comparative occurrence of a phrase or idea between different bodies of text. Co-occurrence analysis examines the prevalence of two (or more) words, phrases, ideas or concepts occurring together within a body of text(s).

The nature of results that may be obtained as a consequence of such analysis appears in Tables 6.5 and 6.6. These two tables exemplify the form of findings that were actually produced in similar studies (Priest and Trayner 2004; Priest 2002, 2008, 2009; Priest and Sarne 2006).

The cells of Table 6.5 show the results of using co-frequency analysis. By comparing similarities and differences between the cells of Table 6.5, two notable features are evident: (1) affirming-type influences manifest to the same extent in 'well-handled' and 'poorly handled cases'. Situational-type influences are slightly more apparent in cases that are 'well-handled' compared to those that are 'poorly handled'; (2) political- and adaptive-type influences are opposite in the extent to which they manifest in 'well-handled' and 'poorly handled' cases.

This analysis suggests that leaders of the 'well-handled' cases are more oriented to a fit between repertoire and situation, whereas

152   Interpretive Research Paradigm in Action

Table 6.5 Co-frequency of types of experiential influences referred to by leaders of 'well-handled' and 'poorly handled' responses to bushfire emergencies

Type of experiential influence	Leaders of 'well-handled' bushfire emergencies	Leaders of 'poorly handled' bushfire emergencies
POLITICAL	Low	High
SITUATIONAL	High	Med
AFFIRMING	Med	Med
ADAPTIVE	High	Low

leaders of the 'poorly handled' cases are more oriented to ensuring political fit, while having low attention to influences on the situational fit of their applied repertoires.

Further analysing the prevalence of combinations of types across sub-samples is helped by using co-occurrence analysis. Table 6.6 shows the results of a co-occurrence analysis of combinations of influence-types as manifest in the sub-samples of the 'well-handled' and 'poorly handled' bushfire emergencies.

In Table 6.6, one reads each row to discern how a particular leader orientation (e.g. SITUATIONAL-ADAPTIVE) is typically expressed in 'well-handled' cases compared to 'poorly handled' cases, and the corresponding right-hand column entry indicates stakeholders' predominant perception of such leaders' orientation (e.g. well-balanced).

When comparing similarities and differences between 'well-handled' and 'poorly' handled cases, Table 6.6 exhibits three notable features.

1. Co-occurrences of POLITICAL-ADAPTIVE influences as well as SITUATIONAL-ADAPTIVE influences exhibit markedly different expression between the 'well-handled' and 'poorly handled' cases.
2. SITUATIONAL-AFFIRMING and AFFIRMING-ADAPTIVE co-occurrences are both strongly expressed in the 'well-handled' cases and less so in the 'poorly handled' cases.
3. POLITICAL-SITUATIONAL co-occurrence is more strongly expressed in the 'well-handled' cases compared to 'poorly handled' cases, and POLITICAL-AFFIRMING only somewhat in the 'poorly handled' cases.

Table 6.6 Co-occurrence of types of influences that are most distinct or most similar across 'well-handled' and 'poorly handled' responses to bushfire emergencies

Combined type of experiential-influence	Leaders of 'well-handled' emergency responses	Leaders of 'poorly handled' emergency responses	Stakeholders' perception* of how a leader regards the type of combined influence
POLITICAL + SITUATIONAL	Med	Low	Well intentioned
POLITICAL + AFFIRMING	Low	Med	Well directed
POLITICAL + ADAPTIVE	Low	High	Well regarded
SITUATIONAL + AFFIRMING	High	Med	Well suited
SITUATIONAL + ADAPTIVE	High	Low	Well balanced
AFFIRMING + ADAPTIVE	High	Med	Well prepared

*The predominant stakeholder perception applies if, and only if, the co-occurrence is Med or higher.

From this illustration, it is evident that co-analysis can help to add meaning to typologies. In this case, the four-part typology noted in Table 6.4, and the somewhat enhanced definitions of the four types of influence arising from it, are a result of this kind of analysis and the information that arises from it.

This emergent four-element typology helps to answer the question: '*What* types of experiences influence a leader's reasoning about the role identities, sense making, decision making and action directives they exhibit while responding to an emergency situation?' However, the typology does not offer any distinctions between such influences and exhibited responses in 'well-handled' or 'poorly handled' agency responses. The analysis does, however, suggest the need to develop a new typology about, for instance, leaders' orientations to repertoire that manifest as what they attend to when assuming particular role identities and operating in particular sense making, decision making and action modes.

The final section of this illustration presents this new typology and then goes on to illustrate how this helps in the development of a theory to answer the question: '*Why* are there more or less effective types of leader responses?'

Answering the 'what' question with more than one typology

Here are examples of questions that may direct further inquiry and analysis.

1 *What* do leaders refer to when accounting for their repertoire preferences during crises compared to routine emergency responses?
2 At *what* time is a leader's response to a critical emergency considered to be most/least effective?
3 *What* is the difference between an institutionally acceptable repertoire and a situationally appropriate repertoire?
4 At *what* time, and *why*, are effective types of leader responses to critical emergencies different to responses in routine emergencies?

These kinds of questions usually trigger further sampling, data generation and analysis. The second typology below, of leaders' orientations to repertoire, arose from these kinds of questions. This is typical of the cycles of questioning, designing and answering when using the Interpretive paradigm.

The typology below describes *leaders' orientations* to choosing and expressing role identities, sense making, decision making and action directives during responses to critical emergency situations. This second typology helps to answer the question: '*What* types of leader responses are more associated with 'well-handled' agency responses compared to 'poorly handled' responses?'

This second typology comprises six caricatures. These six types reflect differences in a leader's orientations that are linked to experiential influences. For each of the caricatures, there is a distinctive orientation that manifests as a different focus in role identity, sense making, decision making and action directives.

1 The BUREAUCRAT acts in an orderly way to protect the organization's identity by using administrative tools as authorities, sanctions and rewards. Organization life is of central importance, and the task is to work diligently and reliably to reinforce the organization's higher purpose, traditions and right to continue being. Seniority is a privileged position to be respected and deferred to. Advice from recognized certified experts carries more weight than advice from unrecognized, albeit more widely experienced,

people. Compliance with systems, policies, rules, procedures and standards is the key to dependable and timely sense making, decision making and action.
2 The POLITICIAN's role is to keep a clear focus on where authority and power is located because, 'at the end of the day', what matters is having a mandate to do what needs to be done. Retaining the attention of the right people, building a reputation for winning, and retaining support or trust is what is needed to get jobs done. Avoiding surprises, scandal and blame requires constant watching. The success of roles, sense making and decision making relies on one's reputation, relationships, engaging and empathizing, widespread and high-level situational awareness, advice on priorities and doability and being able to communicate the right messages via the right channels at the right time and place.
3 The SURVIVOR is always alert to opportunities to advantage his/her career while also benefiting from the reputation, resources or other benefits of his/her closely affiliated professional, volunteer or social units. Awareness, investigations, choices and priorities that determine activities that the leader initiates or becomes involved with typically appear to incorporate some measures that help to protect or advance needs and interests with which the leader identifies. Attention to sources of risk translates into strategies that enhance survival and promotion or protect no-fault reputation. Communications commonly ensure that bosses are kept apprised of choices and achievements that meet important organization or community criteria.
4 The INNOVATOR is known for being the creative but practical problem solver. This manifests as momentary, regular and long-term creative responsiveness that usually provides valued outcomes for well-identified stakeholders. The Innovator is stimulated by significant needs that arise in any setting; high-profile settings may be overlooked in favour of greater needs that are associated with low-profile stakeholders. Quickly and collaboratively developing practical steps is what receives and retains attention and energy. Others commonly experience an Innovator type of orientation as refreshing if new approaches are needed, but puzzling or even frustrating if a committed plan with clear and unchanging actions and outcomes is needed.
5 The MAVERICK type is driven by a long-term vision and the ability to see a new situation in all its detail, much of which is usually far removed from the present situation. The ability to envision a distinctive future that may be very different from the present is

complemented by a clear sense of the major achievements, practical steps, resources and participant roles that together form a doable pathway in the face of serious uncertainty, change and even opposition. The abilities to motivate, excite, encourage, negotiate and drive people, as well as beg, borrow or otherwise acquire resources and adapt to surprises, are all characteristic of the maverick.

6 The CHIEF is, for some, the epitome of the ideal crisis leader, having a commanding grasp of the overall situation and situation detail, a clear decisive and practical action focus, an empathic and engaging communication style, excellent resource network, pertinent hands-on experience and an ability to relate to, and influence, people at all levels. These perceived qualities are satisfactory if, and only if, those who are relying on these leadership skills are themselves unable to improve on the leader's sense making, decision making and action directives, and the consequences of the leader's qualities-in-action deliver the solution hoped for by the team and other stakeholders.

The BUREAUCRAT-, POLITICIAN- and SURVIVOR-type orientations are associated mainly with strong institutional influences. These influences are typical of routine aspects of employer and industry work and training, emergency-based field experience with natural disasters and formal education-and-training courses that are run by registered training providers. The latter three (INNOVATOR, MAVERICK and CHIEF) are associated with influences that reflect not only institutional but strong non-institutional origins, such as community activities, as well as family and personal-interest activities that are unusual and memorable (e.g. lengthy or demanding travel adventures in geographically and ethnically unfamiliar settings; life-changing events or episodes at a family or personal level).

Notwithstanding the common approach to describe typologies in a narrative style, a graphic or tabular style may sometimes help the researcher to identify common or discriminating patterns between types from one or several typologies. Discovering such patterns may then trigger further productive investigations.

An example of this format is shown in Table 6.7. This table summarizes answers to two questions that are directly related to the purpose of the study.

1 *What* does each type of leader orientation most attend to when expressing role identity, sense making, decision making and action directives?

Leaders' Experiences and Agency Effectiveness 157

2 *What* resources does each type of leader draw on when expressing role identity, sense making, decision making and action directives?

Both questions may be answered by coding and analysing co-frequencies of types of attention and types of resources associated with each type of leader orientation.

In Table 6.7, the labels in the left-hand column under the words 'Attention' and 'Resources' stand for aspects that the 'what' research question is concerned with in relation to the types (i.e. leader orientations) that are being elaborated. Each cell entry expresses the dominant or persistent character of each aspect of each type. For example, typical of a BUREAUCRAT-type orientation is a strong and frequent attention to *covering risk* when *directing* actions and, typical of an INNOVATOR-type is a dominant concern for *evidence* when wanting to make *sense* of a new situation.

The three examples below indicate how entries in the upper part of Table 6.7 may be read.

- A BUREAUCRAT type, when SENSING what is going on, will commonly include *compliance* matters.
- A SURVIVOR type, when DECIDING an important matter, will give prominence to approved *criteria*.
- A CHIEF, when DIRECTING action, will usually ensure that *empathy* is a strong part of the message.

Entries in the lower part of Table 6.7 may be read in the same way. The following are examples.

- A POLITICIAN, when THINKING about a challenge, is often concerned about *influencer*'s reactions.
- An INNOVATOR usually initiates ACTION only after *linking* players considered essential to success.
- A MAVERICK will often BEHAVE in ways that *excite* people whose contributions are needed.

Tables help the researcher succinctly present dominant aspects of types as they relate to elements of a regularity or a key research question. But this is not their only use; they may help to identify themes that are shared by some facets of some types. For instance, the meanings of word groups in the cells suggest that the BUREAUCRAT, POLITICIAN and SURVIVOR types exhibit a

Table 6.7 Signature characteristics of types of leader orientation

Attention	BUREAUCRAT	POLITICIAN	SURVIVOR	INNOVATOR	MAVERICK	CHIEF
	Signature attributes of the six types of leader orientation					
IDENTITY and its FOCUS	Direct attention to selected policies	Build profile by & with authority	Secure reputation by exploiting opportunity	Facilitate imagining to close needs gaps	Develop vision to transform ideas	Get real & pragmatic about fixing situations
DATA focus	Structured	Short term	Selective	Strategic	Holistic	Situation
SENSE via	Compliance	Opinion	Risk	Evidence	Value	Resources
DECIDE via	Expertise	Buy-in	Criteria	Consult	Long-term	Priorities
DIRECTING	Cover risks	Reputation	Responsibility	Get buy-in	Persuade	Empathize
PROGRESS	Justify	Benefit	Convenience	Value	Strategic	Operational
OUTCOMES	Protecting	Winning	Surviving	Benefitting	Building	Solving
Resources	Signature resourcing attributes of the six types of leader orientation					
SELECT for	Compliance	Approval	Safety	Value	Future	Solution
THINK with	Regulators	Influencers	Bosses	Researchers	Community	Team
BEHAVE by	Auditing	Engaging	Hide–Shine	Investigating	Exciting	Appealing
ACTION via	Announcing	Lobbying	Frame–Name	Linking	Showing	Driving

predisposition towards satisfying or responding to an (assumed) institutional requirement, whereas several word groups in the cells for the INNOVATOR, MAVERICK and CHIEF types exhibit a communal predisposition that is beyond institutional control. This institutional/communal distinction will be referred to again in the final section of this illustration, where theory construction is discussed.

So far, we have illustrated the development of two different typologies. Each is focused on a particular aspect of the research problem:

- types of *experiential influences* on the resources and repertoires that leaders develop; and
- types of *personal orientations* that leaders exhibit when responding to an emergency situation.

Both these typologies help to answer 'what' questions, and so enable a potentially richer and more insightful understanding of aspects of the research problem. However, understanding is not the same as explanation. In Interpretive research, while better understanding comes from well-answered 'what' questions, helpful explanation comes from well-answered 'why' questions.

Analysis and theorizing

Beyond understanding enabled by typologies Of the two typologies developed so far, that of leader orientation to repertoire is, prima facie, theoretically more potent than that of experience-based influences on leader repertoires. There are two reason for this: (1) the former types are richer in aspects that relate directly to cognitive and behavioural conduct during emergency response activity; and (2) leaders' orientations to repertoire (as opposed to lifelong *experiential influences*) are more directly associated with either a 'well-handled' or a 'poorly handled' emergency response because of the single incident and shift basis on which most leaders are assigned to a particular emergency.

For this reason, the next part of the illustration will focus on the typology of leader orientation to show that descriptions of individual types, and subsets of types, can be enriched by examining associations between types and sample subsets from which the data were generated.

Analysis of associations within and between typologies may lead to a theory that answers 'why' questions about the regularity being studied.

160   Interpretive Research Paradigm in Action

Theorizing and investigating typologies and their associations   In this section, we present the results of testing associations: first, between types of orientations and response outcomes; and second, between combinations of experiential influences and repertoire orientations, on the one hand, and case outcomes on the other.

Identifying strong and weak associations helps to devise a theory to explain 'why' the regularity identified at the start of the research exists. Table 6.8 shows results of a co-frequency analysis that compares the prevalence of types of leader orientations in 'well-handled' or 'poorly handled' bushfire emergencies. As with the previous tables' cell entries, words are used to represent the prevalence of types across sample subsets, although numbers[4] could also be used.

By contrasting the prevalence of each type between 'well-handled' and 'poorly handled' cases, it is clear that the leader orientations that most strongly separate the two groups of cases are the CHIEF and INNOVATOR types, which are prominent in the 'well-handled' cases, and the POLITICIAN and BUREAUCRAT types, which are most clearly associated with the 'poorly handled' cases. The SURVIVOR and MAVERICK types are not clearly associated with either of the case groups. Further purposive sampling, and perhaps also different types of data, may be needed to more clearly place each of these two types closer to one or other of the response outcomes.

Several interesting questions can be posed as a result of this analysis. For instance: to 'what' extent is there a strong association between types of experiential influences and leader orientations, on the one hand, and either 'well-handled' or 'poorly handled' response outcomes on the other? One way to answer this question is

Table 6.8   Co-frequencies of leader orientations in 'well-handled' and 'poorly handled' responses

Type of influence	Prevalence of leader orientations in 'well-handled' emergency responses	Prevalence of leader orientations in 'poorly handled' emergency responses
Bureaucrat	Very Low	Med
Politician	Low	High
Survivor	Low	Med-High
Innovator	High	Low
Maverick	Med	High
Chief	Very High	Low

Table 6.9 Co-occurrences of experiential influences and leader orientations in cases of 'well-handled' and 'poorly handled' responses

Combined types: Experiential-Influence AND Leader-Orientation	Prevalence of leader orientations in 'well-handled' emergency responses	Prevalence of leader orientations in 'poorly handled' emergency responses
Political-Chief	Low	High
Political-Innovator	Med	Med
Political-Politician	Very Low	High
Political-Bureaucrat	Med	Med
Adaptive-Chief	High	Low
Adaptive-Innovator	Med	Med
Adaptive-Politician	Med	High
Adaptive-Bureaucrat	Low	Med

to examine co-occurrences between combinations of types and one or other form of outcome. Table 6.9 shows these combinations in the left-hand column and the results[5] of the co-occurrence analysis in the remaining two columns.

The results of this co-occurrence analysis suggest that, for the purpose of discriminating between 'well-handled' and 'poorly handled' cases, the most discriminating combinations of types are: for 'well-handled cases', the presence of ADAPTIVE-CHIEF and the absence of POLITICAL-CHIEF and ADAPTIVE-BUREAUCRAT; and, for 'poorly handled' cases, the presence of POLITICAL-CHIEF, POLITICAL-POLITICIAN and ADAPTIVE-POLITICIAN, and the absence of ADAPTIVE-CHIEF.

The final step in this illustration is about the development of a tentative theory to answer the question: '*Why* are there more or less effective types of leader responses?'

Theory development is about proposing and testing discriminating insights about associations between subtypes of the typology or typologies *vis-à-vis* elements of the regularity and/or the primary 'why' question. And, because a theory should at least hold across the sample, the testing must be applied to each unit of the sample.

In this illustrated study, leaders' orientations were examined across different sub-samples, including each of the 'well-handled' and 'poorly handled' bushfire emergencies. Some results of initial steps in this direction were presented in the previous sections. Table 6.10

extends the findings of such an examination with co-frequencies for *each* of the four sample cases whose profiles are noted below.

Case 1: A 'well-handled' response by local and interstate teams to a major bushfire in rugged terrain and needing air-support and Remote Area Fire-fighting Teams (RAFTs[6]). The bushfire threatened critical infrastructure. Leaders sampled = 23.

Case 2: A 'well-handled' response by interstate and overseas teams covering open terrain with less than requested resources, following failed fire support infrastructure. The major bushfire threatened small communities. Leaders sampled = 20.

Case 3: A 'poorly handled' response by agency volunteer teams and interstate support teams to a major bushfire in heavily timbered terrain. There was good road access and ground resources but only patchy communications and no air-support. The major bushfire threatened timber mills, water infrastructure and communities with significant historic and cultural sites. Leaders sampled = 19.

Case 4: A 'poorly handled' response by local volunteer agency and community response teams to a major bushfire covering light forest, farmland and wheat silos. The bushfire threatened critical rail, road and bridge infrastructure, small communities and important cultural sites. Leaders sampled = 17.

Profiles of Cases 1 and 2 differ strongly with respect to confounding factors, such as terrain, essential infrastructure and familiarity of firefighting teams with local conditions and each other's resource systems and practices. These factors would normally be expected to significantly challenge leaders responsible for overall response effectiveness. Similarly, the profiles of Cases 3 and 4 strongly differed. For these reasons, the researcher could infer that if certain types are strongly (or weakly) associated with the two 'well-handled' cases, but weakly (or strongly) associated with the two 'poorly handled' cases, then the reason for this is less likely to be associated with any of the confounding factors and more likely to be associated with some aspect of the types themselves. This kind of argument is an essential part of the evolving questioning, designing and analysis that is so characteristic of Interpretive research, which is constantly seeking to identify interesting variations and nuances that add to insightful understanding.

Bearing in mind the contrasting sample design for the four cases, when we compare and contrast the co-frequencies within the two

Leaders' Experiences and Agency Effectiveness 163

Table 6.10 Co-frequency of leader orientations in each sampled bushfire emergency

Type of leader orientation		'Well-handled' Case-1	'Well-handled' Case-2	'Poorly handled' Case-3	'Poorly handled' Case-4
Institutional	*Bureaucrat*	Low	Very Low	Med	Med
	Politician	Low-Med	Low	High	Med
	Survivor	Low	Med	Low	High
Communal	*Innovator*	Med	High	Low-Med	Low
	Maverick	High	Low	Med	High
	Chief	High	High	Low	Med

'well-handled' cases and then within the two 'poorly handled' cases, and finally between the two pairs of cases, it is evident that the CHIEF type, followed by the INNOVATOR type, were most strongly expressed only in the 'well-handled' cases. This is in stark contrast to the POLITICIAN type, followed by the BUREAUCRAT type, which were most strongly expressed only in the 'poorly handled' cases.

An institutional bias in the orientations of the BUREAUCRAT, POLITICIAN and SURVIVOR types is noted in the left-hand column of Table 6.10. This contrasts with the bias towards a community orientation by the INNOVATOR, MAVERICK and CHIEF types.

Theory – developing an argument from results of investigations The last three tables have brought together implications for developing a theory to answer the key question: 'Why are more broadly experienced leaders associated with more effective responses to crises?'

When considering the two broad types of orientations – institutional and communal – it is evident that:

- in the 'well-handled' cases, communal orientations clearly outweigh institutional orientations, suggesting that a communal orientation is a strong differentiator of response outcome; and
- in the 'poorly handled' cases, institutional orientations and communal orientations are similarly expressed, suggesting that

an institutional orientation alone is not a strong differentiator of response outcome.

Considering this evidence, together with the prevalence of each of the six types of leader orientations in the four cases, two conclusions follow:

- the most desirable types of orientation are CHIEF and INNOVATOR; and
- the least desirable types of orientation are BUREAUCRAT, POLITICIAN and, to a lesser extent, the MAVERICK type.

This is a key finding of the study and is summarized as follows:

> This study has provided evidence that strong communally based experiential influences beyond institutional influences, together with the ability to know and apply identities, thinking and behaviour that better respond to the character and context of a disaster, is unique to leaders who are more likely to be associated with effective responses to bushfire crises.

Findings: typology-based answers and theory-based answers

A final aspect of this overall finding that remains to be presented is the answer to the study's principal 'why' question, which concerns situations when the demands of a natural disaster overwhelm the competence, capability and capacity of an agency to respond. The research question as originally stated is: '*Why* do the types of more helpful experience (for the purpose of a leader's reasoning) help to increase perceived first-responder effectiveness?'. This question is about leaders with a breadth of experience beyond institutional experience being more associated with more effective agency responses.

One approach that could be used to answer this 'why' question is to identify attributes that are unique to leaders associated only with effective responses, and different attributes that are unique to leaders associated only with ineffective responses. The resulting profile is the basis of a tentative theory that can help understand the regularity with which this study is concerned. For now, we argue for a theory that is based on the previous analyses and findings and that answers the research question.

To answer this question, it is necessary to either adapt an existing theory or imaginatively construct a theory that accounts for the

Leaders' Experiences and Agency Effectiveness 165

analyses and findings produced thus far. The theory comes from the results noted in the last three tables, up to and including Table 6.10. The CHIEF-type characteristics are most strongly associated with only effective response cases and, to a lesser degree, the INNOVATOR-type characteristics. The 'characteristics to emphasize' column shown in Table 6.11 is an amalgam of the characteristics of these two types. Similarly, the researcher has produced an amalgam based predominantly on the type characteristics of the BUREAUCRAT and the POLITICIAN and, to a lesser degree, the MAVERICK. The result is shown in the 'characteristics to avoid' column in Table 6.11.

Table 6.11 Type characteristics most and least suited to leadership of effective bushfire responses

Attention	Characteristics to emphasize	Characteristics to avoid
IDENTITY and its FOCUS	Share view of immediate challenges and ways to deal with them now	The heroic and grand total solution woven from others' big ideas
DATA focus	Pieces that make biggest difference	All aspects needed for completeness
SENSE via	Tangible usable resources	Ultimate value that fits the rules
DECIDE via	Check priority focus with key people	The best advice for the big ideas
DIRECTING	Emotional commitment	What is legally and reputationally safe
PROGRESS	Action/outcomes people value now	Well-defended progress for long term
OUTCOMES	Make a difference that people value	Reputations and efforts recognized

Resources	Characteristics to emphasize	Characteristics to avoid
SELECT for	Making a difference that counts now	Able to defend intended value
THINK with	Collective focus on facts	Focus people on rules
BEHAVE by	Focus on facts that can be worked with	Collective appeal to those in power
ACTION via	Coordinated and immediate work	Big announcements and gestures

The next step in theory formation is to consider what is involved in the *reasoning attention* and the *reasoning resources* that are strongly expressed and strongly avoided (as noted in Table 6.7). This is an imaginative as well as an analytic task. The statements below are evidence-based propositions for which a constructed theory must account.

Effective leadership – at all levels, from the fire ground through coordination to overall management – involves five forms of reasoning.

- *Attention* is more about the immediate and imminent situation and less about long-term (i.e. post-event) time frames and issues.
- *Data* variety is more about key facts for critical risk factors and less about many facts for all risk factors.
- *Sensing* is more about making holistic actionable albeit incomplete assessments rather than making complete assessments with response steps and resources that are too late or too impractical to action.
- *Deciding* and directing action is more about timely briefings, advice and buy-in using 'local know-how' and less about remote expertise and procedural correctness in decision making and action.
- *Identity* is more about being in touch with the actual situation, and what is available to deal with it, and less about the rules and reputations to account for when dealing with it.

To enact these five forms of reasoning, the author's WIKID*way*™ model (Priest and Sarne 2006, 2011; Priest 2008, 2009), which constitutes the theory, is proposed.

Propositions:

(a) All leaders reason from their wisdom and their know-how.
(b) Wisdom is the basis for the insight that builds as well as connects particular know-how with situations and their contexts.
(c) Different know-how may construct different data, or may notice different data and differently interpret data, about a situation.

Therefore:

(d) The greater the breadth of wisdom and know-how, the greater is the potential for a leader to reason beyond institutional wisdom and know-how, particularly when the response demands of a natural disaster overwhelm the competence, capability and capacity of an agency to respond.

As the leader type characteristics noted in Table 6.11 are consistent with this theory, we argue that the tentative theory above is our answer to this study's primary 'why' question.

Conclusion: a critique of the study, practice implications and further research

A conclusion to such a study would normally be expected to comment on: its strengths and weaknesses; constraints under which the findings may be used; important questions arising from the study; suggestions and reasons for particular paradigm-based approaches to tackling these questions; and suggestions for further research.

For the present purposes, we content ourselves with suggesting how the findings based on the use of the Interpretive paradigm could be taken further using a different paradigm. To do this, we conclude with two questions:

- *Why* are some leaders of critical bushfire emergency responses more effective than others?
- If there are more and/or less effective leaders of critical emergency responses, *how* can they be identified or developed?

In chapter 8, we illustrate a way in which these two questions may be addressed within the Critical Realist paradigm, and this illustration will refer to the background and findings of both the Neo-Positive and Interpretive illustrations (in chapters 4 and 6) that we will assume the reader has read.

7
Principles of Critical Realist Research

Chapter summary

- The first part of the chapter reviews the principles of the Critical Realist research paradigm:
  - the origins of the paradigm are identified;
  - the main characteristics are outlined, including its characteristic logic of inquiry and its view of causal explanation;
  - two traditions – structuralist and constructionist – are compared and their differences reconciled;
  - the philosophical assumptions on which the paradigm is based are reviewed;
  - the nature of social critique, and the need for critics to declare their standpoint, are discussed; and
  - major limitations of the paradigm are noted.
- The second part of the chapter sets out the characteristic steps involved in using this paradigm.

Introduction

Realist philosophies of science are not new. The core realist ontological assumption is that reality is external to and independent of the ideas, experiences and perceptions human beings have of it, or what they imagine it to be; it acts independently and behaves in regular ways. However, there are variations around this core assumption. Blaikie (2007: 14–18) has identified five versions: *shallow*

Introduction

realist, conceptual realist, cautious realist, depth realist and *subtle realist*. Classical positivism is in the *shallow realist* camp, Neo-Positivism in the *cautious realist* camp and some versions of interpretivism fit into the *subtle realist* category (e.g. Hammersley 1992). The version of realism we discuss in this chapter is the sole representative of the *depth realist* position.

If it is accepted that the subject matters of the natural and social sciences are different, there are serious difficulties in transferring realist ontological assumptions, which might be regarded as appropriate in the natural sciences, to the social sciences. This has led to a different kind of realism in the social sciences, namely, Critical Realism. Other labels are associated with this tradition: 'transcendental realism' (e.g. Bhaskar 1978, 1979), 'scientific realism' (e.g. Bhaskar 1986; Pawson and Tilley 1997), 'realism' (Blaikie 1993b; Pawson and Tilley 1997) and 'social realism' (Blaikie 2007, 2010). Here we use Critical Realism for reasons that will become clear.

Critical Realists believe that they have identified the only scientific principles that are capable of adequately explaining any aspect of social life. They reject any form of positivism, both classical or neo, and some realists are unhappy with what they regard as the relativistic tendencies of interpretivism. They not only reject the ontologies advocated in the philosophies of idealism and relativism, especially as the latter is manifest in post-modernism, they also reject the logics of *induction* and *deduction* as being adequate for an explanatory social science.

Critical Realism also differs from our other two research paradigms in its epistemological assumptions, and it adopts the view that observed regularities are eventually explainable in terms of underlying 'real' causal structures and/or mechanisms. Unlike classical positivists, who believed that the only things we can regard as being real are what we can observe with our senses, Critical Realists claim that, while we can observe regularities in the world around us and this is the starting point in any scientific investigation, we may not be able to observe directly the fundamental elements, the causal structures and mechanisms, that produce these regularities. Hence, the task of science is to discover these underlying elements, describe their nature and show how they produce observed regularities.

As with the Neo-Positive paradigm, and to a large extent the Interpretive paradigm, the use of the Critical Realist paradigm begins with an established regularity for which an explanation is sought. Therefore, it is necessary to find evidence for a regularity, say, from previous research or by conducting new research. As this is a descriptive phase of research, the use of either *inductive* or *abductive* logic is appropriate, together with whatever methods of data collection and analysis are judged to be relevant and/or useful.

Origins

The origins of realism in the natural sciences need not detain us here. Our concern is with how Critical Realism has become an emerging research paradigm in the social sciences. The inspiration came initially from Rom Harré's writings in the philosophy of the natural sciences (1961, 1970, 1972). His ideas have been elaborated by two of his students at Oxford, Russell Keat (Keat and Urry 1982) and Roy Bhaskar (1978). Bhaskar's early work was also directed at the elaboration of realist principles in the natural sciences, which he referred to as 'transcendental realism' (1976). Both Harré and Bhaskar went on to apply these principles in the social sciences (Harré and Secord 1972; Harré 1974; Bhaskar 1979) but with some differences. We shall include both their approaches as well as other related versions. (For a more detailed review of Harré's and Bhaskar's ideas, including a comparison of their approaches, see Blaikie 2007: 145–51.)

A number of writers have expounded, elaborated and evaluated Harré's and Bhaskar's ideas. Not surprisingly, one of the first was the other student of Harré. In collaboration with John Urry, Keat produced a seminal work (1982) on the philosophy of social science. Essentially, they compared positivism and realism (read Critical Realism) in the context of the social theories of Marx, Durkheim and Weber. The following quotation captures their view of Critical Realism.

> For realists, adequate causal explanation requires the discovery both of regular relations between phenomena, and of some kind of mechanism that links them. So, in explaining any particular phenomenon, we must not only make reference to those events which initiate the process of change: we must also give a description of that process itself. To do this, we need knowledge of the underlying mechanisms and structures that are present, and of the manner in which they generate or produce the phenomenon we are trying to explain. (Keat and Urry 1982: 30)

Another strong advocate of a realist approach was Benton (1977). He also reviewed what he called 'the three sociologies': positivist sociology in the works of Comte and Durkheim; interpretive sociology in the work of Weber; and Marxist sociology. While acknowledging his indebtedness to Harré in particular, as well as to Keat and Bhaskar, he approached Critical Realism primarily from a Marxist point of view. Consequently, he has been rather critical of what he regarded as Bhaskar's concession to interpretivism, which he considered to be quite unnecessary (Benton 1981:19). Benton's version of realism focuses on structures *per se* rather than their socially constructed character. (For a review of other criticisms of Bhaskar's approach, see Blaikie 2007: 192–5.)

Since the foundations of Critical Realism were laid in the 1970s, it has been developed, elaborated and advocated by a number of social scientists in a variety of ways: realist philosophy of social science (e.g. Outhwaite 1987; Collier 1994); realist social theory (e.g. Archer 1995); and realist social research (e.g. Sayer 1992, 2000; Pawson 1989; Layder 1990, 1993; Pawson and Tilley 1997). Some of these writers, particularly Sayer, Pawson and Layder, beavered away enthusiastically for more than a decade late last century to take realism from the realm of philosophy into social research practice. The Critical Realist research paradigm in this book is a legacy of their work.

Having the term 'critical' in the name of this paradigm may appear to be curious. As already noted, some labels do not include it. Its use derives from the Marxist orientation of a number of the advocates of realist social science, which not only focuses on underlying structures as explanatory strategies but also associates human emancipation with the paradigm (see Box 7.1). We will come back to the emancipatory component of some versions of Critical Realism later in this chapter.

Main characteristics

According to Critical Realism, science is about explaining non-random patterns, or regularities, be they among events or within particular phenomena. The starting point is descriptions of regularities, which extend common observation into systematic exploration, and then critically checking this through research. Exploration requires a researcher to have some idea about what to look for but not a very clear idea of what to expect. This is the descriptive stage. Next is the theoretical stage in which explanations for the non-random patterns and regularities are achieved by hypothesizing a causal or generative mechanism that could produce them (Harré and Secord 1972: 69–71). This involves building a model of the

Box 7.1   Early critical analysis: Marx's critique of capitalist society

As well as offering sociological analyses of aspects of their own societies, Weber and Durkheim were both concerned with laying the methodological foundations for the developing discipline of sociology, albeit in their own particular ways. Writing before them, Marx's project was very different. Whereas Weber offered an explanation for the origins of capitalism, Marx (1852, 1970) offered a critique. While Marx regarded capitalism as having the potential to free people from the limitations of subsistence living, he also saw it as being the source of their oppression. He presented an analysis of how its deficiencies might be overcome.

Marx was concerned with replacing capitalism with a better, more humane type of society in which individuals can achieve their potential. While he regarded the demise of capitalism as being inevitable, because of its internal contradictions, he was aware that action on the part of workers was also necessary.

Marx's primary concern was with human emancipation. His focus was on the relationship between people and the objects they create, in particular, social structures, which he regarded as consisting of many ongoing social relationships. For example, social classes are structured relationships between the owners of the means of production and the workers who provide their labour in the productive process. In time, the creators of such structures cease to acknowledge them as social products and begin to attribute to them 'objective' status; the structures are regarded as having an independent existence. Because workers in particular come to believe that these structures are immutable and beyond their control, they accept the way their actions are constrained and even coerced by them. As a result, workers come to accept their exploitation as being inevitable. They, as well as the capitalists, fail to understand the true nature of these objectified structures; hence, they suffer from 'false consciousness'. The result is that workers are unaware that they have the capacity to change their circumstances. This is reinforced by the fact that the ideology of the ruling class becomes the ruling ideas; it serves their interests and contributes to the oppression and exploitation of the workers.

Marx also argued that the process of production under capitalism separates the workers from the products of their labour, thus leading to alienation. This takes various forms: from productive activity (it doesn't satisfy their needs); from the objects or products of this activity (they do not own them); from fellow workers (they don't work cooperatively and may be in competition, even conflict); and, ultimately, from themselves (from their own human potential). Hence, workers' relationship to the means of production, and the productive process itself, results in their oppressed and alienated lives.

There is much more to Marx's analysis than can be reviewed here. For our purposes, it is his use of social structures in his explanatory accounts, and his concern with emancipation from alienation and oppression, which contributes key characteristics to this paradigm. Whether he used the logic of retroduction to arrive at the existence of these structures, and the mechanisms that operate within them, is an open question. However, it is difficult to imagine how else he could have done this without working backwards from what he had observed, to construct models of what might be producing it, and then testing the models against further observation.

mechanism, if necessary using analogies and metaphors, such that, '*if* it were to exist and act in the postulated way [it] would account for the phenomenon in question' (Bhaskar 1979: 15). The third phase is to search for evidence of the existence of the mechanism. To express this very simply:

- establish the regularity;
- propose an explanatory mechanism; and
- then look for evidence of its existence.

The key issue here is how to discover the mechanism.

The logic of retroduction

Finding explanatory mechanisms is a very difficult problem in the natural sciences where they are not obvious, may never have been observed and their nature is unknown. The researcher has to suggest a mechanism's appearance and behaviour by building a model of it.

Using a caricature of the state of physics about a hundred and fifty years ago will help to illustrate this. Scientists were struggling to understand the nature of matter and to find explanations for many of the things they observed. It was suggested that matter might be made up of atoms. Of course, nobody had ever seen such a thing, although the idea of atoms can be traced back about two and a half thousand years to Greek philosophy. Some ingenious scientists began to imagine what an atom might look like and were even able to draw diagrams of it, using the solar system as an analogy. It had a nucleus with electrons revolving around it; later protons and neutrons were added. On the basis of this model, experiments were conducted that successfully split atoms, and this led to the first nuclear bombs being constructed and exploded. The splitting of the atom and the consequent 'controlled' explosion of atomic bombs provided evidence that the hypothetical model of the atom, which had been creatively produced much earlier, probably existed. However, it was not until the mid-1960s that the first photograph of an atom was produced.[1] It had remained a hidden mechanism until advances in technology made this observation possible.

The logic used to create models of mechanisms is *retroduction* (Bhaskar 1979: 15). This involves working back from what is known to the unknown; of starting with a regularity and then trying to discover an explanation for it; of building a hypothetical model of a possible explanatory mechanism (a description of its appearance and nature) for a known regularity. It involves a great deal of creative imagination (Hempel 1966), intuition (Medewar 1969a), guesswork (Feynman 1967) or the free creation of our minds (Popper 1972). (See Blaikie 2007: 82–9 for a more detailed discussion of *retroduction*.)

The problem of finding explanatory mechanisms in the social sciences is rather different to that in the natural sciences. This is hardly surprising given the differences in the nature of their subject matters and how they can be researched. As social scientists can converse with, rather than just observe, their subject matter, the discovery of relevant explanatory mechanisms is much easier.

The approaches of both Harré and Pawson to realism in the social sciences reinforce this distinction. Finding explanatory mechanisms in the social sciences also requires a high level of creativity, as well as familiarity with both a range of theoretical ideas and the context in which an explanation is sought. It may not be too difficult to identify a likely mechanism, given that its nature and behaviour may be well known and it may be possible, by research, to establish its existence directly rather than indirectly. In some contexts, a number of possible mechanisms might be considered, requiring a choice to be made and justified. Such mechanisms will be illustrated in the next chapter.

Causality in Critical Realism

The main distinguishing feature of Critical Realism is its view of causality. Two competing views have been present in the philosophy of science, identified by Harré as successionist and generative. Philosophers such as Hume (1888) argued that causes cannot be observed, just sequences of events. All that science can do is to infer causality from regularities between events. This is the successionist view, which is reflected in the pattern model of explanation characteristic of classical positivism. In the generative view, establishing regularities is an essential first stage in research, but these regularities need to be explained in terms of something that links two events or concepts, namely, an underlying mechanism. These mechanisms generate the regularity and, if they can be identified, provide an explanation for it. They are not variables; it is their ways of acting, their constitution and behaviour, which is responsible. In other words, there are regularities between events because they are linked by mechanisms.

However, something more is required. In the social sciences, regularities between events, or relationships between concepts, always occur in particular contexts. What we aim to describe and explain is always constrained by time and space. Hence, it is necessary to specify the context in which a regularity occurs and in which the mechanism operates. In specifying the context, the characteristics of the group or location, and the social and cultural conditions, need to be identified (Pawson 1989: 212–17). This version of the research paradigm can be summarized in a simple statement:

Regularity = Mechanism + Context

> The basic task of social inquiry is to explain interesting, puzzling, socially significant regularities (R). Explanation takes the form of positing some underlying mechanism (M) which generates the regularity and thus consists of propositions about how the interplay between structure and agency has constituted the regularity. Within realist investigation there is also investigation of how the workings of such mechanisms are contingent and conditional, and thus only found in particular local, historical or institutional contexts (C). (Pawson and Tilley 1997: 71)

An important element of this statement is the reference to the 'interplay between structure and agency'. This is not only a reference

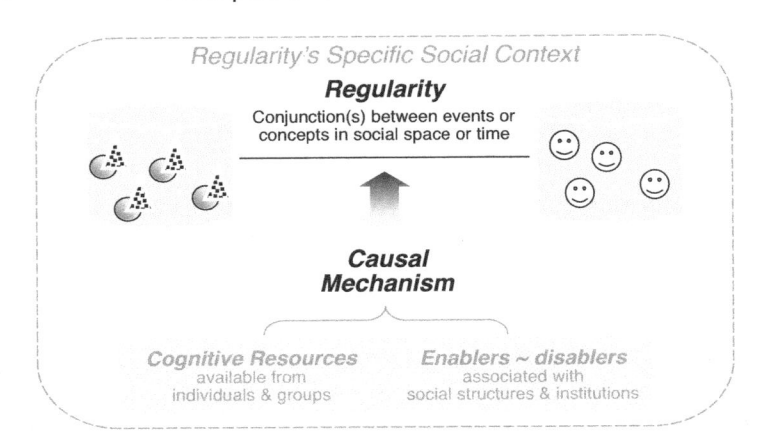

Figure 7.1 Realist explanations of regularities

to Giddens's (1976) notion of the *duality of structure*, but also to the explanatory role played by both socially constructed structures and social actors' actions. Underlying these types of mechanisms is the cognitive activity of these social actors, their goals and motives, the rules they follow and the way these influence their actions.

In causal explanation, be it successionist or generative, time is an ingredient. A regularity is generally more than an association; it implies movement or direction from one event (etc.) to another.[2] It is therefore possible to specify the outcome of a regularity as being 'caused' by the operation of a particular mechanism in a particular context. The Critical Realist model of explanation has been captured in Figure 7.1.

Later, Pawson (2000) described his version of Critical Realism as 'middle-range realism', a not accidental reference to Merton's 'middle-range theory' (1957a). While Merton reformulated Durkheim's theory of egoistic suicide as a deductive (Neo-Positive) argument, Pawson has given another aspect of Durkheim's theory, concerning anomic suicide, a realist gloss. Hence, anomie is not simply correlated with suicide rates; it is the mechanism that produces different rates across different communities. In a manner similar to Harré, he viewed mechanisms in terms of the way people reason and the resources they have available.

It is difficult to provide a concise set of ontological and epistemological assumptions for the Critical Realist research paradigm as its two major founders disagree, particularly on ontological assumptions. So, before trying to do this, it is necessary to review their respective positions. Bhaskar's approach can be characterized as *structuralist* and Harré's as social *constructionist*.

Bhaskar's depth realism

According to Outhwaite (1987: 45–6), Bhaskar's version of Critical Realism consists of four principles.

1 A distinction is made between *transitive* and *intransitive* objects of science. Transitive objects are concepts, theories and models that scientists develop to understand and explain some aspects of reality; intransitive objects are the real entities and their relations that make up the natural and social worlds.
2 Causal relations are regarded as powers or tendencies of things that interact with other tendencies such that an event may or may not be produced, and may or may not be observed.
3 In the domain of the real, definitions of concepts are regarded as real definitions, i.e. statements about the basic nature of some entity or structure (see Table 7.1).
4 Explanatory mechanisms in the domain of the real are postulated, and the task of research is to try to demonstrate their existence.

Hence, there are two key features in Bhaskar's version of 'scientific' realism. The first is the distinction between transitive and intransitive objects of science, and the second is the idea of *ontological depth*.

Critical Realists accept that human observers of the social world cannot conduct research from a neutral position. This means that the social, cultural, demographic and intellectual background, as well as the location of an observer in time and space, influences the way that an observer describes and interprets the social world. Any attempt to understand the social world is conceptually mediated and theory-laden. Hence, social scientific knowledge can develop and change. Bhaskar's solution was to regard this knowledge as being transitive – subject to disputes, revision and even refutation – while the objects of science are intransitive – they are just there (Bhaskar 1986: 24).

While the objects of the natural sciences may have this intransitive character, Bhaskar recognized that social worlds do change. However, changes in our knowledge of the social world may not produce changes in that world; these changes occur independently of observers of it. This is not to deny the possibility that the very act of studying a social life may influence it in some way and bring about change, whether or not a researcher intends it. The important philosophical point is that it exists and can change without the presence of researchers.

The other important feature of Bhaskar's work, but closely related to his idea of the intransitive and transitive dimensions, is his notion

Table 7.1 Domains of reality

	Domain of empirical	Domain of actual	Domain of real
Experiences	✓		
Events		✓	
Mechanisms			✓

of *ontological* depth; a three-level ontology of *empirical, actual* and *real* existences. The empirical (observable) domain comprises observations and experiences of change that manifest in the actual domain. The actual domain comprises the events that arise from the actions of generative mechanisms that are in the real domain but, unlike in the empirical domain, do not require an observer. The real domain comprises objects whose structures and/or generative mechanisms can potentially cause change in events, but whose elements may not readily be accessible or directly observable. Table 7.1 highlights the key characteristics of the three domains of reality.

In his later work, Bhaskar introduced the third *critical* dimension that involves judgemental rationality and constitutes the *metacritical dimension* of discourse 'in which the philosophical and sociological presuppositions of accounts of science are critically, and self-reflexively, scrutinised' (1986: 25). This metacritique aims to identify causally significant absences in thought; what social actors take for granted (tacit knowledge) and what they are unable to express because of the lack of appropriate language. Regarding the latter, social actors cannot perceive or know that for which they do not have concepts. For example, they may experience feelings but not be able to articulate them for lack of relevant concepts.[3] Further, they may experience something like oppression, but not be able to articulate the feelings associated with it, and certainly not be able to identify its association with, say, 'false consciousness'. By giving words to these experiences, and identifying the causes, a social scientist is providing a metacritique that can facilitate self-reflection and a new point of view. The moral component for the social scientist is providing this new point of view and, therefore, creating the possibility for change.

Harré's ethogenic approach

Over a thirty-year period, Harré developed very firm ideas on, firstly, a realist philosophy of science and, secondly, a realist philosophy of social science (1970, 1972, 1974, 1977, 1979, 1983, 2002). His view

Main characteristics

of a realist natural science is very similar to Bhaskar's, but his realist social science is quite different. To a large extent, this is related to their different social ontologies.

From a social research point of view, Harré's most significant work is the one he co-authored early on with Secord (Harré and Secord 1972). The purpose of this book was to promote a paradigm shift in social psychology. The old paradigm that he wanted to reject was some version of positivism. The new paradigm is concerned with explanations based on real processes: the self-monitored rule following that generates social behaviour (Harré and Secord 1972: 21–2).

Harré and Secord (1972) outlined their new paradigm as including the following.

1 Human beings are agents acting according to rules. Social behaviour is mediated by meanings, not responses caused by stimuli. Reasons can be used to explain actions. Lay explanations of behaviour provide the best model for psychological theory (p. 29).
2 People need to be treated as human beings and their commentaries on their actions must be treated as authentic, although revisable, subject to empirical criticism (p. 101).
3 The mechanisms responsible for many of the observed patterns of social interactions essentially involve the interrelations of meanings as perceived by the interactors. The structure of the meaning relations can be discovered by studying the accounts that people give of social interactions in which they have taken part (p. 128).
4 Descriptions of patterns of social interaction should be sought in the reasons, rules, meanings and the like taken into account by the participants and expressed in their ordinary language (p. 132).
5 Social life is made up of episodes, which include not only overt behaviour but also thoughts, feelings, intentions and plans of the participants (p. 147). An episode is any part of social life, involving one or more people, in which some internal structure can be discerned and which has a beginning and an end (p. 153).
6 The ethogeny of an episode is the rules, meanings and so on that are followed by conscious agents and are responsible for its structure (p. 208).

In Harré's ontology, human powers (such as, meaning giving, choice making and rule following) are basic and the social order is an epiphenomenon of this. A person's social capacities are related to their cognitive equipment. However, this is not readily available for inspection by the actor themselves, by other social actors or by social researchers. It is therefore necessary to construct models of the cognitive structure of persons from relevant fragments that a researcher can compile. Social actors do this in the interactions with each other, and social scientists need to do it in order to explain patterns of social life. These models are surrogates for generative mechanisms and it is the social scientist's task to establish their plausibility.

Harré's ethogenic approach requires two types of models to be constructed: models, or abstract descriptions, of social episodes; and models of actors' cognitive resources. In so far as macro-social structures enter the scene, they exist only as models in people's minds and are part of their cognitive resources (Harré 1976).

Reconciliation

The various traditions of social theory also reflect this tension between *structuralist* and *constructionist* accounts of social life. Resolutions of this tension have been presented by a number of theorists going back at least to Berger and Luckmann (1966), and to Giddens (1976) and Bhaskar (1979). Essentially they argue, as Marx had done much earlier, that while social realities are human creations, once established they can take on a life of their own and can and do constrain both those social actors and later inhabitants of that social world. Marx expressed this as follows: 'Men [sic] make their own history, but they do not make it as they please; they do not make it under circumstances chosen by themselves, but under circumstances encountered from the past' (Marx 1852). Giddens identified this as the *duality of structure*, 'that social structures are both constituted *by* human agency, and yet at the same time are the very *medium* of this constitution' (1976: 121).

Bhaskar also referred to the *dual character* of society: 'Society is both the ever-present *condition* (material cause) and the continually reproduced *outcome* of human agency' (1979: 43). In this sense, social structures are different from natural structures. They are the products of previous inhabitants and current social actors simply reproduce and, perhaps, modify them in the process. However, Bhaskar insisted that they have an independent existence, that they exert influence on current human activity and, as such, have a causal role in explanations of social life.

However, Harré and his colleagues regarded Bhaskar's social

structures as reifications; abstractions that are just *assumed* to exist. As such, they can hardly cause things to happen. For Harré, social structures are intimately related to social activities; they are generated from networks of relationships between people as they play roles and perform acts. They are 'secondary formations or products of the activity of people acting according to rules, customs and conventions' (Harré 2002: 115). Therefore, they have no causal efficacy; it is agents, individuals and collectivities, not social structures, which make things happen. It is social rules that facilitate and constrain people to act in certain ways, and it is people who are at the centre of causal powers in the social world.

As we shall see in the later section on 'limitations', these ontological issues have been taken up by a number of writers. In the meantime, let us examine a way of at least partially reconciling these two positions. What is relevant here is the fact that both researchers and social actors work with ontological assumptions. The ontological assumptions that a researcher adopts, whether explicitly or implicitly, have to be distinguished from ontological assumptions social actors adopt, even if unreflectively. It is social actors who are the constructors and maintainers of social realities, and it is highly likely that they reify these realities and 'allow' them to constrain their activities. At the same time, they may act within more 'intimate' and dynamic structures of 'rules, customs and conventions'. A critical issue here, as we have already seen in the Interpretivist paradigm, is what should be the relationship between everyday ontologies and social scientific ontologies.

The differences in ontological assumptions between Bhaskar and Harré lead to differences in explanatory models; the former favours macro structures and the latter micro structures. But both models can be used; it is just a matter of when each one is appropriate. For example, macro structures may be relevant in a situation where one group of actors (the ruling class) is able to impose its political ideology and power onto another group (the proletariat). The latter may experience social reality as being external and very constraining physically, socially and psychologically. To understand the power of such structures, it would be necessary to study all three types or levels of constraint and, in the process, take into account both macro and micro structures and mechanisms. On the other hand, if the focus of research is on social relationships in various types of families, Harré's notion of more dynamic social relationships based on 'rules, customs and conventions', i.e. micro-social structures, may be more appropriate. However, macro structures and mechanisms may also be relevant, even in this situation.

By concentrating on generative mechanisms operating in a particular context, Pawson has managed to avoid the debate about the ontological status of social structures. To do this, he adopted Giddens's view of the relationship between agency and structure and, hence, avoided the structuralist extremes of Bhaskar's position. By focusing on mechanisms rather than (external) social structures, his model of Critical Realist explanation can be used with any version of Critical Realism.

Assumptions

At the risk of some simplification of the differences just discussed, the following ontological and epistemological assumptions can be used to characterize this paradigm.

Ontological assumptions: depth realist

a) Social reality is viewed as a socially constructed world in which either social episodes are the products of the cognitive resources that social actors bring to them (Harré) or social arrangements that are products of material but unobservable structures of relations (Bhaskar).
b) Unlike natural structures, social structures are less enduring and do not exist independently of the activities they influence or social actors' conceptions of what they are doing in these activities.

Epistemological assumptions: neo-realism

a) Knowledge of the causes of observed regularities is derived from the structures and/or mechanisms that produce them.
b) The discovery of these structures and mechanisms may necessitate the postulation or selection of entities and processes that go beyond surface appearances.
c) This view of causation allows for the possibility that competing or cancelling mechanisms may be operating independently when no event or change is observed.

Relationship to critical theory

Critical Realism is commonly associated with critical theories of society and the related emancipatory research intentions commonly

Relationship to critical theory

referred to as critical research. This association is not without foundation as both traditions have an emancipatory component. The key representatives are Bhaskar (1986) and Habermas (1970, 1972).

Bhaskar (1986) argued that social science has an emancipatory potential. By offering explanations of social phenomena that go beyond what can be observed and what social actors know, realist social science can provide a point of view that can challenge what is taken for granted. The possibility is created for offering a critique of lay accounts and taken-for-granted ways of viewing and understanding social life. If social research can identify misconceptions, what Marx called 'false consciousness', and ways of avoiding alienation and suffering, change is possible.

Critical theory came out of the Frankfurt School in Germany in the 1930s and became popular outside Germany in the late 1960s. It was founded on the idea that human reason is the highest potential of human beings and that this facility makes it possible to criticize and challenge what goes on in social life. The early critical theorists saw humans as free, autonomous agents who are able to create and control their own lives provided they are not subjected to any form of alienation. As they regarded capitalism as being a major source of alienation they, like Marx before them, focused their critiques on it. They were also opposed to positivism for its support of the status quo.

Habermas was particularly concerned with a critique of positivism, mainly from the point of view of interpretivism and hermeneutics. He accepted that as there are fundamental differences in the subject matters of the natural and social sciences, different methods or modes of experience must be used; in the natural sciences, it is 'sense experience' (direct observation) but in the social sciences it is 'communicative experience' (understanding of meaning used by social actors). He accepted that we cannot escape working with ontological and epistemological assumptions in our search for knowledge, and that these assumptions reflect particular 'interests'. These interests determine what will count as the object of knowledge, the categories relevant to this and the procedures for discovering and justifying knowledge.

This led Habermas to propose three different kinds of scientific inquiry: *empirical-analytic* sciences (positivist); *historical-hermeneutic* sciences (interpretive); and *critical theory*. Each kind of science has different underlying interests and focuses on different aspects of social life, 'work', 'interaction' and 'power', respectively. (For a more detailed review of Habermas's approach to critical theory, see Blaikie 2007: 135–40.)

It is this emancipatory component that Critical Realism and critical theory share, largely because of their common Marxist origins. According to Sayer: 'The quest for emancipation ... involves addressing normative questions and the feasibility of alternatives' (2000: 158).

The critic's standpoint

A key issue in any emancipatory programme is the standpoint adopted by the critic.

> In the last 20 years many researchers have come to accept that social science must be critical of the practices it studies, whether their topics be mainly economic, political or cultural. Any social science claiming to be critical must have a standpoint from which its critique is made, whether it is directed at popular illusions which support inequality and relations of domination or at the causes of avoidable suffering and frustration of needs. But it is strange that this critical social science largely neglects to acknowledge and justify these standpoints. (Sayer 2000: 172)

Hence, in examining any critique of an area of social life it is necessary to examine the standpoint that is adopted in order to know whether the critique can be justified. Questions such as the following need to be asked.

> [D]oes it privilege the position of a particular group ... ? Does it imply a society without difference? If it implies greater equality, on whose terms is equality to be defined? Secondly, it involves assessing whether the alternative is feasible and desirable. We have to ask whether remedying one set of problems would generate others (it usually does), and whether these would be worse than the original problems. (Sayer 2000: 163)

Bhaskar's view that all knowledge has a critical potential, because it can change the way people see themselves and the world around them, does not just apply to his version of Critical Realism. The important question is whether this criticism is simply seen as a *potential* or whether it is adopted as a *fundamental* role of a Critical Realist social science.

A number of sociologists (e.g. Berger 1963; Giddens 1982) have accepted that sociology has intrinsic critical potential, but they do not adopt it as an essential part of practice. The problem with the potential critique position is that the outcome is not predictable and may not necessarily be desirable. It is not enough to enlighten people, or facilitate their self-enlightenment, about the sources of their illusions and/or oppression; this may just lead to unhappiness and despair. For emancipation to be effective, the structures and mechanism that produce the problems must be removed or neutralized (Sayer 2000: 160).

The problem with making critique part of research practice is establishing a basis for a particular kind of critique. Unlike the younger critical social sciences of feminism and green theory, which have dealt explicitly with the problem of standpoint, Bhaskar seems not to have provided a clear idea of how a particular standpoint can be justified. He relied on the argument that not only can science not be free of values (the identification of a problem involves value judgements, as do decisions about what are adequate descriptions and good explanations) but also that science can be involved in assessing the relative merits of different values (Sayer 2000: 160).

Habermas, on the other hand, dealt with the problem of standpoint by arguing that rather than relying on evidence produced by observation to arrive at 'the truth', a 'rational consensus' should be possible through critical discussion in 'an ideal speech situation' (Habermas 1976: 107–8; McCarthy 1982: 308; Giddens 1985). Participants in such a discussion need to be free of all constraints or distorting influences, conscious strategic behaviour and more subtle barriers to communication derived from self-deception. All participants must not only have the same chance to speak, but they must also be free to question and refute claims of other speakers. Any such discourse is based on the assumption that what a speaker says is understandable and true, and that the claims made are sincere and appropriate for the speaker to make. Hence, truth involves the promise of reaching a consensus. Habermas's solution is an ideal that is difficult to achieve but it is also a pragmatic solution to a vexed philosophical and scientific problem.

To reiterate, social scientists have to stand somewhere, with regard not only to the assumptions that they adopt in their research, but also to what they do with their findings. It is not possible to argue for neutrality, as this is also a standpoint, and one that is difficult to justify morally. Not only is social scientific knowledge not absolute, it can have consequences, positive or negative, for social actors, whether or not they are involved in the knowledge production. Social science can have a role in improving social life; better that this be an active role that might help to ensure positive outcomes.

Limitations of the Critical Realist paradigm

In spite of the claims by advocates of Critical Realism, that this paradigm is a fundamental improvement over Neo-Positivism and Interpretivism, it still has its critics, particularly of Bhaskar's version. (For a more detailed review of many of the criticisms that follow, see Blaikie 2007: 192–5).

For a start, we have the 'family' squabbles between Harré and Bhaskar and the resulting differences in the directions they have taken in applying realist principles to the social sciences. A number of critics (e.g. Benton 1981; Keat and Urry 1982; Stockman 1983; King 1999) have argued that Bhaskar's conception of external social structures renders them as theoretical and unobservable. This criticism would not be serious if Bhaskar had not at the same time accepted that social structures are socially constructed and maintained. These two ideas seem to be incompatible, although we have already suggested a resolution. There is a failure to recognize the bearing that this has on the manner in which the social world is studied (Stockman 1983: 209). This criticism does not apply to Harré's version.

Layder (1985) has taken this point further. While Bhaskar accepted that knowledge is transient and reality is intransient, Layder claimed that our ontological claims must also be transient because they are theoretical. Even though we may believe in a real, external world, we have no direct access to it; we can only theorize about it, and our theories may not be accurate. 'In maintaining the existence of intransitive structure which is irreducible to individuals, Bhaskar paradoxically argues that society is dependent on individuals and yet also independent of them and that social action is both intentional and unintentional and objective' (King 1999: 269). Arguing from a hermeneutic point of view, King's solution is to go back to Harré's ontology.

According to Stockman (1983), there is a difference in the accessibility of mechanisms in the natural and social sciences, something that Bhaskar seemed not to recognize. In the natural sciences, scientific instruments may detect the effects of mechanisms, but the situation is more complex in the social sciences. The only instrument the social scientist has is an ability to communicate with social actors. However, this criticism can be turned on its head.

Conclusion

The Critical Realist research paradigm provides an alternative to the other two better-known research paradigms. The distinction between the intransitive and transitive dimensions of knowledge, the notion of ontological depth, the mode of causal explanation and an emancipatory component, are its distinguishing features. However, the paradigm has a number of versions that we wish to accommodate.

We believe that the different views about the role and ontological status of social structures need not be seen as insurmountable but, rather, as alternatives that can both be used, depending on the nature of the research problem and the context in which it is investigated.

Similarly, we regard the emancipatory component as being a matter of degree. At one end of the spectrum, it may be regarded as an essential and integrated component of a research project. At the other end of the spectrum, it may not be seen as particularly relevant, even though the inherent critical potential of social scientific research is recognized. Just as with the issue of the status of social structures, where a researcher chooses to be located on this spectrum, for a particular research project, will depend on a number of factors, including the nature of the research problem, the context and aims of the research and the researcher's personal goals and preferences.

It is the key feature of this research paradigm, namely, its concern with a particular mode of explanation based on generative mechanisms, which will determine its selection. It provides social researchers with a distinctive and very useful alternative to Neo-Positive and Interpretive modes of answering 'why' research questions.

Characteristic steps of the paradigm

For a given social phenomenon the task of defining or selecting important 'what', 'why' and/or 'how' questions usually first requires preliminary work to identify particular problems, or parts of a problem, that most deserve attention. At this stage, any paradigm may be a candidate. However, once preliminary work identifies the need to investigate a causal mechanism for an important regularity and, perhaps, suggests how a situation or practice may change as a result of understanding what generates the regularity, then a Critical Realist inquiry is, prima facie, the obvious candidate.

Unlike the process of reflexive exploration characteristic of the

Interpretive paradigm, the Critical Realist paradigm's interest in a well-defined regularity, and a carefully and thoroughly described causal mechanism, provides a very clear focus for the researcher's sampling, data gathering and analysis. This is a process of refined acquisition rather than the reflexive exploration characteristic of the Interpretive paradigm.

Seven phases

Research that is framed within a Critical Realist research paradigm may be considered as comprising seven phases.

1 *Describe the phenomenon and a research problem in context.* To do this, first characterize manifestations of the phenomenon and the specific context in which it occurs, together with notable patterns that are associated with the phenomenon. A context's description will typically specify the particular social space-time and the substantive topical focus. Next, highlight specific events, processes and conditions, as well as any attributed impacts, which social actors associate with the problem.
2 *Describe the problem's key regularity.* If a regularity is not clearly specified, then the researcher must answer a 'what' question about the regularity's features, the conditions under which it manifests and the importance associated with its occurrences. This will involve fieldwork as well as a literature review. Once the regularity is well defined, the next step is to formulate the research questions.
3 *State the research questions.* The questions will typically be about 'why' the regularity arises and, perhaps, 'how' knowledge of its causal mechanism may be used to facilitate change.
4 *Critically review literature.* A central task is to construct and describe a causal mechanism's structure, content and dynamics. If well done, it will clearly set out the way the mechanism operates with human reasoning interacting with human mental and behavioural resources to produce the effects that are symptomatically reported as the regularity. This requires a theoretical imagination as well as a deep understanding of the regularity's substantive and contextual setting. Literature plays three key roles in this step.

   - It can be expected to provide the researcher with substantive background that is relevant to the phenomenon in context and the regularity.
   - It is a rich source of theoretical ideas in the form of models and

Characteristic steps of the paradigm

metaphors that can help inform development of a candidate causal mechanism.
- It may suggest sources and methods for assembling evidence for the existence of a causal mechanism that the researcher may propose.

5 *Construct a causal mechanism.* The context will already have been characterized and described. However, central to designing and describing a causal mechanism, its triggering, its operation and its effects, is the manner in which it and its context communicate and inter-operate. Describing these elements helps to focus the task of getting evidence for the existence of the mechanism. Designing and describing a causal mechanism must also account for the structure, resources, rules or conditions, processes and associated symptomatic outcomes that constitute the mechanism's operation and consequences. Again, the clearer the specifications, then the better focused is the task of finding evidence and arguing for the mechanism's existence.

6 *Develop and evaluate evidence* to qualify the existence of the proposed causal mechanism. Two classes of evidence are required. One concerns the actual and symptomatic attributable effects of the mechanism when it is operating and when it is silent. This class of evidence also seeks to associate the mechanism's operation with the regularity. The second class of evidence concerns the triggering of the mechanism and the relationship between the mechanism's context and its own structure, content and processing.

7 *Interpret, report and critique the research.* There are two tasks at this stage of the research. First, qualify and communicate the significance of the findings, as well as their limitations and practice implications. Second, evaluate the philosophical, methodological and practical strengths, contributions, weaknesses and limitations of the study's design and conduct, as well as suggest directions for further research.

The remainder of this section will focus on the two phases that are most clearly characteristic of the Critical Realist paradigm; the construction of a causal mechanism and the development and evaluation of evidence.

Constructing a causal model or causal mechanism

A causal mechanism typically comprises a structure or organized collection of types of resources, boundaries, interrelationships, processes, rules and corresponding operational effects associated with the social actors who are directly part of, or are impacted by, the regularity.

Because the researcher is setting out to invent and describe a cause of observable patterned social effects, it will often be the case that what people say, how they behave and what they do will be the actual consequences of the mechanism's operation and these, in turn, will collectively manifest as the observable social effect. The types of resources and processes involved in operationally causing the utterances, behaviours or actions that lead to the patterned observable effects will be cognitive in nature. These include memories, mental models, heuristics, intuition, judgement and reasoning skills and habits. Identifying and classifying, as well as describing these types of resources, together with the ways in which they interact and the conditions under which this happens, is what is needed when developing a causal model or mechanism.

The cues to start this process are provided by the detailed descriptions of the context and the regularity. By working backwards from these descriptions and their particular elements and conditional relationships, and asking 'What kinds of resources and interactions are causally consistent with the observed pattern?', the researcher is able to provisionally develop classes of cognitive resources and processes which, when triggered, operate together to produce actual outcomes and consequent observable effects. This trial-and-error process depends on ideas from literature as well as the researcher's imagination, general knowledge and specific substantive knowledge of the current research problem.

There are four key steps to devising a candidate causal model or mechanism. These steps are repeated iteratively until the model appears to warrant the likely expense and time needed to acquire and evaluate evidence for its existence.

1 Refine descriptions of the context, the regularity and conditions under which the regularity manifests. Also, identify and describe actual outcomes (i.e. signals and conditions) that appear to be directly associated with the regularity.
2 Propose and describe classes of cognitive resources that are, prima facie, necessary for the production of the outcomes and consequent regularity described in the first step.
3 By referring to resources described in the second step, and the conditions noted in the first step, describe cognitive processes and their start/stop rules that operate on the resources to produce the outcomes and consequent regularity described in the first step.

Characteristic steps of the paradigm 191

4 'Desk check' and, if needed, adjust the causal model so it is increasingly effective when accounting for and anticipating the regularity in terms of people's reasoning and actions that are part of their everyday social life, as well as outlier or exceptional aspects and events in their social life.

Several questions that help to 'desk check' a tentative causal model before searching for evidence of its existence are noted below.

- Is it capable of producing the kinds of effects that can be detected in the actual and empirical domains?
- Are the model's types of resources and their interrelationships described sufficiently that the produced effects can be anticipated and accounted for?
- Is the model sufficiently specific with well-defined elements and relationship rules between and within elements of the model's structure, resources and processes?
- Does the model's structure and rules of operation involve learning and start/stop conditions that account for causal activity?
- Is it comprehensive – covering a well-defined range of cognitive, emotional and behavioural resources and processes?
- Is there good literature support for the model's elements that will enable well-defined data to be assembled, analysed and interpreted?
- Is it a contingent mechanism – capable of constrained as well as self-adjusting activity?
- If there are phase effects between operation and detectable effects, are the phase conditions defined and knowable?

The search for, and interpretation of, evidence

Evidence requirements must address the need for confirming and disconfirming evidence and facilitate judging where the weight of evidence falls.

It is assumed that this phase does not occur until the proposed causal mechanism has been thoroughly 'desk checked'. This is because the task of finding evidence for a proposed causal mechanism may, depending on the scope of the research, be expensive and time consuming and also involve ethical, legal and logistical considerations.

Finding and interpreting evidence is about developing an argument for the existence of directly inaccessible structures, as well as intellectual and behavioural resources and processes, which constitute the causal mechanism. Therefore, indirect means of assembling evidence focus on collecting and interpreting data about symptomatic events, patterns, artefacts and observations. Cross-checking directly observable effects and patterns against other primary and secondary sources, such as interviews and records, are indicative of the means by which evidence is progressively checked and assembled.

Sampling and data gathering

The researcher's core task is to use the proposed causal mechanism to inform the preparation of a rich description of the context and instances of the absence or presence of the elements of the proposed mechanism in action. The argument for affirming evidence rests on the preponderance of confirming data and the absence of contradictory data, notwithstanding the possibility of as yet undefined alternative explanations.

In order to expose the types of resources, processes and organization that constitute the tentative causal mechanism, it is essential to be able to access authentic, appropriately wide-ranging, rich and nuanced accounts, as well as rich descriptions of informants' biographical backgrounds: their mental, emotional, behavioural resources and processes; their contextual experience; and other contextual material that facilitates comparison and interpretation of data.

Harré and Secord (1972) suggested that the researcher focus on: social actors' decisions, behaviours, actions and interactions; social actors' thinking and behaviour and their reflections on their reasons for such thinking and behaviour in particular situations; and critical analysis of social actors' accounts compared to the researcher's observations and other sources of activity associated with the regularity of interest.

Analysis

Analysis of data involves detailed and high-level work. In detailed analysis the aim is to identify and classify occurrences of each of the causal model's concepts and relationships (e.g. operational procedures and conditions, including starting and stopping rules) according to whether or not it is implicitly or even explicitly referred to in informants' detailed accounts or in other data. At this level of analysis, informants' concepts about their mental resources and reasoning are compared to specific elements of the proposed causal mechanism in order to establish the evidence for each specific element.

In high-level analysis, the researcher interprets the various sources of data in order to compare and contrast multiple conditional manifestations of the regularity with data that point to social actors' expressed use of the types of resources and processes that are also elements of the proposed causal mechanism. By classifying occurrences and the strengths of occurrences of the causal mechanism's elements, interrelationships and start/stop triggers according to social actors' accounts, a pattern of affirming and/or disconfirming evidence is assembled.

Based on these analyses, the researcher weighs the evidence as to whether the causal mechanism exists, as well as noting matters for further research.

When to stop

A practical stopping rule is that as a proposed model's simplicity (i.e. elegance) and comprehensiveness increases, then less supportive evidence that is counter-intuitive is needed and more dismissive evidence that is counter-intuitive is required. This is not a clear-cut rule but it is a guide.

Review questions

We invite you to use the review questions in the Appendix not only to test your knowledge of the paradigms but also to help stimulate the process of designing and conducting your own research.

Further reading

Bhaskar, R. (1979). *The Possibility of Naturalism*. Brighton: Harvester. Not easy reading in places but contains the core ideas of Critical Realism. Chapter 1 is the most useful, and chapter 2 to p. 69, is also relevant.

Blaikie, N. (2007), *Approaches to Social Enquiry*, 2nd edn. Cambridge: Polity. Provides elaborations of many of the ideas covered in this chapter. See, particularly, pp. 82–9, 110–17, 135–40, 145–57, 183–7, 189–91 and 192–5.

Harré, R. (1974). Blueprint for a new science, in N. Armitage (ed.), *Restructuring Social Psychology*. Harmondsworth: Penguin.

Harré, R. (1977). The ethogenic approach: theory and practice. *Advances in Experimental Social Psychology* 10: 283–314. These two articles provide overviews of Harré's more focused ideas.

Harré, R. and Secord, P. F. (1972). *The Explanation of Social Behaviour.* Oxford: Blackwell. Lays out in detail Harré's earliest version of a realist social science.

Keat, R. and Urry, J. (1982). *Social Theory as Science.* London: Routledge & Kegan Paul. The whole book still has much to offer and chapter 2 on 'Realist Philosophy of Science', especially pp. 27–36, captures the main features of a realist approach.

Outhwaite, W. (1987). *New Philosophies of Social Science. Realism, Hermeneutics and Critical Theory.* London: Macmillan. This brief work is also well worth reading right through. In particular, pp.19–60 provide an accessible summary of realism in social science, with particular reference to Bhaskar, Benton and Harré. Pages 77–91, on 'Realism and Critical Theory', complement the discussion of the topic in this chapter.

Pawson, R. (2000). Middle-range realism. *Archives Européennes de Sociologie* 41: 283–325. This article is the most developed statement of his position and is essential reading for any serious researcher.

Pawson, R. and Tilley, N. (1997). *Realistic Evaluation.* London: Sage. Of all the recommended reading listed here, this one is by research practitioners who have translated and integrated the various versions and principles into usable procedures. It draws heavily on Pawson's earlier work (1989) but presents his position more accessibly in a more developed form.

Sayer, A. (2000). *Realism and Social Science.* London: Sage. The Introduction and chapter 1 (pp. 2–28) provide an excellent, well-written overview.

8
The Critical Realist Research Paradigm in Action

Chapter summary

- This chapter's first illustration is a variant on the illustration about environmentalism in chapter 4 and discusses the task of establishing a causal explanation.
- The second illustration follows the chapters 4 and 6 illustrations about Neo-Positive and Interpretive research into crisis leadership in a bushfire emergency. This illustration focuses on:
  - the meaning and implications of 'why' and 'how' research questions;
  - the process of developing and describing a causal mechanism; and
  - the process of assembling and evaluating evidence about a causal mechanism.

1 Gender and Environmentalism

Introduction

This illustration of the Critical Realist research paradigm is derived from the same research programme as the illustration of the Neo-Positive research paradigm in chapter 4. There the concern was with the association between age and environmentalism; here it is the companion association between gender and environmentalism. As we shall see, the evidence for this association is not consistent and seems to be limited to specific aspects of environmentalism.

In the Neo-Positive illustration, environmentalism was viewed broadly as attitudes and behaviour related to environmental problems and their solutions. Here, environmentalism is viewed more narrowly and focuses on just two measures of it: 'level of avoidance of the use of environmentally damaging products'; and 'level of confidence in the capacity of science and technology to solve environmental problems'. The reason for this restriction will become clear shortly.[1]

Initially, the illustration will look like it is going to use the Neo-Positive paradigm, but it will soon diverge to become Critical Realist. The point of divergence occurs when a decision is made to seek a causal explanation (using a generative mechanism) rather than one based on a connected set of paired associations (i.e. a deductive theory).

While this illustration is informed by previous research, it is a research design that would enable an investigation of the association between gender and environmentalism to be conducted at a greater depth than this previous research achieved.

The problem

Research during the second half of last century examined associations between a range of socio-demographic variables and various measures of environmental attitudes and behaviour. As we saw in chapter 4, 'age' is the standout variable. Gender, on the other hand, received less attention and, when it was included, the associations were generally much weaker and inconsistent. Something else appears to be involved. However, rather than looking for moderating or confounding variables, as could be done when the Neo-Positive paradigm is used, possible mechanisms that might be responsible for producing the association will be investigated. Therefore, the research problem is an intellectual puzzle: the need to better understand the association between gender and environmentalism.

Research questions

The research problem can be transposed into two research questions.

Q. 1 *What* is the form of association between gender and environmentalism?
Q. 2 *Why* does this form exist?

Review of extant literature

Two studies in the United States in the 1980s presented findings that indicated that this association is rather complex. McStay and Dunlap (1983) provided moderate support for gender differences, with females having a higher level of concern for the environment than males, even when controls for age, education, income and area of residence were applied. However, they found evidence to suggest that women, in contrast to men, were more likely to engage in behaviour concerned with environmental quality that is personal rather than public. Similarly, Blocker and Eckberg (1989) found that women were likely to be concerned about local environmental issues and men about general ones.

In Australia, Blaikie (1992) found that, while there were consistent associations between gender and various measures of environmentalism, with females having more responsible attitudes and behaviour than males, the strengths of these associations were generally weak. However, the strongest association was with a scale of three attitude items that measured 'confidence in the capacity of science and technology to solve environmental problems'; women were less confident than men. In the same study, Blaikie and Ward (1992) found that for the specific aspect of environmental behaviour concerned with 'level of avoidance of the use of environmentally damaging products', men were more likely than women to say that they do *not* do this.

Therefore, we have two quite specific regularities, one concerning the role of science and technology in finding solutions, and the other concerning practical, everyday contributions to the solution of environmental problems. The former is in the public domain and the latter in the private domain. This can be expressed in the following regularity: Women are less confident than men about global solutions and more involved than men in local solutions. This is our answer to the first research question and now needs an explanation.

A possible explanation

Working back from this regularity, using retroductive logic, it could be suggested that the avoidance of the use of environmentally damaging products might be a reflection of household responsibilities rather than gender per se. This is supported by the global/local differences noted in the literature.

The following four propositions (see Blaikie 2010: 245) elaborate these ideas and point in the direction of a possible explanatory mechanism.

- Women who are primarily involved in home making and child rearing will have a higher level of environmentalism, and a greater concern with local environmental issues, than men who are primarily breadwinners and pursue careers in the public sphere.
- Women who have a significant involvement in the public sphere will be more like 'traditional' men in their level of environmentalism and locus of concern about environmental issues.
- Men who have had, and continue to have, a significant involvement in the private sphere, with household and child-care/rearing responsibilities, will be more like 'traditional' women in their level of environmentalism and locus of concern about environmental issues.
- Women who have never had child-rearing responsibilities will, in similar social contexts, have a lower level of environmentalism than women with these responsibilities.

If these propositions were to be used in a Neo-Positive study, they could be investigated by locating appropriate samples of relevant populations (women and men in both 'traditional' and fully or partially 'reversed' roles) and then variables, such as types and levels of involvement in the private and public spheres and types and levels of environmentalism, could be measured and analysed. The result would be the establishment of more elaborate regularities (descriptions) within the umbrella of gender and environmentalism.

The Critical Realist paradigm requires a deeper kind of explanation. The four propositions need to be imaginatively translated into a hypothetical model of a causal mechanism operating in a specified context to produce an outcome consistent with the observed regularity under consideration. It is to this process that we now turn.

In line with the approaches to Critical Realism of Harré and Pawson, what we need to hypothesize is 'social mechanisms ... about people's *choices* and the *capacities* they derive from group membership ... reaching "down" to the layers of individual *reasoning* ... and "up" to the collective *resources* on offer' (Pawson and Tilley 1997: 66). Hence, mechanisms involve both human agency (choices and reasoning) and social structures (capacities and resources) (see Giddens 1979, ch. 2; 1984, ch. 1).

Gender and Environmentalism 199

Thus when we explain a regularity generatively, we are not coming up with variables or correlates which associate one with the other; rather we are trying to explain how the association *itself* comes about. The generative mechanisms thus actually *constitute* the regularity; they *are* the regularity. . . . A mechanism is thus not a variable but an *account* of the make-up, behaviour and interrelationships of those processes which are responsible for the regularity. A mechanism is thus a theory – a theory which spells out the potential of human resources and reasoning. (Pawson and Tilley 1997: 67–8)

It is necessary to consider such explanatory mechanisms as operating in specific contexts, as *'the relationship between causal mechanisms and their effects is not fixed, but contingent.* . . . In realist terms, it is the *contextual conditioning* of causal mechanism which turns (or fails to turn) causal potential into a causal outcome' (Pawson and Tilley 1997: 69). Therefore, the main task of a researcher using the Critical Realist paradigm is to hypothesize the kind of reasoning of, and the resources available to, people in the context in which the regularity is evident.

Possible explanatory mechanisms

What choices and capacities are relevant to explaining gender differences in types and levels of environmentalism? Adults with home-making and child-rearing responsibilities have a primary concern with the health and welfare of family members. Choices and decisions are made that deal with these concerns, and anything that poses a threat will be resisted. These threats are both global and local and are associated with such things as: climate change; air quality; water quality and availability; and food quality, purity and security. Families have limited capacities to deal with such threats at a public or global level. They can sign petitions, join demonstrations and vote for politicians who are willing and able to address such issues. At the local level, they can take actions that contribute to a reduction in these threats, limited though they may be. For example, they can: avoid using products that damage the ozone layer and contribute to climate change; reduce household waste that contributes unnecessarily to landfill and the consequent production of methane gas; control what they put into sewage and drainage systems that can pollute waterways and require expensive methods of water treatment; limit their water usage to reduce the need to extend water storages and reliance of energy hungry desalination plants; and limit their use of methods of heating, cooling and transport that rely on the use of fossil fuels, which are major contributors to climate change. There are many choices that can be made, and it is possible that the reasoning behind them is to promote the health and welfare of the family.

These assumptions can be summarized in a hypothetical mechanism, which operates in a particular context, and produces the observed regularity.

> The main feature of the *context* is the presence or absence of responsibility for children. The generative *mechanism* is the reasoning and choices associated with threats to the family from environmental problems. The *outcome* is attitudes and actions that are seen to contribute to the amelioration of these threats.

Such mechanisms are not unknown, nor are they hidden below the surface of everyday life. This type of reasoning, and these kinds of choices, confront adults with family responsibilities in any society, although the level of awareness of the impacts of environmental issues, global and local, will vary, as will the knowledge and awareness of the capacities of, and resources available to, individuals to respond to them.

Therefore, gender is only relevant in understanding differences in environmentalism in so far as roles are gendered in traditional ways. What is important are the roles associated with responsibilities for the care of family members, particularly children, in a specific context, not who occupies these roles. As roles within families are increasingly degendered, and both parents have a significant participation in the public sphere, we would expect reasoning to change and a wider range of resources to be available. Instead of being limited to local solutions (but these should not be undervalued), both parents will have wider horizons for their reasoning and responses. In other words, as the gendering of family-related roles is reduced, the association between gender and environmentalism may disappear.[2]

To summarize: the contexts in which adults with responsibilities for children are located, and the roles they have both within and outside the family, create either opportunities or limitations on their reasoning about possible and actual impacts of environmental problems on the family and about contributions that they can make to reducing them. This reasoning, within the context of available resources, makes it possible to explain the choices they make,

Gender and Environmentalism

and the actions they take. Adults whose roles are entirely or mainly located within the family will reason and respond differently to adults with family responsibilities whose roles include a significant involvement in the public sphere.

This statement is hypothetical in the sense that research is required to investigate whether it reflects the way people in such contexts think and act. However, it is not a hypothesis of the kind used in the Neo-Positive paradigm; it is not a statement of a relationship between two concepts. Rather, it is about a possible generative *mechanism* operating in a particular *context* that produces a certain kind of *outcome*.

The other finding of interest in the 1992 study was the attitude concerning the 'level of confidence in the ability of science and technology to solve environmental problems'. It was suggested earlier that this regularity might also reflect the local/global differences in gendered roles. It is therefore possible to see this regularity as being part of the one just discussed. However, there is another line of investigation that could be pursued.

An obvious gender difference that might be relevant here is educational subject choices. Is this view of the role of science and technology a consequence of the fact that fewer women than men include mathematics and the sciences in their education, and choose occupations that are less dependent on these disciplines? Has this produced a lower level of understanding of the value of these disciplines? Or do women tend to see scientific and technological solutions as being too removed from everyday life, or as being masculine rather than feminine? We leave it to the reader to contemplate a possible regularity-context-mechanism-outcome model to formulate these ideas.

Concepts

Unlike in the Neo-Positive paradigm, it is not necessary to identify key concepts or to define and operationalize them. Rather, concepts are present in the hypothetical model and these, and others, will play a sensitizing role in the investigation of the explanatory model. In this illustration, the following concepts will play this role:

Traditional and modern families
Environmental issues and problems
Home making and child rearing
Family health and welfare
Reasoning and resources

Establishing and confirming the model

It is important to note that, while a researcher may set out with a hypothetical model of an explanatory mechanism, in the end this has to be confirmed with the social actors in the context under investigation. The initial model is only a guide for the investigation. The aim is to see whether the hypothesized mechanism fits with the way social actors reason and make choices in this type of context.

A sample could be drawn from men and women who are married, or living in a stable relationship, and who have responsibility for dependent children. As it will not be possible in advance to know what roles adults play within and outside the family, quota sampling could be used to select couples in 'traditional' and 'modern' family roles, as well as an intermediate 'transition' category. A preliminary, unstructured interview phase could be used to identify the couple's dominant role type and to allocate them to the three family-type categories. In addition, quota sampling could be used to include a range of background variables, using three categories based on general socio-economic status (using standard indicators) and three categories based on location (city, country town/village and rural areas). A cube matrix based on these three criteria will have 27 cells. With three couples in each cell, a total sample of 81 couples would be required.

A combination of unstructured and 'realist' interviews (see Pawson 1995, 1996; Pawson and Tilley 1997) could be used. Unstructured interviewing would be appropriate in an exploratory phase to obtain social actors' accounts of their environmental concerns, and the actions they have taken in response to them, as well as the extent to which the couples' roles are gendered. This first phase should provide an answer to the first research question. A second round of interviews, with the same couples, could use 'realist' interviewing to investigate research participants' reasoning and choices in this context. This requires:

> a teacher–learner relationship to be developed between researcher and informant in which the medium of exchange is the CMO [context, mechanism, outcome] theory and the function of that relationship is to refine the CMO theories. The research act thus involves 'learning' the stakeholder's theories, formalizing them, 'teaching' them back to the informant, who is then in a position to comment upon, clarify and further refine the key ideas. (Pawson and Tilley 1997: 218)

Gender and Environmentalism 203

In this kind of interviewing, the researcher sets out with a hypothetical model of the mechanism and the context but has to learn about the research participant's reasoning and choices from *them*. From this dialogue, the hypothetical model stated earlier will either be confirmed or will need to be refined. This will provide an answer to the second research question.

Summary

This illustration has focused on the reasoning and choices made by social actors in a particular context, with the aim of identifying the explanatory mechanism that will answer the 'why' research question. Retroductive logic was used to arrive at this mechanism. To establish whether this *is* the mechanism, it is necessary to use an interviewing technique that requires social actors to educate the researcher about their reasoning and choices in this context.

The model hypothesizes that underlying the concept of 'gender' is a variety of ways of reasoning and choosing that, in this particular context, have more to do with level of responsibility for the care of children and whether roles occupied are predominantly in the private rather than the public domain. While, traditionally, this distinction has been associated with the gendered division of labour, changes in the roles in which males and females now engage may render the older gender differences irrelevant.

One of the intentions behind the selection of this illustration has been to provide a contrast between the Critical Realist and Neo-Positive research paradigms. Because the two research problems addressed in each illustration have emerged from the same research programme, together they constitute the use of research paradigms in a multiple mode; different research questions from the same research programme have been investigated using different research paradigms. These possibilities will be taken up in the next chapter.

A concluding note: the critical aspect of the use of this research paradigm remains latent rather than manifest in this illustration. There are many global and local environmental threats that adults with responsibilities for raising the next generation have to contend with. Climate change is obviously significant, with present and potential impacts on this and future generations. And there are other problems: sceptical and even climate change-denying politicians in power; vested interests that lobby governments to reduce or even cancel policies that are designed to address climate change and other environmental problems; corporations that place profit ahead of social responsibility; new resource extraction methods that cannibalize productive food-producing farmland and create the potential for groundwater contamination; oil spills that lead to serious pollution and expensive restoration; industrial contamination of land and waterways; salinity problems that are caused by intensive irrigation; and excessive food miles caused by supermarkets sourcing cheaper products from lower-cost economies when the same products are available locally.

Investigating how adults with child-rearing responsibilities reason about and act towards such overwhelming problems may seem to be trivial by comparison. Similar studies on the reasoning of politicians and business leaders would provide a more extensive understanding of what needs to be done to address these problems. The framework outlined in this research proposal could be used as a starting point.

2 Why Leaders' Broader Experiences Support Better Outcomes of First Responders in Crises

Introduction

The chapter 6 component of this Crisis Leadership research programme illustrated the construction of a typology of experiential influences and a typology of leader orientations. They help to better understand leaders' choices of repertoire (i.e. their role identities, sense making, decision making and action orientations) when responding to four bushfire emergencies. An analytic imagination then led to arguing from evidence that more effective agency responses were associated with leaders whose lived experiences were not predominantly or exclusively institutional. The theoretical propositions about crisis leadership illustrated in chapter 6 are restated here:

Propositions:

(a) All leaders reason from their wisdom and their know-how.
(b) Wisdom is the basis for the insight that builds as well as connects particular know-how with situations and their contexts.
(c) Different know-how may construct different data or may notice different data and differently interpret data about a situation.

Therefore:

(d) The greater the breadth of wisdom and know-how, the greater is the potential for a leader to reason beyond institutional wisdom and know-how. This is particularly relevant when the response

Leaders' Experiences and Outcomes

demands of a natural disaster overwhelm the competence, capability and capacity of an agency to respond.

This theory is based on associations established within the Interpretive paradigm but it raises some further questions.

Q. 1 *Why* are some leaders of critical bushfire emergency responses more effective than others?
Q. 2 *How* can better leaders of crisis responses be identified or developed?

Answering these questions appears to offer prospects that go beyond understanding and into the realm of benefits for society. This illustration indicates a way to address these two questions from within the Critical Realist paradigm, and it assumes that the reader is familiar with the background and findings of the Neo-Positive and Interpretive illustrations in chapters 4 and 6.

Road map for this illustration

The Critical Realist paradigm is concerned with constructing and then finding evidence for an underlying causal mechanism that explains a regularity in a particular context. As the clarity, bounds, nuances and discriminating detail of descriptions of a context and a regularity increase, the researcher has a greater variety of characteristics to refer to when assembling and analysing data in order to establish evidence for the existence of the proposed causal mechanism. The four aspects, of context and regularity, together with causal mechanism and then evidence, are the crux of a Critical Realist study. In this illustration, these four aspects account for the bulk of the work that is presented here. However, other aspects of a typical Critical Realist study are still needed in order to sufficiently describe such research.

The Critical Realist paradigm in action is discussed and illustrated here in the following sections.

- The phenomenon of interest and the research problem
- Context and regularity
- Purpose and population
- Relevant literature
- Construct a causal mechanism
- Evidence – data and analysis
- When to stop

The phenomenon of interest and the research problem

Background details of the phenomenon are set out in chapter 4 (pp. 80–5). In the earlier illustrations (chapters 4 and 6), we considered, on the one hand, associations between a leader's wisdom, insight, know-how and interpretation of data and, on the other, the identities that a leader may adopt, as well as the sense making, decision making and action directives they undertake, as part of crisis-response leadership. In this illustration, we draw on these concepts and associations when explaining patterns between professional and life experiences and the outcomes of critical bushfire responses to which leaders contribute.

Because the regularity under investigation is about leaders' experience and crisis-response outcome, we remind the reader of the essence of the meaning that leader experience and response outcome have. A leader's lived experiences are those arising directly from agency employment and volunteer work, as well as from all other experiences in a leader's life, including distinctly different employment, community, family and personal activities. Experiences span straightforward everyday routines, developmental activities such as education or job change, through to profoundly challenging experiences, such as crises and disasters. An agency's crisis-response outcome reflects stakeholders' post-emergency assessments of inertial, expected and actual outcomes as consequences of the agency's response actions.

Context and regularity

An important first step in a Critical Realist study is to establish a clear description of the context and the regularity to be explained. The context of this illustration is confined to major bushfire crises in Australia since 2013. This is because the study needs first-hand accounts from people with fire-response leadership roles who are able to recall subtle detail about their roles, sense making, decision making and action orientations, as well as access to detailed records to inform probing and clarification of leaders' accounts. Other reasons for selecting major bushfire events in Australia for this study are that: they are frequent and span all major states, so it is easier to get a wide diversity of leader inputs; the organizing, systems, resourcing and legal arrangements for rural fire-agency responses are comparable across Australia; and the movement of professional and volunteer fire agency personnel between agencies and between states

Leaders' Experiences and Outcomes 207

(e.g. Tasmania, Victoria, South Australia, Western Australia and New South Wales) is comparatively low. These aspects reduce confounding factors that would otherwise present significant countervailing influences on the argument about evidence for the existence or otherwise of the proposed causal mechanism.

So, simply stated, the context for the mechanism is:

> Leading emergency services responses to critical post-2013 bushfires in Australia, where the initial scale and pace of a bushfire exceeded the abilities of combined emergency services agencies to adequately respond in order to avert unacceptable loss of lives and/or disruption or loss of significant economic social and environmental activity, resources, assets and infrastructure.

When considering this context, it is important not to overlook the wicked-problem characteristics (e.g. the fast-changing, complex, ambiguous, conflicted nature) of critical bushfire emergencies and their response demands. Remaining aware of this is essential to devising a plausible causal mechanism and then finding evidence for it.

In this illustration, the regularity that we consider is: 'In responses to critical natural disaster emergencies, leaders with broader life experience are more associated with perceived response effectiveness than are leaders with narrower but deeper professional experience alone.' This was introduced in the companion illustrations in chapters 4 and 6.

Purpose and population

Two of the most challenging aspects of a Critical Realist research project are: proposing a causal mechanism for a regularity; and describing how particular data in context may be obtained and analysed in a way that constitutes evidence for the mechanism's existence and its mode of operation. In considering these two aspects, the researcher will adopt the *depth realist* ontological assumptions, although the researcher may, at different times throughout the study, be expected to work with other ontological assumptions.

In this illustration, adapted for this book, the population of interest comprises the mix of critical bushfires in Australia since 2013, together with their agency-response leaders at all levels; from captains and brigade leaders at field level through IMT leaders and up to state coordinators, chief officers and commissioners responsible for state and national response coordination. Not all bushfires are included here but only those whose scope and speed overwhelmed agencies' response ability shortly after each incident was declared.

Relevant literature

Referring to literature is helpful when: describing contexts and populations as well as variously modelling the regularity of interest; scanning for ideas that help to devise potential causal mechanisms; defining criteria against which a potential causal mechanism will be selected; searching for and arguing the merits of evidence for the existence of the selected causal mechanism; arguing for the bounds (quasi-generalizability) of the contexts in which the regularity and causal mechanism hold; and critiquing the research and suggesting further research problems, questions and settings and their importance. The literature already noted in chapters 4, 6 and 7 is sufficient for the purpose and scope of this illustration.

Construct a causal mechanism

The causal mechanism outlined here is based on the WIKID*way*™ model that emerged from research and consulting (Priest 2008, 2009; Priest and Sarne 2006, 2011). This work focused on (in)effective leadership and management reasoning[3] in technology-enabled business performance, business and organization crisis response and managing natural disaster response.

The causal mechanism to be described comprises structures, resources, interrelationships and operational triggers. It will be used to account for how and why different experience influences, and is influenced by, contextually located sense making and decision making as part of bushfire-crisis response.

The reader is reminded that chapter 4 refers to and elaborates the part that exposure, noticing, internalizing and performing play when a person transforms an experience into their reasoning resources (Wisdom, Insight, Know-how, Interpretation and Data) that shape their sense making and decision making.

The model and its elements The WIKID*way*™ model (www.InfoServ.com.au) is about a particular reflexive relationship between: (a) evolving social world associations, activities and their effects; and (b) five types of evolving reasoning resources and their interaction. In this relationship, the latter are a product of, and a cause of, the former. This dualistic relationship is summarized in the statement:

[Social world [Associated activity [Patterns]]] ↔
[Wisdom [Insight [Know-how [Interpretation [Data]]]]]

The symbol ↔ means 'reflexively interacts with'. The nested brackets indicate successive frames of reference within which meaning, understanding, explanation or even role or purpose is revealed. For instance, Know-how [Interpretation [Data]] indicates that Know-how operates as a frame of reference and resource for Interpretation, which shapes the defining and meaning of Data. The statement suggests that a causal explanation for an evolving pattern or regularity in a social world may be constructed in terms of a reflexive interaction between people's reasoning resources that comprise cognitive, emotional and behavioural processes and content.

In the social world of leading responses to bushfire crises, it is proposed that the regularity between broader experience and more acceptable response outcomes may be causally explained in terms of the operation of the WIKID*way*™ model. The model may be conceptualized at two levels. The first schematic (Figure 8.1) depicts the connection between a leader's reasoning resources and their context. These resources are activated by start/stop rules or events, and the regularity is the aggregate of the effects produced directly as a result of the resources in action. The second schematic (Figure 8.2) depicts five types of interrelated reasoning resources that a leader draws on – Wisdom, Insight, Know-how, Interpretation and Data.

Figure 8.1 depicts the boundary of the context as a dotted line. This is to reinforce the idea that a leader's five types of reasoning resources are part of the context. This figure also depicts two important dynamics that characterize the causal nature and effects of leaders' reasoning. First, reasoning typically starts and stops according to triggers, which are typically detectable conditions, events or states. Second, reasoning produces effects whose symptoms are detectable by the context's social actors. It follows, therefore, that reasoning may modify the context and, as a result, possibly change future triggering of this activity. This is highlighted at ❶ in Figure 8.1. In this way, the nature of a leader's reasoning and the modes of operation remain stable but the specific content and processes, when subject to the same contextual triggers, may later produce different effects.

Figure 8.2 depicts the five interrelated types of resource that are

210   Critical Realist Research Paradigm in Action

CONTEXT
A particular social and physical world
Social actors in a physical setting are part of a phenomenon that exhibits a regularity

Causal Mechanism
Reasoning resources' processes and contents

Start/stop triggers
Systems and conditions that exist in the context.

Effects
of causal mechanism's operation

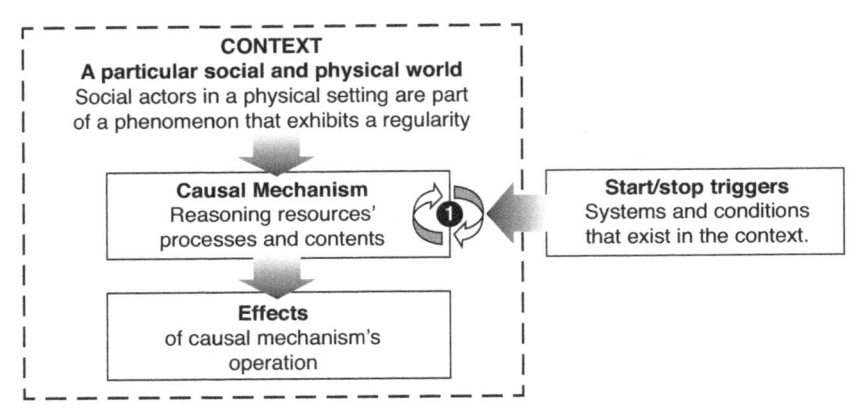

Figure 8.1   A causal mechanism in context

Wisdom
(WorldViews + Situations → Approaches)

Insight
(Wisdom + Know-How → Perception)

Know-How
(Knowledge + Application → Competencies)

Interpret
(Data + Know-How → Meanings)

Data
(LocalWorld + Proxies → DataInstances)

Start/stop triggers

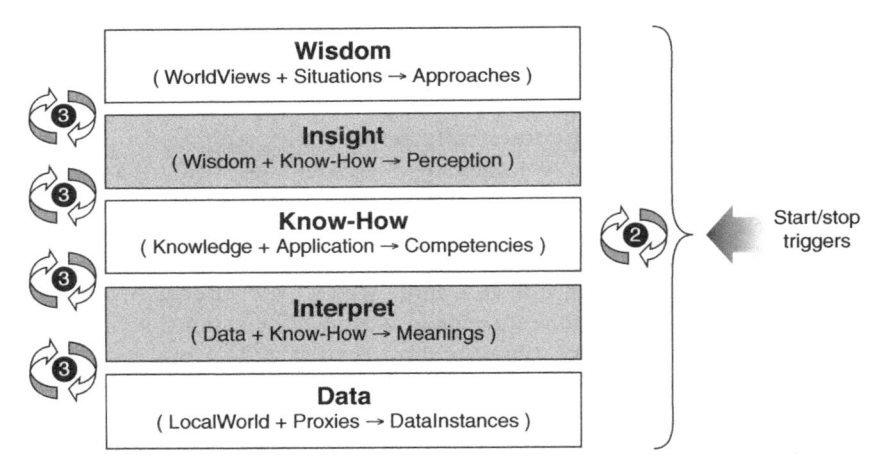

Figure 8.2   Five types of interrelated reasoning resources

involved in a leader's reasoning. Each type of resource is a distinctive collection of substantive contents and processes that a person may use when they are involved in sense making and decision making, such as when a leader is determining responses to a bushfire crisis confronting a remote rural community.

In broad terms, these five types of resources are as follows.

- *Wisdom* is about local and global ways of 'looking' at things in a particular social world and being able to use the resulting views to inform understanding as well as to guide effective and acceptable

ways to operate in the social world.
- *Insight* is about seeing a more fundamental nature of something, some activity and/or some situation; it is also about discerning signature characteristics and caricatures, as well as what is surprisingly present or surprisingly absent.
- *Know-how* is a combination of knowledge and ways to use knowledge ranging across substantive knowledge and competence in the application of knowledge to social and material worlds.
- *Interpretation* is about choosing and using particular know-how in order to define or select and then make sense of, and/or make decisions about, instances of data that represent aspects of the social or material world.
- *Data* refer to proxies and their instances as representation that epitomize or just symbolize a particular aspect of a social or material world.

Each of the five types of resource evolves as a result of feedback from the contextual effects of its interaction with the other reasoning resources. In this way, broader and deeper experience expands the potential for reasoning. And, if associated braiding occurs, then improved reasoning and, hence, improved sense making and decision making may follow.

Figure 8.2 also highlights two important dynamics that characterize the way reasoning operates. Firstly, trigger conditions may change as a result of contextually located lessons about the effectiveness of a leader's previous sense making and decision making. This is highlighted at ❷ in Figure 8.2. Secondly, the mechanism for reasoning may change the reasoning resources that comprise Wisdom, Insight, Know-how, Interpretation and Data, and possibly the way they cooperate, but not the structure of the mechanism of reasoning. This is partly because of a feedback relationship between choices and effects and also because of the stochastic influence of context factors not included in the mechanism. This is highlighted at ❸ in Figure 8.2.

The dynamics associated with Figures 8.1 and 8.2 describe the dialectic nature of reasoning: (1) making sense and making decisions; and (2) modifying its own resources based on the effectiveness of the sense and decisions made. In this way, compared to narrowly defined experience, wide-ranging experience introduces and enables broader reasoning resources and activity. This feed-forward and feed-back character is distinctive in three ways: asynchronous evolution; cross-dependence; and braiding.

- *Asynchronous evolution* refers to the tendency for each of the five types of reasoning to first change with learning, then with performance and then with their history of use. Thus, a change in a reasoning resource may not immediately be followed by a change in its use.
- *Cross-dependence* refers to the tendency for use of one reasoning resource to influence content change in another resource. Similarly, content change in one resource may influence the use of another resource. Such influence may be direct or inverse.
- *Braiding* is the process by which each reasoning resource and its use co-validates others according to the experience of their use.

Thus, the history of each reasoning resource and its uses shapes future resources and uses. So, for radically different experiences, the starting points of sense making and decision making are quite different; so too are the effects and the nature and treatment of feedback.

The causal and explanatory power of the mechanism of reasoning rests on this dualistic nature. Note, also, that the structure of reasoning remains constant, although its processes and content evolve with an individual's contextual experiences.

Implication The WIKID*way*™ model has the explanatory potential of a causal mechanism to explain the regularity previously noted between *leaders' broader experience* and *better crisis-response outcomes*.

The model is plausible for the following reasons.

- It is specific – with well-defined elements and relationship rules between and within elements.
- It is comprehensive – it accounts for a wide range of cognitive, emotional and behavioural processes and contents identified in the literature as fundamental to a person's reasoning, actions and interactions, which are part of taking on and performing roles, as well as sense making and decision making.
- It involves learning and start/stop rules that account for causal activity.
- It is a contingent mechanism – capable of constrained as well as self-adjusting activity.
- It is capable of producing the sorts of effects that can be detected in the actual and empirical domains.

In the next section, we discuss how we propose to assemble data and argue the evidence for the existence of the proposed causal mechanism of reasoning.

Evidence from data and analysis

Notwithstanding Critical Realism's distinctive stratified ontology, social realities in the Critical Realist paradigm reflect social actors' concepts and activities in their particular world. For this reason, the epistemological account of a Critical Realist study can be expected to include, or appear in parts to be similar to, aspects of Interpretive inquiry, such as abstracting and theorizing (which rely heavily on Interpretivism's dominant logic of *abduction*, with support from *induction* and *deduction*, in noticing and testing patterns and theoretical possibilities).

In order to find out about and argue for evidence of a causal mechanism, Harré and Secord (1972) suggested that one way the Critical Realist researcher may explain a particular pattern in a part of social life is to dig into what people do and think in relation to relevant noteworthy events and practices. Specifically, they suggest that the researcher focuses on:

- the decisions, behaviours, actions and interactions that individuals voluntarily describe as being central to the parts they play in their social world;
- the thinking (assumptions, methods, rules, concepts, meanings, understandings) that individuals describe as underpinning their own decisions, behaviours, actions and interactions; and
- critically cross-analysing these participant accounts against other observed aspects in order to test the strength (i.e. consistency and scope) of data in relation to the proposed or emergent explanatory model that may partly arise from this type of focused effort.

The aim of this focus is to find evidence for the hidden cognitive, emotional and behavioural processes and content that make up the causal mechanism; the evidence arising indirectly through, for instance, observation and in-depth interviewing with reference to other sources, such as records, to help probing and cross-checking.

Sampling – overall considerations This study's evidence requirements must address the need for confirming and disconfirming evidence. Assiduously searching for both types of evidence, and judging confirming and disconfirming evidence, are bases for drawing a conclusion about the merits of the proposed causal mechanism.

Leaders' reasoning resources and dynamics are what the proposed mechanism focuses on when explaining the regularity between leaders' experience and fire responses. Therefore, selecting bushfires and associated leaders as sources of evidence must be on the basis of ready access to authentic and richly detailed accounts of responder roles, sense making, decision making and action orientation. The researcher must also consider access to agency and community records and other primary sources that will help to probe, qualify and cross-check the meaning of leaders' accounts.

While Australia's catastrophic February 2009 Black Saturday bushfires were, at the time, rich sources of data, it is now too long ago to access sufficient numbers and variety of relevant leaders whose memories and records will meet these conditions. When this illustration was drafted in 2016, potentially good sources of data from which evidence could be constructed were recent bushfires in any of Australia's states spanning the summer seasons of 2013, 2014 and 2015. Compared to the Black Saturday fires, leaders of agency responses to these fires are more likely still to be accessible, and their memories almost certainly fresher. Also, access to detailed documentation and other sources for the purpose of probing, qualifying and cross-checking the meaning of leaders' accounts of particular incidents, challenges, dilemmas, processes and emotions as they unfolded could be expected to be much improved compared to the situation with the Black Saturday fires or even earlier. Sampling more recent fires and leaders involved in related response efforts is more likely to ensure access to people's biographical backgrounds covering formative family, community, close friends, school aspects of childhood and early work years, as well as further training through teenage years and early/middle adult life.

Finding confirming and disconfirming evidence requires samples that offer access to data about suitable fire events and leaders who exhibit all combinations of leader types and outcome types. A suitable sample will include: leaders at all levels with recent and detailed memory of their responder roles, sense making, decision making and action orientation; leaders at all levels associated with major fires that were widely regarded as 'well-handled' and others associated with major fires that were 'poorly handled'; leaders with significant broad life experience and others with narrow and deep institutional experience; critical bushfires for which detailed records of fire progress and response choices exist and are accessible; and critical bushfires for which detailed context and impact background documents and informants exist and are available.

Finding such a sample can be challenging. So, more recent fire events would comprise the initial sample and, as profile data are

Leaders' Experiences and Outcomes 215

gathered and analysed, the sample would progressively be reduced to ensure a more appropriate mix of cases and a more manageable research workload.

Depending on the number of acceptable-profile fire events and associated leaders, it may also be desirable to do the sampling, data gathering and analysis using a team of researchers. Unlike an exploratory Interpretive study, this approach is quite practical because the proposed causal mechanism being well defined would give all researchers a common orientation from which data would be sought, assessed and compared.

Classes of data Four classes of data are required: (1) data about leaders' cognitive, emotional and behavioural processes and content; (2) data about leaders' biographical and institutional experience; (3) data about the particular bushfire(s) that a leader's accounts relate to; and (4) data for each particular bushfire that reflects stakeholders' assessments of crisis-response effectiveness.

Three broad approaches to obtaining these data from the sample will guide the data-analysis efforts.

Depth interviews   These are directed explorations with:

(a) each leader – the purpose being to explore the private cognitive, emotional and behavioural processes and content that leaders disclose and elaborate when they account for what they and others report as their public-situation roles, sense making, decision making and action orientation; and
(b) fire event stakeholders (e.g. local community leaders, local infrastructure and service provider representatives, resident and business representatives) – the purpose being to elicit stakeholders' assessments of the effectiveness of an agency's overall fire response.

Profile interviews   These are structured-elaboration interviews in which:

(a) leaders, their close family members and close colleagues profile the variety, scope and impact of the leader's professionally formative and broader life-changing experiences; and
(b) subject matter specialists in government departments (e.g. Forestry, Land Management, Meteorology), fire response agencies (e.g. rural fire fighting agencies) and research groups

(e.g. cooperative research centres) profile the scale, impact threat and response challenges of each fire in the sample.

Corporate and research records   These types of records relate to fires or leaders in the sample and are hard copy (e.g. institutional reports), electronic (e.g. emails, digital voice records, digital video images, e-maps, blogs, social media posts), personal diaries, legal inquiries (e.g. commissions or inquests), as well as researchers' working papers and published peer-review journal articles. They are used to help profile each fire in the sample, probe leaders' accounts and elaboration of their reasoning and conduct as part of their fire-response roles, and probe and qualify stakeholders' assessments of agencies' overall response effectiveness.

For all these sources, the researcher's core task is to use the proposed causal mechanism to inform the preparation of a rich description of the context and instances of the absence or presence of the elements of the proposed mechanism in action. The argument for affirming evidence rests on the preponderance of confirming data and the absence of contradictory data, notwithstanding alternative explanations remaining possible.

Getting participants' accounts   Non-directed elaboration is an approach in which the researcher does not disclose to participants the specific model elements and their relationships. That is, the interviewer does not mention wisdom, insight, know-how, interpretation or data, or their meanings and interrelationships. However, the interviewer will state a broad intention to better understand a leader's awareness of their cognitive, emotional and behavioural states, and activities when they are involved in situational sense making and decision making and when they assume or change particular roles, as well as their situational sense making and decision making during the course of the fire response. Similarly, when interviewing leaders and their colleagues and family about what it is in the leader's life that has significantly contributed to making the leader the person they are, the interviewer will not explicitly state or elaborate the specific notions of experience that are part of the proposed causal model. Rather, they will invite interviewees to comment on and further elaborate cues that they voluntarily offer, which might relate to life-changing experience and memorable and formative professional experience.

Hence, the idea is to encourage interviewees to talk and elaborate issues pertinent to the model without specifically flagging concepts and meanings that are part of the model. The researcher has the model in mind but the interviewees do not. The researcher shows interest in and encourages interviewees to reflect on and elaborate matters that can either help to put flesh on the bones of the model or contradict what the model asserts as a causal activity that gives rise to the regularity. This approach differs from that advocated by Pawson (1996).

Analysing data This is a three-layered process involving micro- (low-level) analysis, meso- (middle-level) analysis and macro- (high-level) analysis.

Micro-analysis involves the researcher in a hermeneutic examination of each leader's account of why and how their role choices, sense making, decision making and action orientation during a particular bushfire evolved as they did. The aim is to identify and classify occurrences of each causal-model concept and relationship (i.e. heuristics and operating rules, including starting and stopping rules) that can systematically be associated with the leader's account.

At this level of analysis, the researcher seeks to identify a leader's personal concepts about what they draw on and how they approach the way they reason, and then relate these to specific elements of the proposed causal mechanism. Once this has been done, the researcher is able to produce a summary of the occurrences and the strength of correspondences between each bushfire leader's account of the bases for their role choices, sense making, decision making and action orientation, and elements of the proposed causal mechanism.

The results of this level of analysis may be imagined as a set of two-dimensional tables. Each table corresponds to a particular combination of leader and bushfire. Each entry in a table shows the frequency and intensity of association between a bushfire leader's particular reasoning processes and contents on the one hand and an element of the causal model on the other hand. An element of a causal model is a resource, a relationship between two resources or an operating rule (such as an 'if–then' statement or a condition such as an on/off trigger about some aspects of the mechanism's active state).

Meso-analysis requires that the researcher interprets the various sources of data about each leader's specific professional experiences, and broader life experiences, in order to associate with each of these two types of richly described experiences a simple ranked label. For instance, each leader's professional experience and broader life experience may each be classified according to a seven-point Likert-type scale. Similarly, the researcher may interpret various stakeholder sources of data about each fire's perceived overall fire-response assessment using a similar type of scale. The common modes of bias usually associated with a Likert-type scale do not apply, as the task is performed by the one trained researcher. Therefore, comparisons of ranks between types and level of experience are possible, as are comparisons of ranks between fire response assessments.

Macro-analysis classifies occurrences of the causal mechanism's elements, interrelationships and start/stop triggers according to leader experience and associated fire-response types from which the occurrences are derived. A three-dimensional table of model-component occurrences, experience type and fire-response type is a result of this level of analysis. This type of analysis enables development of a table showing relative-experience mix and corresponding fire-response mix for all leaders and all fires in the sample. Compared to the use of narrative text alone, such a table makes it easier to apprehend the prominence or otherwise of the regularity and its co-occurrence with elements of the proposed causal mechanism. Because the presence and absence of associations are both apparent, such a compound image constitutes the argument for existence of the proposed causal mechanism, as well as visually presenting the strength of the argument.

Three major assumptions apply in this form of multi-level analysis: the protocols for data gathering and analysis are well defined and consistently applied across the evolving sample; the researcher(s) purposively maintain(s) a detailed awareness of the model's concepts, proposed dynamics and causative actions, and checks for their existence in all the primary data; and the researcher(s) conducting the analysis will be trained and will consistently apply protocols for judging and comparing ranked metadata.

When to stop

Establishing evidence for the existence of the proposed causal mechanism is not simply a consequence of a thoroughly designed, well-resourced and carefully executed study. It may be the case that the proposed causal mechanism does not exist or that its existence is well masked or even supported by unrecognized confounding factors. Because the researcher is also using participant accounts to access participants' 'hidden' reasoning resources, participants' reflections and expressions can be expected to at least partly model aspects of social worlds other than the social world in which each leader operated when responding to sampled fire events. Hence, distinguishing authentic from transitive data and meanings remains a challenge with the approach outlined here. For these kinds of reasons, a researcher cannot be sure when to conclude data gathering, analysis and development of pattern-based evidence.

A practical stopping rule is that, as a proposed model's simplicity (i.e. elegance) and comprehensiveness increases, then less supportive evidence that is counter-intuitive is needed and more dismissive evidence that is counter-intuitive is required. This is not a clear-cut rule but it does offer guidance for progressively designing studies, and assembling evidence and argument, to either accept or reject a potential causal model and mechanism.

9
Multiple Paradigm Research

Chapter summary

- The purpose of this chapter is to introduce the idea that a research programme that uses more than one research paradigm has the potential to generate better answers to 'why' research questions.
- This chapter begins with a reiteration of the key research principles that have been elaborated, developed and illustrated in the previous chapters.
- It then picks up a notion that has been implicit in the illustrations, i.e. that it is possible to use more than one research paradigm in a research project.
- By returning to some of those illustrations, it shows how research paradigms can be used in parallel or in sequence, thus constituting two versions of multi-paradigm research.

Introduction

Throughout the book, we have stressed the need to conduct social research with explicit philosophical assumptions and logics of inquiry, and with consistency between these and decisions made about other elements of a research project. We have also stressed that a research problem needs to be translated into one or more research questions. Some research projects may require only one question, particularly in situations in which little is known of the phenomenon and some description of it is required (say, a 'what' question). In the reverse situation, the phenomenon may have already been well described but an explanation is required for a previously discovered pattern or regularity (say, a 'why' question). What is more likely is that an investigation will require a number of research questions. All the illustrations in chapters 4, 6 and 8 are like this.

We have also indicated that answering 'what' questions is different to answering 'why' questions; the requirements for producing a description are different from producing an explanation. 'What' questions are answered by collecting or generating relevant data and then, using either *induction* or *abduction*, producing generalizations from the data that will answer the question. However, when 'why' questions are involved, explanatory ideas have to be produced, either top-down or bottom-up, and finding and testing these ideas is the challenge.

When researchers make a commitment to only one paradigm, they limit their potential to produce the best possible answers to their 'why' questions. Like the advocates of mixed-method research, but for rather different reasons, we also strongly support the use of a variety of methods of data gathering/generation and analysis. Nevertheless, to reiterate a point made in chapter 1, the choice of methods is not the fundamental issue in social research, and there is not a one-to-one relationship between research paradigms and types of methods. This means that, in choosing a research paradigm to answer a particular research question, a researcher is *not* making a commitment to use particular methods, or even only one.

Apart from the initial institutional sexual abuse of children and young people illustration, introduced in chapter 2, each of the illustrations has used just one research paradigm. However, hints were given that, in some of these, more than one research paradigm could have been used. It should also now be obvious that the three crisis leadership illustrations in chapters 4, 6 and 8 comprise a research programme with a range of research questions answered using the three research paradigms. It constitutes what we call 'multi-paradigm research'; typically, questions answered within one part of a research programme, using just one of the paradigms, raises further questions that can be answered using one of the other research paradigms, and so on.

Because of the complexity of the research problem in the illustration on institutional sexual abuse of children and young people, a number of research questions were required. Three of these questions are used here to illustrate how such a set of questions can be answered using different research paradigms; it becomes a multi-paradigm study with paradigms being selected for their ability to provide, in the researcher's judgement, the best way to answer each question. The consequence of using research paradigms in this way is that neither the research nor the researchers can be labelled in terms of a single paradigm, in the way that 'qualitative' and 'quantitative' are commonly used.

We have deliberately referred to the use of a number of research paradigms within a research project as 'multiple or multi-paradigm', rather than 'mixed-paradigm'. There is an important reason for this. While we have argued that some research questions lend themselves to the use of more than one paradigm, we are not proposing that paradigms be mixed to answer a single research question. Given the differences in their ontological and epistemological assumptions, mixing makes no sense. There is nothing to prevent a researcher attempting to answer a particular research question in more than one way, using a different paradigm on each occasion. Whether the answers turn out to be the same, similar or different is an open question and one that may stimulate further questioning and investigation.

It is important to note that the use of multiple paradigms has nothing to do with the popular idea of triangulation.[1] Having answers to a research question from more than one point of view may be useful, but paradigms cannot be combined to produce a more complete answer. However, they can be used *in parallel* or *sequentially*.

Two types of multi-paradigm research

In the *parallel*-use type, an array of research questions is answered using a variety of research paradigms. Leaving aside the necessary sequence in answering related 'what' and 'why' questions, where the former has to be answered before it becomes evident what the latter needs to explain, the order in which a set of 'why' questions is investigated is usually not important.

In the *sequential*-use type, research questions form a chain in which answers to the first raise the next question, and so on. Successive questions can be answered using the same or different paradigms. Both 'what' and 'why' questions can be approached, even alternating between them, as answering a 'why' question can raise further 'what' or 'why' questions. Sometimes, later questions can go off at a tangent, and maybe even stimulate another research programme. There is potential for this in the first Neo-Positive illustration. In the sequential-use type, researchers can be learning as they go, with the answer to one question raising further questions. Perhaps this is the ideal way for new knowledge to be generated. In practice, a researcher may have to meet certain requirements that constrain this ideal, such as finishing a thesis within a certain time. In such cases, it may be safer to deal with a set of research questions in parallel.

Two illustrations

Two illustrations of multi-paradigm research are provided here. These presentations will be very much briefer than those in the previous illustrations as the focus is not on the origin, nature and use of paradigms but on how they can be used in combination.

As indicated above, the first illustration takes up other aspects of the institutional sexual abuse of children and young people illustration and shows how paradigms can be used in parallel. The second illustration draws together the three crisis leadership illustrations in chapters 4, 6 and 8 and shows how they constitute an example of sequential multi-paradigm research. This is not to suggest that a change of paradigm must be made at each stage, just that it may be useful to do so.

1 Sexual Abuse of Children and Young People in the Catholic Church

Introduction

When this research project was introduced in chapter 2, an illustration was provided of how one research question could be answered using all three research paradigms. Here it will be used to demonstrate how three 'why' research questions can each be answered using one of the paradigms.

As the questions are dealt with independently, this illustration is an example of the *parallel* use of multi-paradigm research. In this case, the questions cover different aspects of the research problem.

Research questions

As indicated in chapter 2, this illustration will address three of the research questions that were introduced there.

Q. 2 *Why* have the perpetrators of child sexual abuse engaged in these activities?
Q. 4 *Why* have victims remained silent for so long?

Q. 5 *Why* have church leaders and administrators not dealt with perpetrators in appropriate legal and responsible humanitarian ways?

Choice of paradigms to answer three research questions

While the assumption behind this illustration is that a different research paradigm will be used with each of the three research questions, in practice a decision might be made to use the same paradigm for all the questions. The issue is, what would lead you to make that decision, or the choice of a combination of paradigms? A cursory glance at these three questions does not suggest an obvious choice of research paradigm. The choices that follow, and the justifications for them, are illustrative only. (Factors that influence the choice of research paradigm are discussed in chapter 10.)

Q. 2 *Why* have the perpetrators of child sexual abuse engaged in these activities?

This question addresses the first regularity.

> *Choice*: Neo-Positive paradigm.
> *Reasons for choice*: It lends itself to deductive theorizing and hypothesis testing; perpetrators may be reluctant to be interviewed in depth and may not be open because of guilt and shame. They have not been very forthcoming in public inquiries conducted in Australia. Would they respond to structured interviews? Would some other method of data collection be better?
> *Possible explanatory ideas*: The Church is a haven for paedophiles; celibacy has consequences; an underlying deviant culture may be tolerated; there is a disjunction between public rituals and private practices; forgiveness is always available through confession.

Q. 4 *Why* have victims remained silent for so long?

This question addresses the second regularity.

> *Choice*: Interpretive paradigm.
> *Reasons for choice*: In spite of the guilt and shame, there is evidence that victims are starting to speak out, sometimes decades after the events. Sensitive in-depth interviewing may be disturbing but also therapeutic. Victims may appreciate the opportunity to unburden themselves in a safe and anonymous environment.

Crisis Leadership: A Multi-Paradigm Research Programme

Possible explanatory ideas: Powerlessness; threats of serious consequences if this deviant behaviour is revealed; not being believed and being made to feel guilty; combinations of fear, guilt, shame and self-blame; lack of knowledge, power and opportunities to expose what happened to them.

Q. 5 *Why* have church leaders and administrators not dealt with perpetrators in appropriate legal and responsible humanitarian ways?

This question addresses parts of the third and fourth regularity.

Choice: Critical Realist paradigm.
Reasons for choice: Like perpetrators, so far most church leaders and administrators seem to have been reluctant to reveal their part in the secrecy and in the way they have dealt with perpetrators. The explanatory mechanisms may be similar to those used in answering question 3. Evidence for their existence may have to be pieced together from a variety of sources. Straightforward hypothesis testing with systematically collected data, as is appropriate in the Neo-Positive paradigm, may not be possible.
Possible explanatory ideas: Hierarchy of goals – maintenance of the institution takes precedence over pastoral care of members; resistance to intrusion of legal procedures; meaning of the vow of celibacy; interpretations of celibacy, homosexuality and sin.

It should be clear from this discussion that researchers need to be very familiar with the field of research and the possible opportunities and limitations for data gathering/generation. We invite you to consider other choices of paradigms and to justify them.

2 Crisis Leadership: A Multi-Paradigm Research Programme

The three crisis leadership illustrations in chapters 4, 6 and 8 comprise a research programme with a range of research questions that are answered *sequentially*, using the three research paradigms. The illustrations together constitute what we call multi-paradigm research.

The three research illustrations started with the following problem:

The frequency and severity of Australian bushfire emergencies that will outstrip the response ability of emergency agencies has increased and is expected to further increase over the coming decades.

Associated with this problem is an apparent regularity:

> In these critical emergencies, the decisions and actions of leaders with significant external experience (i.e. challenging lived experience that goes beyond their significant agency experience) are more associated with outcomes that achieve public approval than are the decisions and actions of those leaders with only significant agency experience.

Two questions that immediately arise from this are:

Q. 1 To *what* extent are leaders' external challenging lived experiences associated with response-effectiveness in critical emergencies?

Q. 2 If leaders' external experiences are increasingly associated with response-effectiveness in critical emergencies, then *why* is this so?

The first question invites a qualitative, quantitative or mixed description. In any event, a description is not necessarily paradigm dependent, so the illustration in chapter 4 focused on answering the 'why' question. Several approaches may have been taken, but answering the question within a Neo-Positive paradigm was chosen. The main reasons for this choice are: (1) this is an early-stage inquiry and there is considerable literature on leadership and crises, so deducing a theory to test is, prima facie, plausible; and (2) in-depth inquiries may need to investigate leadership failures at senior levels, as well as challenge well-entrenched philosophies, systems and interests, so an Interpretive inquiry can be expected to be more demanding.

The 'why' question was approached by first deducing, from pairs of statements, the 'maverick theory' of leadership that anticipates the regularity. Each pair of statements reflects a plausible relationship between concepts of leadership identity, reasoning and actions, and concepts that are central to the regularity – experience and outcomes. All that remained was to test the theory in order to corroborate or dismiss it. Answering the 'why' question from a Neo-Positive perspective helped to characterize the regularity and offer a plausible reason for its presence. However, this approach offered no evidence for the merits of, or deeper understanding about, the pairs of statements on which the theory is based. After all, the statements in the theory are only posited associations between concepts.

So, the Neo-Positive study provided some answers but also raised questions that sought deeper understanding about the nature and

Crisis Leadership: A Multi-Paradigm Research Programme 227

cause of the regularity. It also seemed that developing deeper understanding would help to develop ideas about causality rather than the reverse happening. With this in mind, the following two questions, which arose from the Neo-Positive illustration, were discussed in chapter 6.

Q. 3 *What* types of formal and also broader leadership experience are more or less helpful for leaders' reasoning in a crisis?
Q. 4 *Why* do the types of more helpful experience help to increase perceived first-responder effectiveness?

An Interpretivist treatment of the two questions is strongly indicated for the following three reasons: (1) what constitutes a challenging life experience, or an intense and formative organization experience, is a personal and social construction, and language and observation seem to be how a researcher may understand these experiences and the part they play in a leader's reasoning and actions; (2) literature on crisis leadership, challenging life experiences and reasoning (sense making and decision making) is disparate, so in-depth exploration can be expected to make a useful contribution; and (3) there is considerable literature about particular natural disaster events and the circumstances leading up to them as well as their aftermath, so this may provide valuable contextual material when exploring crisis leaders' reasoning and their reflections on the bases for their situational thinking and action.

Exploring issues and meanings can be expected to be stimulated by discussion of, for instance, the wicked nature of crisis situations, dichotomies (e.g. control + surprise, compliance + invention, procedure + intuition, clarity + confusion), dilemmas (e.g. conflicts between organization-moral, agency-community, career-personal, legal-ethical interests and principles), life-changing experiences and a leader's various identities (e.g. family, community, agency). The chapter 6 component of the research programme illustrated an Interpretive approach which, through the development of typologies and their conditional associations, generated theoretical understanding that answered the 'what' and 'why' questions.

As was the case with the Neo-Positive study, further questions emerged. In the case of the Interpretive study, two new questions were:

Q. 1 *Why* are some leaders of critical bushfire emergency responses more effective than others?

Q. 2 *How* can better leaders of crisis responses be identified or developed?

The 'why' question could be answered within any of the paradigms discussed in this book. A theory could be deduced and tested in the manner outlined in chapter 4, or another in-depth exploratory Interpretive study could be undertaken. However, as answering the accompanying 'how' question assumes some causal understanding, the 'why' question above invites treatment within a Critical Realist paradigm.

In the case of the Critical Realist paradigm illustration, a causal mechanism was adapted from related work and the researcher's knowledge of the substantive practice domain and context. Once a candidate causal mechanism was conceived and thoroughly described, it remained to find contextually salient evidence for the existence of the mechanism.

Deep substantive knowledge, and a lively and flexible theoretical imagination, are both very important ingredients when tackling 'why' and 'how' questions from the perspective of a Critical Realist paradigm. This reinforces, where possible, the value of undertaking exploratory depth studies ahead of seeking a causal explanation.

10
And Another Thing . . .

Chapter summary

- By way of review, this chapter returns to a number of important topics and adds some supplementary ones:
  - techniques that can be used in the neglected craft of theory construction and generation;
  - some ideas that can stimulate creativity in social research;
  - the issue of the porousness of some paradigm boundaries, particularly between the Interpretive paradigm and the constructionist version of the Critical Realist paradigm; and
  - possible influences on a researcher when a choice of research paradigm is made.
- Finally, the main theme of the book is revisited.

Introduction

This final chapter covers a number of supplementary topics, both further elaborations of issues introduced previously and some new ones that would have intruded or added too much complexity earlier.

The neglected craft of theory construction

Philosophical resistance

The founder of the version of Neo-Positivism that is presented in this book, Karl Popper, and some other philosophers who adopted or concurred with his views, regarded processes of theory construction as of no interest to philosophers of science. Popper distinguished between the *logic of knowledge* (referred to as logics of inquiry here) – the method by which theories are justified – and the *psychology of knowledge* – the process by which a new idea is conceived.

> The initial stage, the act of conceiving or inventing a theory, seems to me neither to call for logical analysis nor be susceptible to it. The question of how it happens that a new idea occurs to a man [sic] ... may be of great interest to empirical psychology; but it is irrelevant to the logical analysis of scientific knowledge. ... [T]here is no such thing as a logical method of having new ideas, or a logical reconstruction of this process. (Popper 1959 [1934]: 31, 32)

Popper made this statement in spite of the title of the book in which it appears, *The Logic of Scientific Discovery*. He argued that every discovery contains an 'irrational element' or 'creative intuition'. Reichenbach and Braithwaite presented similar views. Reichenbach (1948: 382) argued that philosophers of science cannot be concerned with reasons for suggesting hypotheses, only with reasons for accepting them, and Braithwaite proposed that it is a matter of 'the individual psychology of thinking and the sociology of thought' (1953: 20–1), neither of which is the concern of the philosopher.

This reluctance to consider the processes that researchers use to produce explanatory ideas is more than just a matter of drawing discipline boundaries. The rationale behind Popper's approach to the philosophy of science was his abhorrence of the logic of *induction*. In so far as theory construction might involve the use of *induction*, he wanted no truck with it. Unfortunately, Popper's dogmatic stance is of no help to the practising social scientist.

Medewar was critical of Popper's position in two books with titles that declare where he stood; *Induction and Intuition in Scientific Thought* (1969a) and *The Art of the Soluble: Creativity and Originality in Science* (1969b). He, like Popper, was concerned with explanation in the natural sciences and advocated the use of *deductive* rather than *inductive* logic, but what he had to say applies equally well to the social sciences.

> The major defect of the hypothetico-deductive scheme [read Neo-Positivist research paradigm], considered as a formulary of scientific behaviour, is its disavowal of any competence to speak about the generative act in scientific inquiry, 'having an idea', for this represents the imaginative or logically unscripted episode in scientific thinking, the part that lies outside logic. The objection is all the more grave because

an imaginative and inspirational process enters into all scientific reasoning at every level; it is not confined to 'great' discoveries, as the more simple-minded inductivists supposed. (Medewar 1969a: 55)

At the time that Popper and Medewar were writing, the only logics of inquiry being considered were *induction* and *deduction*, and many social scientists today seem to also confine their attention to them. However, the other logics discussed here, *abduction* and *retroduction*, are both concerned with theory construction.

The key task of the paradigms

The use of imagination and creativity are required in all three research paradigms. The generation of typologies in the Interpretive paradigm requires the use of creative imagination; and this is also necessary in the next step of generating an explicit theory from these types. The construction of hypothetical causal mechanisms in Critical Realism requires a great deal of imagination and creativity, as does the construction of deductive theories in the Neo-Positive paradigm, whether by the researcher or someone else. Researchers cannot expect to rely on others to have done this work for them. Even if ideas are borrowed from existing theories, they may have to be reformulated to suit the task at hand.

Any scientific attempt to explain some phenomenon requires not only the capacity to use some form of logic, and technical skills in data collection or generation and data analysis, but it also involves a high degree of creativity. The following discussion offers some ideas on what is involved in such an activity and how these abilities might be developed.

Dialogues in social research

Habermas A useful way to generate explanatory ideas is to think of the process as involving one or more monologues or dialogues. As we saw in chapter 7 (p. 183), Habermas (1970, 1972) argued that different modes of experience are used to understand the natural and social worlds; 'sense experience', or direct observation, in the natural sciences and 'communicative experience' in the social and human sciences. Natural scientists engage in a *monologue* with their subject matter, while social scientists can engage social actors in *dialogue*. Given that research participants have already pre-interpreted their social and cultural reality, social researchers need to discover these interpretations and use them as ingredients in social scientific accounts. This gives the social sciences a distinct advantage over the natural sciences in the task of generating explanations. Giddens (1984) extended this idea in his notion of the *double hermeneutic*.

In the Neo-Positivist paradigm, explanatory ideas are derived from the literature on both theory and research. This process is characterized as a monologue as the researcher does the 'talking', as it were, but the literature is silent. The literature cannot be engaged in conversation in the way that people can. As we shall see, there is a middle ground between monologue and dialogue.

Hermeneutics This characterization of the process is rather too simple. The reading of any literature involves a monologue with the author as well as the content. The hermeneutic tradition (see Blaikie 2007: 117–24, 151–7 for a review), with its concern for the understanding of texts, initially ancient but now any written or recorded material, grappled with the problem of grasping an author's intentions and meanings.

There have been various and diverse attempts to deal with this problem. Early on, Schleiermacher (1768–1834) proposed the idea of the *hermeneutic circle* in which a reader attempts to construct the life context in which the mental activity of writing the text took place and in which it makes sense. The hermeneutic circle involves trying to grasp this unknown context in order to understand the meaning of individual words. The meaning of individual words can only be understood in the context of a whole sentence, but the meaning of the sentence is dependent on the meaning of individual words. This is the circle in which the reader of ancient texts was engaged. There is a dialectical interaction between the whole and the part, between context and concept, each giving the other meaning (Palmer 1969: 87).

More recently, Gadamer (1989) has extended these ideas in his notion of the *fusion of horizons*. He argued that it was necessary to grasp the 'historical tradition' (culture or worldview), the way the world was understood at the time a text was written. This involves looking beyond what is said to what is being taken for granted while it is being said. It is about bridging the gap between our familiar world and the meaning that resides in an alien world.

While the hermeneutic tradition developed as a response to the desire to understand ancient texts, it has considerable relevance to any contemporary academic discipline that relies on textual material, particularly if it was produced by authors who are not accessible.

Social scientists face the same issues every time they transcribe an interview and then want to analyse it, presumably without the luxury of being able to go back to the research participant to discuss the meaning of every word and sentence.

When a researcher chooses to work within the Neo-Positive research paradigm, engagement with the literature has similar challenges to those discussed in hermeneutics. Compared to the task faced by natural scientists in trying to 'read' nature, to characterize the reading of textual material as a monologue is rather simplistic. Texts have been produced by writers who imbue them with meaning; nature does not have an author in this sense. Therefore, as the reading of texts involves an attempt to communicate with an absent or passive partner, this process lies somewhere between a monologue and dialogue.

An important feature of the reading of texts, which is particularly highlighted in the reading of a set of interview transcripts, is that the position from which the reader approaches texts can change. When a reader returns to a text after a period of time, it is highly likely that the reading will be different. This is because the reader's understanding of the subject matter may have changed in the meantime. After a number of transcripts have been worked on, and the reader returns to them, the second and subsequent readings are very likely to be from a different point of view. In a sense, this process has a dialogic character.

It is important to recognize that Neo-Positive researchers do not confine themselves to the literature in the search for explanatory ideas. Dialogue with experts may also be involved (supervisors, colleagues, conference participants). In addition, dialogue with social actors may form a preliminary stage in such research (different from pilot studies and instrument testing), but this then becomes a multi-paradigm study with an Interpretive first stage.

The Interpretive research paradigm *must* use communicative dialogue with people. However, Habermas's distinction between the use of monologue in the natural sciences and dialogue in the social sciences needs further elaboration. The creative process in abstracting social scientific typifications from everyday typifications is dependent on a complex set of dialogues.

The dialogic method

Blaikie and Stacy (1982) advocated the use of the *dialogic method* and presented a set of four dialogues: with the social participants; with the everyday constructs that emerge from the dialogues with participants; with the accumulating information (what is recorded in field notes, is held in the researcher's memory or is being observed at any time – conversations, statements, behaviour), as well as emerging typologies; and with 'outsiders' such as supervisors/advisors, research collaborators and/or colleagues.

From his experience in using this dialogical method, Drysdale (1985) offered some elaborations and suggestions for refining the four dialogues. What is presented here is an amalgam of the ideas from these two sources.

The first dialogue occurs between the researcher and social actors whose world is being investigated. The researcher aims to enter this world to learn about this 'form of life'. This involves engaging in the conversations of everyday life, to learn the language and culture in order to negotiate this social world. This dialogue occurs in the initial stages of research but may continue throughout its duration. It is important to note that engaging with other 'forms of life' is not confined to traditional anthropological research; it may be necessary in one's own society.

The reverse of this kind of dialogue usually occurs later in the research – when a typology or theory is being validated – and may be different in character. The researcher presents to the research participants the typologies and theory that have emerged to see to what extent they recognize the researcher's accounts of their social world. This is a complex dialogue that may result in researchers finding it necessary to make refinements to their accounts and maybe engage in further dialogue and refinement.

The second dialogue begins as soon as a researcher starts the first dialogue. For example, if a series of in-depth interviews has been conducted, it is inevitable that, as soon as two have been completed, comparisons will be made; what is learnt from the first one will stimulate reflection on the second, and vice versa. As further interviews are undertaken, this reflexive process can become complex and possibly very confusing. This process is similar to what occurs when any textual material is revisited.

One way to deal with this is to have periods of immersion in the social world followed by periods of withdrawal for detached reflection; do a few interviews and then stop and think about what has been learnt. Or, do more than one round of interviews, with periods of reflection between them. As this process continues, the researcher's grasp of the phenomenon becomes more detailed and nuanced; each successive involvement will be from a more 'sophisticated' vantage

The neglected craft of theory construction 235

point. This will change the way in which the next involvement is handled: the formulation of the problem will become sharper; there will be new ideas to test; and new 'data' will be observed, noticed or considered to be potentially relevant.

This second dialogue is different from the first, as it is not conducted with other people; it goes on in the head of the researcher. It involves conversations with oneself about what has emerged from the first dialogue. It is hard to imagine that social research can be conducted without this process occurring, regardless of the research paradigm used. All scientists must engage in this dialogue in some way in the course of their research. However, such a phenomenon does not fit neatly into the linear reconstructions that are used in reports of research. It is our view that this must be recognized and facilitated.

The third dialogue is particularly relevant in the use of the Interpretive research paradigm. It is an extension of the second and demands the use of all aspects of a researcher's skills, knowledge and creative ability. The aim is to produce a number of clusters of characteristics, a typology, but, initially, without any idea of what the finished product might look like; it is a process of giving meaning to concepts that are not yet known; it is like doing a jigsaw puzzle without having much idea of the shape of the pieces or what it will look like when finished. The process is complex, fragmented, difficult to manage and sometimes disorienting. It is at the heart of *abductive* logic.

In the second and third dialogues, the move from everyday to social scientific typifications is not just a matter of changing relevances from the requirements of everyday life to the production of social scientific knowledge. There is a process involved here in which the researcher needs to be aware of the possibility, perhaps inevitability, of using taken-for-granted limitations that narrow the scope of creative thinking. By the time a researcher is engaged in the third dialogue, an emerging typology is going to be crammed with fuzzy possibilities; with a multitude of mini-hypotheses, some only half formed, some contradictory and some half forgotten. It is easy to choose to concentrate on one, dismiss the others and fudge the anomalies (Drysdale 1985).

A fourth dialogue occurs between the researcher and one or more 'outsiders', hopefully with people who have knowledge of, and empathy with, the 'dialogic method', and who may be involved in the research but do not participate in the fieldwork. This dialogue should occur at regular intervals throughout the period when typologies and theory are being generated. The experiences of the fieldwork, and the involvement in the other dialogues, are such that without this dialogue it may be difficult for a researcher to have confidence in the ideas that are emerging. This dialogue can also help to resist the temptation to impose some kind of order on the data too quickly in the hope of relieving the uncertainty or anxiety.

Drysdale has added some other dialogues with:

- the research paradigm as well as the dialogic method itself – of being reflexive about the process;
- methods that have been selected to collect and generate data;
- oneself, which can involve personal growth and the development of self-understanding, something that is vitally necessary for an Interpretive researcher to be able to understand others, and research participants in particular; and
- past personal and research experiences – with types of people and social situations that have been encountered, and with what worked and what didn't work in previous research.

Drysdale also identified some difficulties with which a researcher has to contend:

- when it is that a researcher can say that they understand;
- with the way research participants can change during the course of their involvement in the research;
- with the role the research participants attribute to the researcher;
- with strategies participants adopt (e.g. being vague) as a way of coping with the process; and
- of a researcher being involved, perhaps totally immersed, in a social world and then being unable to critically evaluate that involvement.

In order to deal with some of these difficulties, Drysdale developed a technique of his own to search for themes in the early stage of moving from everyday typifications to social scientific typifications. He called this *the glancing technique* and likened it to the difference between central and peripheral vision. While the cones in the centre of the eye work well in moderate-to-good light, the rods on the periphery of the eyes work better in low light. Concentrating on central vision in low light eventually leads to night blindness. This is analogous to the researcher who concentrates on what they normally look at and neglects possibilities outside of this. The researcher needs to learn to glance left and right, up and down, and not to focus entirely on looking forward. However, the question is how to do this? Drysdale made some suggestions.

- Find ways of distracting yourself from normal thinking patterns – to think beyond your own biographical experiences and assumptions.
- Take time to listen to interview recordings and to read or reread transcripts with no specific intent in the hope that something will happen.
- Engage in unrelated activities, such as listening to idle conversations, reading a newspaper or a novel or poetry, watching television, as well as reading academic material and having discussions with peers and supervisors.
- Glance constantly even if it is not a familiar mode of operating and might even be uncomfortable.
- When nothing seems to be emerging, despair is setting in and it may even seem pointless, just keep going as this may release the mind for 'glancing'.
- In reading transcripts, pay attention to odd or unusual word order in familiar texts.
- Trust your own understanding as being credible.

He claimed that *the glancing technique* has the potential to help a researcher set aside preconceptions and the intrusive influence of existing concepts and theories.

Critical Realist paradigm

Critical Realism can make use of both monologues and dialogues. In the *structuralist* tradition in this paradigm the monologic approach is appropriate, while the *constructionist* approach requires a more dialogic approach. The search for hypothetical causal mechanisms is similar to the search for theoretical ideas required for propositions in a deductive theory. But ideas may also be gleaned using the same *abductive* process characteristic of Interpretivism. Pawson's (1996) realist interviewing, which can be used to both search for mechanisms and establish their existence, is very dialogic.

Creative theoretical imagination

A creative theoretical imagination is an essential part of a researcher's toolkit. During several decades of practice work and research, mainly in leadership development, business innovation and organization performance, one of the authors has developed a systematic approach to stimulate a creative theoretical imagination and a practical creative imagination (Priest and Sarne 2003, 2011). The approach involves a particular form of deconstructing and reconstructing descriptions of observations, ideas, problems, activities, products and the like with reference to purposefully selected knowledge bases as well as regular and unusual practical experiences.

A porous paradigm boundary

A careful examination of Harré's version of Critical Realism presented in this book and in his later writings shows that his views have considerable affinity with our Interpretive paradigm. He seems to have a foot in both camps. While this could be seen as invalidating two of our research paradigms, it is certainly not the case.

We have pointed out in a number of places throughout the book that the three paradigms are typifications; abstractions from a range of philosophical and methodological positions as well as research practice. We are not legislating for these three paradigms but have presented them as well-established alternatives that can be used as strategies for solving research problems and answering research questions. Researchers are, of course, free to use or even invent other research paradigms. However, there is one critical requirement, namely, that the ontological and epistemological assumptions adopted should be made explicit; they need to be compatible and they need to be appropriate for the task at hand. Harré's approach to social research is a perfect example of this.

For a discussion of how Harré's use of models relates to Weber's and Schütz's use of ideal types, and for a discussion of a problem with paradigm boundaries, go to www.InfoServ.com.au.

Influences on choice of research paradigm
Internal influences

The choice of research paradigm is the most critical decision a social researcher has to make. Ideally, the most important influences on this decision are those that are internal to the research. A researcher's aim should always be to find the best possible answer to a research question. However, judgements about this are not always

Influences on choice of research paradigm

straightforward and it may not be possible to be clear about this at the outset of the research. The key internal considerations are:

- the purpose of the research;
- the nature of the research problem;
- the context in which it is located;
- the type and form of the research questions;
- the type and quality of suitable data;
- whether these data are accessible; and
- how the results will be interpreted and used.

However, there is also a range of other influences.

Current contextual influences

All social research is conducted within academic, social, economic, political, cultural and technological contexts, and these can have an influence on the choices made in designing a research project, including the choice of research paradigm.

The academic context includes the discipline(s) within which a researcher works. Some disciplines have dominant preferences for both how research should be conducted and the ontological and epistemological assumptions that should be adopted. There can be consequences for a researcher who chooses to deviate from these preferences.

Where disciplines are ecumenical about research approaches and paradigms, academic schools or departments can have dominant views. Academic journals in which a researcher hopes to publish might also have preferences for the types of research they publish. In general, it is researchers' peer groups and reference groups that are important here, and the consideration has to be the price they are prepared to pay for not conforming to what is expected. Hence, a researcher is very likely to have their career and employment prospects in mind even when choosing a research paradigm.

The political culture in which the research is conducted can also be relevant. For a start, this can influence the kinds of research question that researchers believe are acceptable and which will not create problems for them. This is the case in many developing societies where research that even remotely raises questions about political leadership and forms of government can have serious consequences. How research questions should be answered, including the methods used, can be constrained by the cultural and political context.

Here is a summary of some important contextual influences.

- Societies are different in their cultures, economies, polities, ethnic compositions and geographical locations and thus produce different research problems.
- The character of academic disciplines varies from country to country, from region to region.
- The institutions in which research is undertaken develop different traditions of social research.
- Differences in academic education and research training can produce different kinds of researchers.
- Level of acceptability or popularity of different methods of data collection/generation and analysis differs between institutions, disciplines, regions and countries.
- What research can be undertaken is influenced by the availability, extent and type of research funding.
- By their preferences and possible prejudices, funding bodies and groups or organizations that commission research, can influence research approaches, styles and methods.

Historical contextual influences

Social research is always conducted at a particular time. While this may appear to be a statement of the obvious, the point in time at which research is undertaken, as well as the location of the researcher, have a significant effect on points of view that are adopted. In the course of a career in social research, it is highly likely that a researcher will experience changes in the way research is designed, funded and conducted. This will be magnified if the researcher moves between institutions and particularly between countries.

One of the authors of this book first undertook social research in the 1960s, in a country that was far removed from the dominant centres of social research in Europe and North America, and at a university in which the discipline of sociology had just been introduced. The way a research problem was approached at that time and in that place was not only different from other locations but was also very different from what novice researchers are now likely to do in that place or elsewhere. Later experience in conducting social research in other countries helped to make these differences even more obvious.

It follows that the period of history through which a researcher lives has a large bearing on what is researched and how it is undertaken. Many types of change will occur.

Influences on choice of research paradigm

- Societies constantly change.
- The social problems they throw up change.
- What is regarded as legitimate/appropriate/relevant research problems change.
- The state of knowledge in any field develops and changes.
- Theories evolve, new ones are proposed and their popularity comes and goes like fashion.
- Methods are improved and new ones introduced.
- The acceptability or popularity of certain methods changes.
- Disciplines also come and go, as does their popularity.
- The way each generation is educated changes and develops.
- Entry to and trajectories within academic and research careers change.
- The way social research is funded can lead to changes in priorities.

As these various influences associated with current and historical contexts can be very powerful and coercive, they can leave researchers with little room to manoeuvre and, hence, with limited scope to follow their own preferences.

Personal preferences

While recognizing the importance of these contextual influences on paradigm choice, throughout the book we have concentrated on the internal considerations. However, there is another set of influences that is more specifically personal in nature. A researcher is likely to have particular theoretical, methodological and even ideological commitments that can influence the selection of a research problem, the research questions that are entertained and how they are answered and, ultimately, paradigm choice. Of course, these personal preferences are the result of all or many of the influences already discussed, but they are the ones with which a researcher deals and of which she or he needs to be aware.

Researchers bring a particular set of experiences and skills to a research project. The choice of paradigm might be influenced by what has been used and has been found to work in the past – a paradigm that is familiar and in which relevant skills have been developed. The preference may be to stay within a research comfort zone, regardless of the nature of a research problem.

Researchers also bring with them different cognitive, language and social capacities. Here are some examples of these differences.

- Some researchers will have developed the capacity to think very logically and in a linear manner, while others have inherent thought processes that are very different, even chaotic.
- Some researchers have the capacity for imaginative and creative thinking, while others prefer or need to rely on others to do this work.
- Some researchers are only comfortable with all stages of research planned in advance and with predictable processes and outcomes, while others may be able to tolerate the uncertainty and insecurity of a developmental process with an unpredictable end point.
- Some researchers are comfortable with and skilled at mathematical manipulation and presentation of data, while others are only comfortable with using discursive language.
- And, finally, some researchers are comfortable with being intimately involved in other people's lives as part of their research, while others prefer to conduct their research at a distance.

The relevance of these differences is that paradigm choices can be made for the wrong reasons. For example, preference for the use of particular methods and even software – quantitative or qualitative – can influence the choice of research paradigm, with the result that the answers to research questions may be unnecessarily restricted. Perhaps it is better for such researchers to choose or accept research problems that are amenable to their limited range of preferences!

Conclusion

The two main themes of the book should be very evident by now: that going beyond description to explanation is the major challenge in social research, and that the most fundamental choice a social researcher has to make is which research paradigm to use to answer research questions. In order to deal with these themes, we have offered three paradigms that have their roots in the work of the main founders of sociology and that have, in various versions, been echoed in philosophies of social research and in major traditions of social theory. Their explicit use as alternatives in social research, as against positions to adopt and defend, has been paid lip service by some writers but, in our view, has not been given the central place that we believe they should have. Our task has been to try to rectify this state of affairs.

Conclusion

There are two traditions of social research that we have deliberately avoided discussing. One is experimental research, which manipulates inputs and conditions in order to establish the cause of particular outcomes. While some social or, more particularly, individual (e.g. psychological or medical) problems may lend themselves to this kind of research, it is not a mainstream strategy for dealing with the majority of *social* problems. Critics have argued that the artificiality of such procedures renders their relevance to real-world social problems of limited utility. The second tradition is particularly common, i.e. applying sophisticated mathematical manipulation to both large and small data sets, with assumptions and models about the influence of some variables on others, to establish causal arguments. The extent to which such procedures are driven by theory, or just increasingly sophisticated number-crunching techniques, requires careful consideration. Both of these traditions have positivist underpinnings but different to those presented in the Neo-Positive paradigm.

As we have seen, descriptive research is not necessarily easy, but it is much less demanding than explanatory research; in other words, it is usually easier to answer 'what' than 'why' research questions. We have argued that answering 'what' questions is a fundamental starting point in any social research. We have shown how this can be done by using either *inductive* or *abductive* logic, and that this does not require the choice of one of the research paradigms, only an awareness of the ontological and epistemological assumptions being used.

The major challenge in any scientific discipline is to explain what is going on: to answer 'why' research questions. Our three research paradigms offer different ways of achieving this aim: in the Neo-Positive paradigm by using *deductive* logic to construct and test theories; in the Interpretive paradigm by using *abductive* logic to generate theory; or in the Critical Realist paradigm by using *retroductive* logic to search for causal mechanisms.

Appendix: Review Questions

In chapter 2, the three research paradigms were described in terms of 22 characteristics (see Tables 2.1 and 2.2). Here we provide a set of questions covering many of these characteristics for each research paradigm. There are a number reasons for doing this.

1 They can be used to review each paradigm and to see whether the main characteristics and procedures have been understood.
2 They raise practical issues, related to each research paradigm, with which novice researchers can be confronted (answers to most of the questions can be found in this book or in Blaikie 2007 and 2010).
3 Experienced social researchers need to ask themselves many of these questions as they design and conduct research.
4 The questions can also provide useful discussion points for (post) graduate students and their supervisor/advisors, or for research collaborators.

Starting questions relevant to all three research paradigms

Initial decisions and actions

- Is the research problem clear and is it researchable?
- Has a regularity related to this problem already been established or do I have to conduct research to do this?
- If so, how do I get it and what should it look like?
- Under what conditions does the regularity hold?
- What research question(s) will make the problem researchable? Why these questions?

Questions peculiar to the Neo-Positive research paradigm

- Do the research questions, and any sub-questions, clearly relate to the phenomenon, the research problem and the regularity?
- What research paradigms could be used to answer these questions and why?
- What limitations does the paradigm choice place on the answers, particularly the ontological assumptions?
- Do the epistemological assumptions fit the character of the research problem?
- Can I be confident that the dominant logic of this paradigm will produce satisfactory answers to the research questions?
- What different tasks and associated logics are needed, and are they doable?
- What are the purposes of a literature review in each research paradigm?
- What should I read, when should I read it, when do I stop and how do I evaluate what I have read?
- What connections do these references have to the study and why?
- How should a literature review be written up? Should it be a chronological review, elaborate themes, follow debates, or . . . ?

Questions peculiar to the Neo-Positive research paradigm

Process issues

- Is it possible to answer the questions with a linear design path?
- Within such a path, what are the main components that need to be addressed to answer the research question(s)?
- What does an outside, top-down stance require of me? How will I do it?
- Where do the component propositions that are needed in the theory come from – observation, previous research, existing theory or do they need to be invented?
- How can I be confident that these components will do the job?
- When is a theory well formed, testable, able to explain the regularity and worth the effort of testing?
- What will I do if the testing of the theory does not produce the type of answers I expect?

Concepts, theory and hypotheses

- What concepts in the propositions in the theory need to be measured?
- What are their common meanings? Is there more than one for each concept? Do I use established definitions or do I define them myself?
- To operationalize a concept, do I create new measures or use existing ones?
- What are the consequent trade-offs and implications of the chosen measures for previous and later choices in the research?
- Given that by adding one or more propositions to the theory to extend its scope, more than one hypothesis can be deduced from it, on what basis do I choose which to test?
- Am I happy to just test component propositions in the theory or to test a new hypothesis derived from the theory in the same setting in which the regularity was established?
- Do I want to see if the theory will stand up to testing in other contexts? If so, what other contexts would provide a rigorous test of the theory?

Data generation/collection and analysis

- What types and forms of data do I need to answer the research question(s) – primary, secondary and/or tertiary?
- In what forms do I need the data – numerical or textual or both?
- What levels of measurement will be used – nominal, ordinal, interval or ratio – and how do these decisions impact the chosen methods of data collection and analysis (see Blaikie 2003)?
- Will data obtained by asking research participants about aspects of their social life, or by putting them in experimental situations, produce reliable information about what actually goes on?
- Will secondary data be useful or necessary? If so, how should I interpret the traces that people leave about their social lives, and what will be the limitations?
- What kind of population will be appropriate to test the theory? Does it need to be the same as that used to establish the regularity?
- Will it be necessary to sample the population and, if so, what kind of sample and how do I get it?
- What is a sufficient response rate, what do I need to do to ensure this and what are the consequences of not getting it?

Questions peculiar to the Interpretive research paradigm

- How do I get access to these data and what do I do if I cannot achieve this?
- How do the circumstances in which the data are to be/were collected influence what I get/got and how I interpret the findings?
- Has the research been planned in full awareness of the analysis I will need to do to get the desired answers to the research questions?

Questions peculiar to the Interpretive research paradigm

Process issues

- Is it necessary to first clearly define a research problem, and then establish a regularity?
- When is a regularity sufficiently defined to enable clearly focused research questions to be developed?
- What is meant by a non-linear, iterative research design, and am I going to be able to handle it?
- What does an inside, bottom-up stance require of me? Am I comfortable with that? How will I do it?
- Considering the role(s) participants will inevitably attribute to me, what effects will that have on how they relate to me, on the data generated and on the conduct of the research?
- How do I get started if I have to rely on research participants to teach me about their social world?
- What do I need to do to be sure that I understand the language research participants use to tell me about their social life?
- How do I deal with differences I discover in the ideas that research participants have about themselves, others and their social situations?
- Once I have a satisfactory grasp of the relevant everyday typifications, and have recorded them, how am I going to make the transition from these to social scientific typifications?
- How much use can I make of existing social scientific concepts in doing this?

Concept, theory and hypotheses

- What sensitizing concepts will be useful?
- Will I be willing and able to let go of these as I begin to discover everyday typifications?

- If I don't have to start my research with a hypothesis to test, how will I know where to begin?
- How do the working hypotheses used to explore questions that arise in the course of data generation and analysis differ from the kinds of hypotheses used in the Neo-Positive research paradigm?
- What criteria are appropriate to check if a tentative theory has merit and is worth reporting?
- Do I need to have a way of testing an emergent theory? When do I stop theorizing?

Data generation/collection and analysis

- How does working with textual data differ from working with numerical data?
- Do I need to rely entirely on primary, qualitative data?
- Am I limited to the use of interviewing and/or participant observation? Should and can they be used in combination?
- What will determine the choice of population or samples; the problem background, the regularity, the research questions, or what?
- When is a sample sufficient in size and/or content?
- What kinds of situation could arise during the course of the research that will require the use of different or further sampling?
- On what bases may findings from different samples be combined or contrasted?
- Are there criteria to guide the progressive generation of data, or a different approach to the data, as a study 'unfolds'?
- What would lead a researcher to take a different approach to the data being generated?
- When should data generation stop?
- How may data from everyday typifications be characterized?
- What levels of analysis are involved in moving from everyday concepts to social scientific concepts?
- Why is it necessary to deconstruct meanings of categories and their typifications, and how is this done?
- What does synthesizing types from components of meaning involve?
- How is this different from producing categories from everyday typifications?
- How do you know when you have a satisfactory typology?
- What is the difference between having one or more typologies and a theory?
- What process can be used to generate a theory from typologies?

Questions peculiar to the Critical Realist research paradigm

- What factors and criteria should be considered when critiquing an Interpretive study?

Questions peculiar to the Critical Realist research paradigm

Process issues

- Does it matter how the regularity, the context and the mechanism are described?
- When is a context and a regularity sufficiently well described?
- Apart from imagination, what is required to devise a hypothetical causal mechanism?
- How plausible is it that the proposed mechanism gives rise to the regularity?
- What kinds of evidence will be needed to argue for the existence of the proposed mechanism, and what will I do if I can't find it?
- What kind of stances will this require of me? When do I use them?

Concept, theory and hypotheses

- What role will concepts and theory play in describing the regularity, devising a possible mechanism and producing evidence?
- Is it going to be necessary to take social actors' typifications into account? If so, when and how?
- Where will the ideas for this mechanism come from – observation, previous research, existing theories or do they have to be invented?
- Hypotheses play a singular and particular role in the other two research paradigms, but in this paradigm they play multiple roles. What are they?

Data generation/collection and analysis

- What kind of evidence will be needed to establish the existence of the mechanism?
- How systematic will the evidence need to be?
- What strategies can be used to allow for finding both confirming and disconfirming evidence for the existence of the mechanism?
- If both are found, on what basis is the explanatory strength of the mechanism to be judged?
- Are there reasons for seeking evidence for the mechanism from other contexts and, if so, on what basis could they be selected?

Concluding questions common to all three research paradigms

- What do I have to do to satisfy critics who expect me to have produced 'objective' results? What does it mean to be 'objective'? Are the same arguments relevant to all three research paradigms?
- What does 'validity' and 'reliability' mean? Do I need to worry about them? If so, how do I establish them?
- Will 'member checking' do as an alternative? Under what circumstances?
- What context(s) do I want my results to apply to, and what do I do to achieve this?
- What audiences are to be addressed, and what reporting style will be appropriate?
- What can I do to discourage the inappropriate use of the results beyond the context(s) from which they were obtained?
- How do I devise work-arounds when my ideal research design hits roadblocks?
- How do I judge and report the inevitable compromises that have to be made in these circumstances?

Notes

Introduction

1 Blaikie (2003) has dealt with this latter theme in the limited context of the analysis of quantitative data. Here, the approach is theoretical and logical, rather than data centred.

Chapter 1   Fundamental Choices in Social Research

1 The philosophical, theoretical and methodological approach taken in this book has much in common with that advocated by Derek Layder (1998). He also has an eclectic view of ontological and epistemological assumptions and a strong recognition of the role they play in social research. See, particularly, his 'New Rules of Method' (pp. 176–8) for a concise summary.
2 Typifying includes the inductive step of characterizing particular instances of data as members of a category. *Abstraction* involves the *inductive* step of characterizing patterned associations between categories as classes that are related through a hierarchy or network, and *deduction* verifies that existing and new instances of data remain consistent with the classes and their relatedness.
3 The main founder of this approach, Max Weber, who stressed the meaningful nature of social action, also argued for a value-free social science. It has been later contributors who have moved in the direction of value relativism.

Chapter 2   Road Maps for Research

1 At the time of writing, a government Royal Commission is being conducted in Australia into the sexual abuse of children and young people in a wide range of institutions and organizations, e.g. religious, military,

educational and welfare (government and non-government). Reports on the activities of this Commission, and investigative journalism, are constantly appearing in various media. On the very day this note is being written, Pope Francis, while on a visit to the United States, spoke about this abuse and met with victims in an effort to change the way the Catholic Church has been dealing with it. At the time the manuscript for the book was being finalized, the film *Spotlight*, based on the *Boston Globe*'s investigation, was showing in cinemas.
2 The difficulties in getting such people to agree to be interviewed are not to be underestimated.

Chapter 3 Principles of Neo-Positive Research

1 In this context, 'observation' is not restricted to what we can 'see' or perceive but includes the use of measuring instruments that are extensions of the human senses. The notion of 'experience' also has the same possibility.
2 In this paradigm, the idea of a causal explanation is rejected as not being possible. Instead, it is argued that all that is possible is to establish regular patterns of associations between events or objects.
3 The notion of relation in this paradigm is no more than a well-defined and plausible association.
4 The above process implies, but is not limited to, a regularity as a relationship between a pair of concepts. For instance, a structural equation or a stochastic model linking proxy variables in a deductively generated theory are also possibilities, and a whole lot more. When a regularity is about a relationship between two concepts, a simple form is one in which proxy variables for the concepts have a direct or inverse association with each other.
5 A plausible association is one that does not involve counter-intuitive conceptual leaps or is already well established in the literature.

Chapter 4 The Neo-Positive Research Paradigm in Action

1 A version of this research topic was used to illustrate a particular kind of research design in Blaikie (2010: 240–3). The purpose here is different, viz. to illustrate the Neo-Positive research paradigm.
2 The two items in this sub-scale are: 'People in developed societies are going to have to adopt more conserving lifestyles in the future' and 'Controls should be placed on industry to protect the environment from pollution even if it means things will cost more.'
3 The three items in this sub-scale are: 'Through science and technology we can continue to raise our standard of living'; 'We cannot keep counting on science and technology to solve our problems'; and 'Most problems can be solved by applying more and better technology'. The first

and third items were scored in the reverse direction so that a high score indicates a low level of confidence, and vice versa.
4 It is important to note that we are dealing with mean scores here and that individual scores in each age cohort are distributed around the mean. For evidence of this variability in the young aged cohort, see Blaikie (1993a).
5 A natural disaster emergency becomes a critical emergency (i.e. a crisis) when the required ability of agencies to respond exceeds their capacity and gets worse as the pace and/or scope of the emergency increases.
6 First-responder organizations typically include emergency agencies (fire, search and rescue, police, ambulance), mandated infrastructure providers (communications, transport, energy, water, health) and approved NGOs (e.g. Red Cross).
7 When a leader assumes a particular identity to deal with a crisis, the degree of fit between the identity's expectations and the character and challenges of the unfolding crisis may or may not match.
8 In the Australian system of government, Royal Commissions are the highest form of inquiry on matters of public importance. Typically chaired by retired senior judges, in recent decades they have included inquiries into institutional sex abuse and major natural disasters such as bushfires.
9 In Australia in 2009, an IMT leader would usually be a Level-3 incident controller as defined in the Australasian Inter-Service Incident Management System (AIIMS) model (AFAC 2004). AIIMS is Australia's and New Zealand's nationally recognized framework for coordinating and managing an all-agency response to natural disaster emergencies. It articulates a hierarchical control, planning, public information, operations and logistics-based approach to emergency management.
10 Identity-clarity reflects the extent to which a person's identities are situationally congruent or the person is able to confidently function within a situationally appropriate identity while setting aside or suspending dealing with their other typical and expected identities and identity conflicts.
11 Conflicts typically arise between agency identity, community needs, political and economic viability, role legitimacy and authority, and avoiding liabilities.
12 Identity congruence increases as the fit between role expectations and situation challenges increases.

Chapter 5   Principles of Interpretive Research

1 Some writers (e.g. Rex 1974: 29) have argued that Weber's limitation of meaningful action to rational action is too restrictive. Schütz (1976), for example, was prepared to accept any action of which a social actor is aware.

2 This is the mode of explanation used in classical positivism but has now been replaced by the use of the logics of *deduction* and *retroduction*.
3 See Blaikie (2007: 179–80; 2010: 93–4) for further elaboration.
4 Many of the ideas in this section were initially discussed in Blaikie and Stacy (1982, 1984) and Stacy (1983).
5 The use of 'ideal' here is unfortunate as it can convey the idea that the description of a type represents a desirable state. Weber also used 'pure', which at least suggests an abstraction that accentuates certain important features. This is really Weber's meaning. We prefer to use just 'types' and 'typologies' but cannot avoid the language that these early writers used, or at least what their translators thought they meant!
6 As an alternative to this, Fallding (1968) suggested that the accentuation should be based on what the people observed accentuate, where *they* put the emphasis. But Weber was not usually in a position to do this.
7 It is neither necessary nor possible here to discuss whether Weber's thesis is satisfactory or not. It is his pioneering use of the Interpretive research paradigm and ideal types to explain an observed regularity that is relevant.
8 While using Weber's concept of *ideal* type, Schütz's ideas are clearly more closely related to Becker's notion of *constructed* type.
9 Rex's concerns can be overcome with this kind of reinterpretation.
10 A discriminating typology is typically one that exhibits several layers of depth, with subtle yet important distinctions at each layer, thus exposing the dynamics that manifest as the regularity that characterizes the life-world being studied.
11 Interrelationships are, for instance, co-relations or co-occurrences within or between typologies or subtypes and elements of the research questions or even the regularity itself.
12 Open interviews are in-depth and unstructured and are specifically designed and conducted in ways that encourage the interviewee to set out and elaborate what they have noticed and interpreted. This means the interviewer provides as few cues as possible – only outlining the purpose of the interview and starting with broad open-ended questions and occasional non-committal encouragements for elaboration or clarification.

Chapter 6   The Interpretive Paradigm in Action

1 Familiar direct reports are selected from three groups of associates, each of whom has long and close professional and/or personal knowledge of the leader's background: those to whom the leader has reported; those who have reported directly to the leader; and those who have mentored or otherwise advised or served as wise counsel.
2 The 'fog' is a colloquial reference to 'operating in the clouds – with no real appreciation of local conditions'. In this study, it was a term used

by some emergency services leaders to refer to the perceived practice of some senior police officers who relied solely on reports from mid-level police who passed on filtered reports gleaned only from low-level police officers in the field, and who were seen to have spent little time getting direct updates from other emergency services personnel.
3 Choosing may be a deliberate (e.g. calculated) act or may be a subconscious (e.g. intuitive) act.
4 In Table 6.8, the cell entries could be allocated according to a seven-point scale for co-frequency prevalence, where 1 = Very Low, 2 = Low, 3 = Low-Medium, 4 = Medium, 5 = Medium-High, 6 = High, 7 = Very High. Regardless of whether text or numbers are used, a question for both forms of representation concerns an effective way to represent contrasts. For instance, if using numbers, is a contrast of 2, such as 7−5, the same as a contrast of 5−3?
5 Apart from a five- or seven-point numerical scale, measures in research, such as criteria-based scales or scales based on degrees of significance or likelihood may also be devised depending on the purpose (www.InfoServ.com.au).
6 RAFTS are specially trained to rappel into rugged terrain and conduct dry fire back-burning and mitigation work.

Chapter 7   Principles of Critical Realist Research

1 I (Blaikie) know this because, when I was an undergraduate student studying the philosophy of science, one day my tutor, in great excitement, produced a copy of this photograph. I have to say that you needed special knowledge to be able to interpret the photograph, as it didn't look anything like the drawings.
2 When a pattern is in the form of an association between two variables, movement from one to the other may or may not be implied. If it is, this does not constitute causation, only a time order.
3 In Thomas Hardy's novel *Far from the Madding Crowd*, Bathsheba was asked by one of her suitors, Boldwood, how she felt about him. She said: 'I cannot tell you. It is difficult for a woman to define her feelings in language which is chiefly made by men to express theirs' (Hardy 1994 [1874]: 327).

Chapter 8   The Critical Realist Research Paradigm in Action

1 An earlier version of this illustration can be found in Blaikie (2010: 243−8). It was concerned specifically with the *retroductive* logic of inquiry (research strategy), rather than the more general notion of research paradigm.
2 The situation for sole parents is more complex and may not be as amenable to this kind of explanation.

3 Reasoning spans cognitive, emotional and behavioural resources. Resources are comprised of processes and substantive content. Processes typically cover heuristics, rules of thumb, logical methods, monologues and dialogues and such like. Substantive content typically covers memories, preferred and variously trusted sources, meanings, models and representations, sensitivities and blind spots, values, beliefs, world views and the like.

Chapter 9 Multiple Paradigm Research

1 For a critique of the use of triangulation in mixed methods research, see Blaikie (1991; 2010: 218–27).

References

Abbagano, N. (1967). Positivism, in P. Edwards (ed.), *The Encyclopedia of Philosophy*, Vol. 6. New York: Macmillan, pp. 414–19.

Adorno, T. W., Albert, H., Dahrendorf, R., Habermas, J., Pilot, H. and Popper, K. R. (1976 [1969]). *The Positivist Dispute in German Sociology*, trans. G. Adey and D. Frisby. London: Heinemann. (First published in German.)

AFAC (2004). *Australasian Inter-service Incident Management System*, 3rd edn. Melbourne: The Australasian Fire Authority Council.

Alexander, J. C. (1982). *Positivism, Presuppositions, and Current Controversies*. London: Routledge & Kegan Paul.

Archer, M. S. (1995). *Realist Social Theory: The Morphogenetic Approach*. Cambridge: Cambridge University Press.

Arcury, T. E. and Christianson, E. H. (1990). Environmental worldview in response to environmental problems: Kentucky 1984 and 1988 compared. *Environment and Behaviour* 22: 387–407.

Bacon, F. (1889 [1620]). *Novum Organon*, trans. G. W. Kitchin. Oxford: Clarendon Press. (First published in Latin.)

Barnes, B. (1982). *T. S. Kuhn and Social Science*. London: Macmillan.

Baronov, D. (2015). *Conceptual Foundations of Social Research Methods*, 2nd edn. London: Routledge.

Bartsch, S. (2004). *Structural and Functional Properties of Collocations in English*. Tübingen: Narr.

Bauman, Z. (1978). *Hermeneutics and Social Science*. London: Hutchinson.

Becker, H. (1940). Constructive typology in the social sciences. *American Sociological Review* 5: 40–66.

Becker, H. (1950). *Through Values to Sociological Explanation*. Durham: Duke University Press.

Benton, T. (1977). *Philosophical Foundations of the Three Sociologies*. London: Routledge & Kegan Paul.

References

Benton, T. (1981). Realism and social science: some comments on Roy Bhaskar's 'The Possibility of Naturalism'. *Radical Philosophy* 27: 13–21.
Berger, P. L. (1963). *Invitation to Sociology*. New York: Doubleday.
Berger, P. L. and Luckmann, T. (1966). *The Social Construction of Reality*. Garden City, NY: Doubleday.
Bhaskar, R. (1978). *A Realist Theory of Science*, 2nd edn. Hassocks: Harvester Press.
Bhaskar, R. (1979). *The Possibility of Naturalism: A Philosophical Critique of the Contemporary Human Sciences*. Brighton: Harvester.
Bhaskar, R. (1986). *Scientific Realism and Human Emancipation*. London: Verso.
Blaikie, N. (1977). The meaning and measurement of occupational prestige. *Australian and New Zealand Journal of Sociology* 13: 102–15.
Blaikie, N. (1978). Towards an alternative methodology for the study of occupational prestige: a reply to my reviewers. *Australian and New Zealand Journal of Sociology* 14: 87–95.
Blaikie, N. (1991). A critique of the use of triangulation in social research. *Quality and Quantity* 25: 115–36.
Blaikie, N. (1992). Nature and origins of ecological world views: an Australian study. *Social Science Quarterly* 73: 144–65.
Blaikie, N. (1993a). Education and environmentalism: ecological world views and environmentally responsible behaviour. *Australian Journal of Environmental Education* 9: 1–20.
Blaikie, N. (1993b). *Approaches to Social Enquiry*. Cambridge: Polity.
Blaikie, N. (2003). *Analyzing Quantitative Data: From Description to Explanation*. London: Sage.
Blaikie, N. (2007). *Approaches to Social Enquiry*, 2nd edn. Cambridge: Polity.
Blaikie, N. (2010). *Designing Social Research*, 2nd edn. Cambridge: Polity.
Blaikie, N. and Stacy, S. J. G. (1982). The dialogical generation of typologies in the study of the care of the aged. Paper presented at the X World Congress of Sociology, Mexico City.
Blaikie, N. and Stacy, S. J. G. (1984). The generation of grounded concepts: a critical appraisal of the literature and a case study. Paper presented at the European Symposium on Concept and Theory Formation, Rome.
Blaikie, N. and Ward, R. (1992). Ecological worldviews and environmentally responsible behaviour. *Sociale Wetenschappen* 35: 40–63.
Blocker, T. J. and Eckberg, D. L. (1989). Environmental issues and women's issues: general concerns and local hazards. *Social Science Quarterly* 70: 586–93.
Braithwaite, R. B. (1953). *Scientific Explanation*. Cambridge: Cambridge University Press.
Brannen, J. (1992). *Mixed Methods: Qualitative and Quantitative Research*. Aldershot: Avebury.

Brannen, J. (2005). Mixed methods: the entry of qualitative and quantitative approaches into the research process. *International Journal of Social Research Methodology* 8: 173–84.

Brinkmann, S. and Kvale, S. (2015). *InterViews: Learning the Craft of Qualitative Interviewing*, 3rd edn. Thousand Oaks: Sage.

Bryant, A. (2002). Re-grounding grounded theory. *The Journal of Information Technology Theory and Application* 4: 25–42.

Bryant, C. G. A. (1985). *Positivism in Social Theory and Research*. London: Macmillan.

Bryman, A. (1988). *Quality and Quantity in Social Research*. London: Unwin Hyman.

Bryman, A. (2006a). Paradigm peace and the implications for quality. *International Journal of Social Research Methodology* 9: 111–26.

Bryman, A. (2006b). Integrating quantitative and qualitative research: how is it done? *Qualitative Research* 6: 97–113.

Bryman, A. (2007). *Mixed Methods Research*. London: Sage.

Bryman, A. (2014). June 1989 and beyond: Julia Brannen's contribution to mixed methods research. *International Journal of Social Research Methodology* 17: 121–31.

Buttel, F. H. (1979). Age and environmental concern: a multivariate analysis. *Youth and Society* 10: 237–56.

Catton, W. R. and Dunlap, R. E. (1978a). Environmental sociology: a new paradigm. *American Sociologist* 13: 41–9.

Catton, W. R. and Dunlap, R. E. (1978b). Paradigms, theories and the primacy of the HEP-NEP distinction. *American Sociologist* 13: 256–59.

Catton, W. R. and Dunlap, R. E. (1980). A new ecological paradigm for a post-exuberant sociology. *American Behavioral Scientist* 24: 15–47.

Chalmers, A. F. (1982). *What is This Thing Called Science?* 2nd edn. St Lucia: University of Queensland Press.

Charmaz, K. (2000). Grounded theory: Objectivist and constructivist methods, in N. Denzin and Y. Lincoln (eds), *Handbook of Qualitative Research*. Thousand Oaks: Sage, pp. 509–35.

Charmaz, K. (2005). Grounded theory in the 21st century: applications for advancing social justice studies, in N. Denzin and Y. Lincoln (eds), *The Sage Handbook of Qualitative Research*, 3rd edn. Thousand Oaks: Sage, pp. 507–35.

Charmaz, K. (2006). *Constructing Grounded Theory: A Practical Guide Through Qualitative Analysis*. London: Sage.

Charmaz, K. (2007). Constructionism and the grounded theory method, in J. Holstein and J. Gubrium (eds), *Handbook of Constructionist Research*. New York: Guilford, pp. 397–412.

Charmaz, K. and Mitchell, R. G. (2001). Grounded theory in ethnography, in P. Atkinson, A. Coffey, S. Delamont, J. Lofland and L. H. Lofland (eds), *Handbook of Ethnography*. London: Sage, pp. 160–74.

Clarke, A. E. (2005). *Situational Analysis: Grounded Theory after the Postmodern Turn.* Thousand Oaks: Sage.

Collier, A. (1994). *Critical Realism: An Introduction to Roy Bhaskar's Philosophy.* London: Verso.

Comte, A. (1970 [1830]). *Introduction to Positive Philosophy.* Indianapolis: Bobbs-Merrill. (First published in French.)

Conklin, J. (2006). *Dialogue Mapping: Building Shared Understanding of Wicked Problems.* Chichester, England: Wiley Publishing.

Corbin, J. and Strauss, A. (2008). *Basics of Qualitative Research: Techniques and Procedures for Developing Grounded Theory*, 3rd edn. London: Sage.

Creswell, J. W. (2013). *Research Design: Qualitative, Quantitative and Mixed Methods Research*, 4th edn. Thousand Oaks: Sage.

Creswell, J. W. (2014b). *A Concise Introduction to Mixed Methods Research.* Thousand Oaks: Sage.

Creswell, J. W. (2015). *Educational Research: Planning, Conducting, and Evaluating Quantitative and Qualitative Research.* Boston: Pearson.

Creswell, J. W. and Plano-Clark, V. L. (2011). *Designing and Conducting Mixed Methods Research.* Los Angeles: Sage.

Cruz, M. G., Sullivan, A. L., Gould, J. S., Sims, N. C., Bannister, A. J., Hollis, J. J. and Hurley, R. J. (2012). Anatomy of a catastrophic wildfire: the Black Saturday Kilmore East fire in Victoria, Australia. *Forest Ecology and Management* (November): 1–18.

Deese, J. E. (1965). *The Structure of Associations in Language and Thought.* Baltimore: Johns Hopkins Press.

Denzin, N. K. and Lincoln, Y. S. (eds) (2011). *The Sage Handbook of Qualitative Research*, 4th edn. Los Angeles: Sage.

Douglas, J. (1967). *The Social Meanings of Suicide.* Princeton: Princeton University Press.

Drysdale, M. (1985). Beliefs and behaviours of the community with regard to social justice: an application of the dialogic method. MA thesis, Royal Melbourne Institute of Technology, Melbourne.

Dunlap, R. E. (1980). Paradigmatic change in social science: from human exemptions to an ecological paradigm. *American Behavioral Scientist* 24: 5–14.

Dunlap, R. E. and van Liere, K. D. (1978). The new environmental paradigm: a proposed measuring instrument and preliminary results. *Journal of Environmental Education* 9: 10–19.

Dunlap, R. E. and van Liere, K. D. (1984). Commitment to the dominant social paradigm and concern for environmental quality. *Social Science Quarterly* 65: 1013–28.

Durkheim, E. (1938 [1895]). *The Rules of Sociological Method*, trans. S. A. Solovay and J. H. Muller. New York: The Free Press of Glencoe.

Durkheim, E. (1970 [1897]). *Suicide: A Study in Sociology*, trans. J. A. Spaulding and G. Simpson. London: Routledge & Kegan Paul. (First published in French).

Endsley, M. R. (1995). Toward a theory of situation awareness in dynamic systems. *Human Factors* 37: 32–64.
Fallding, H. (1968). *The Sociological Task*. Englewood Cliffs: Prentice-Hall.
Feyerabend, P. K. (1970). Consolations for the specialist, in I. Lakatos, and A. Musgrave (eds), *Criticism and the Growth of Knowledge*. Cambridge: Cambridge University Press, pp. 197–230.
Feyerabend, P. K. (1978). *Against Method: Outline of an Anarchistic Theory of Knowledge*. London: Verso.
Feynman, R. (1976). *The Character of Physical Law*. Cambridge: MIT Press.
Fox, N. J. and Alldred, P. (2015). New materialist social inquiry: designs, methods and the research assemblage. *International Journal of Social Research Methodology* 18: 399–414.
Friedrichs, R. W. (1970). *A Sociology of Sociology*. New York: Free Press.
Gadamer, H.-G. (1989). *Truth and Method*, rev. 2nd edn. New York: Crossroads.
Garfinkel, H. (1967). *Studies in Ethnomethodology*. Englewood Cliffs: Prentice-Hall.
Giddens, A. (ed.) (1974). *Positivism and Sociology*. London: Heinemann.
Giddens, A. (1976). *New Rules of Sociological Method*. London: Hutchinson.
Giddens, A. (1979). *Central Problems in Social Theory*. London: Macmillan.
Giddens, A. (1982). *Sociology: A Brief but Critical Introduction*. London: Macmillan.
Giddens, A. (1984). *The Constitution of Society*. Cambridge: Polity.
Giddens, A. (1985). Jürgen Habermas, in Q. Skinner (ed.), *The Return of Grand Theory in the Human Sciences*. Cambridge: Cambridge University Press, pp. 121–37.
Giedymin, J. (1975). Antipositivism in contemporary philosophy of social science and humanities. *British Journal for the Philosophy of Science* 26: 275–301.
Glaser, B. (1978). *Theoretical Sociology*. Mill Valley: The Sociology Press.
Glaser, B. (1992). *Basics of Grounded Theory Analysis: Emergence vs. Forcing*. Mill Valley: The Sociology Press.
Glaser, B. (2001). *The Grounded Theory Perspective: Conceptualization Contrasted with Description*. Mill Valley: The Sociology Press.
Glaser, B. and Strauss, A. (1967). *The Discovery of Grounded Theory*. London: Weidenfeld and Nicolson.
Greene, J. C. (2007). *Mixed Methods in Social Inquiry*. San Francisco: Jossey Bass.
Grunwald, J. and Bearman, C. (2011). *Breakdown in Coordinated Decision in Teams Fighting Large-Scale Bushfires in Australia*, Melbourne: Bush Fire CRC.
Guba, E. G. (ed.). (1990). *The Paradigm Dialogue*. Newbury Park: Sage.
Habermas, J. (1970). Knowledge and human interests, in D. Emmett and A. MacIntyre (eds), *Sociological Theory and Philosophical Analysis*. London: Macmillan, pp. 36–54.

Habermas, J. (1972). *Knowledge and Human Interests*, trans. J. J. Shapiro. London: Heinemann.
Habermas, J. (1976). *Legitimation Crisis*, trans. T. McCarthy. London: Heinemann.
Hacking, I. (1983). *Representing and Intervening: Introductory Topics in the Philosophy of Natural Science*. Cambridge: Cambridge University Press.
Halfpenny, P. (1982). *Positivism and Sociology: Explaining Social Life*. London: Allen & Unwin.
Hallebone, E. and Priest, J. (2009). *Business and Management Research: Paradigms and Practices*. Basingstoke: Palgrave Macmillan.
Hammersley, M. (1992). *What's Wrong with Ethnography?* London: Routledge.
Hardy, T. (1994 [1874]). *Far from the Madding Crowd*. London: Penguin.
Harré, R. (1961). *Theories and Things*. London: Sheed & Ward.
Harré, R. (1970). *The Principles of Scientific Thinking*. London: Macmillan.
Harré, R. (1972). *The Philosophy of Science: An Introductory Survey*. London: Oxford University Press.
Harré, R. (1974). Blueprint for a new science, in N. Armitage (ed.), *Restructuring Social Psychology*. Harmondsworth: Penguin, pp. 240–9.
Harré, R. (1976). The constructive role of models, in L. Collins (ed.), *The Use of Models in the Social Sciences*. London: Tavistock, pp. 16–43.
Harré, R. (1977). The ethogenic approach: theory and practice. *Advances in Experimental Social Psychology* 10: 283–314.
Harré, R. (1979). *Social Being: A Theory for Social Psychology*. Oxford: Blackwell.
Harré, R. (1983). *Personal Being*. Oxford: Blackwell.
Harré, R. (2002). Social reality and the myth of social structure. *European Journal of Social Theory* 5: 111–23.
Harré, R. and Secord, P. F. (1972). *The Explanation of Social Behaviour*. Oxford: Blackwell.
Hayes, P and Omodei, M. (2011). Managing emergencies: key competencies for incident management teams. *The Australian and New Zealand Journal of Organisational Psychology* 4: 1–10.
Hempel, C. G. (1952). Typological methods in the natural and social sciences. Reprinted in M. Natanson (ed.), *Philosophy of the Social Sciences*. New York: Random House, 1963.
Hempel, C. G. (1966). *Philosophy of Natural Science*. Englewood Cliffs: Prentice-Hall.
Hertz, R. and J. B. Imber (eds) (1995). *Studying Elites Using Qualitative Methods*. Thousand Oaks: Sage.
Hindess, B. (1977). *Philosophy and Methodology in the Social Sciences*. Hassocks: Harvester.
Homans, G. C. (1964). Contemporary theory in sociology, in R. E. L. Faris (ed.), *Handbook of Modern Sociology*. Chicago: Rand McNally, pp. 951–77.

Honnold, J. A. (1981). Predictors of public concern in the 1990s, in D. Mann (ed.), *Environmental Policy Formation*, Vol. 1. Lexington: Lexington Books, pp. 63–75.
Honnold, J. A. (1984). Age and environmental concern: some specification of effects. *Journal of Environmental Education* 16: 4–9.
Hume, D. (1888). *A Treatise of Human Nature*. London: Oxford University Press.
Hyde, M. (2013). *2013 Tasmanian Bushfires Inquiry*, Vol. 1. Hobart: State of Tasmania.
Johnson, P. and Duberley, J. (2000). *Understanding Management Research*. London: Sage.
Kaplan, D. (ed.) (2004). *The Sage Handbook of Quantitative Methodology in the Social Sciences*. Thousand Oaks: Sage.
Keat, R. and Urry, J. (1982). *Social Theory as Science*, 2nd edn. London: Routledge & Kegan Paul.
King, A. (1999). The impossibility of naturalism: the antinomies of Bhaskar's realism. *Journal for the Theory of Social Behaviour* 29: 267–88.
Kolakowski, L. (1972 [1966]). *Positivist Philosophy: From Hume to the Vienna Circle*. Harmondsworth: Penguin. (First published in Polish.)
Kuhn, T. S. (1962). *The Structure of Scientific Revolutions*. Chicago: University of Chicago Press.
Kuhn, T. S. (1970a). *The Structure of Scientific Revolutions*, 2nd edn. Chicago: University of Chicago Press.
Kuhn, T. S. (1970b). Logic of discovery or psychology of research, in I. Lakatos and A. Musgrave (eds), *Criticism and the Growth of Knowledge*. Cambridge: Cambridge University Press, pp. 1–23.
Kuhn, T. S. (1970c). Reflections on my critics, in I. Lakatos, and A. Musgrave (eds), *Criticism and the Growth of Knowledge*. Cambridge: Cambridge University Press, pp. 231–78.
Kvale, S. (1996). *Interviews: An Introduction to Qualitative Research Interviewing*. Thousand Oaks: Sage.
Lakatos, I. (1970). Falsification and the methodology of scientific research programmes, in I. Lakatos and A. Musgrave (eds), *Criticism and the Growth of Knowledge*. Cambridge: Cambridge University Press, pp. 91–195.
Lakatos, I. and Musgrave, A. (eds) (1970). *Criticism and the Growth of Knowledge*. Cambridge: Cambridge University Press.
Lassman, P. (1974). Phenomenological perspectives in sociology, in J. Rex (ed.), *Approaches to Sociology: An Introduction to Major Trends in British Sociology*. London: Routledge & Kegan Paul, pp. 125–44.
Layder, D. (1985), Beyond empiricism: the promise of realism, *Philosophy of the Social Sciences* 15: 255–74.
Layder, D. (1990). *The Realist Image in Social Science*. London: Macmillan.
Layder, D. (1993). *New Strategies in Social Research*. Cambridge: Polity.
Layder, D. (1998). *Sociological Practice: Linking Theory and Research*. London: Sage.

Lazarsfeld, P. F. and Barton, A. (1951). Qualitative measurement in the social sciences: classification, typologies and indices, in D. Lerner and H. D. Lasswell (eds), *The Policy Sciences: Recent Developments in Scope and Methods*. Stanford: Stanford University Press, pp. 155–92.

Lincoln, Y. S. and Guba, E. G. (1985). *Naturalistic Inquiry*. Beverly Hills: Sage.

Loomis, C. P. (1950). The nature of rural social systems: a typological analysis. *Rural Sociology* 15: 156–74.

Lowe, G. D. and Pinhey, T. K. (1982). Rural–urban differences in support for environmental protection. *Rural Sociology* 47: 114–28.

Lowe, G. D., Pinhey, T. K. and M. D. Grimes (1980). Public support for environmental protection: new evidence from national surveys. *Pacific Sociological Review* 23: 423–45.

Mannheim K. (1952). The problem of generations, in *Essays on the Sociology of Knowledge*. New York: Oxford University Press, pp. 276–320.

Marsden-Smedley, J. (2013). *Tasmanian Wildfires January–February 2013: Forcett-Dunalley, Repulse, Bicheno, Montumana, Molesworth and Gretna*. Hobart: Tasmania Fire Service.

Martindale, D. (1959). Sociological theory and the ideal type, in L. Gross (ed.), *Symposium on Sociological Theory*. New York: Harper & Row, pp. 57–91.

Markus, L. M. (1997). The qualitative difference in information systems research and practice, in A. S. Lee, J. Liebenau and J. I. De Gross (eds), *Information Systems and Qualitative Research*. London: Chapman & Hall, pp. 11–27.

Marx, K. (1852). The Eighteenth Brumaire of Louis Bonaparte, in R. C. Tucker (ed.) (1970), *The Marx–Engels Reader*. New York: Norton. pp. 436–525.

Marx, K. (1970 [1859]) *A Contribution to the Critique of Political Economy*. New York: International Publishers.

Masterman, M. (1970). The nature of the paradigm, in I. Lakatos and A. Musgrave (eds), *Criticism and the Growth of Knowledge*. Cambridge: Cambridge University Press, pp. 59–89.

McCarthy, T. (1982). *The Critical Theory of Jürgen Habermas*. Cambridge: MIT Press.

McKinney, J. C. (1957). The polar variables of type construction. *Social Forces* 35: 300–6.

McKinney, J. C. (1966). *Constructive Typology and Social Theory*. New York: Appleton-Century-Crofts.

McStay, J. R. and Dunlap, R. E. (1983). Male–female differences in concern for environmental quality. *International Journal of Women's Studies* 6: 291–301.

Medewar, P. B. (1969a). *Induction and Intuition in Scientific Thought*. London: Methuen.

References

Medewar, P. B. (1969b). *The Art of the Soluble: Creativity and Originality in Science*. Harmondsworth: Penguin.

Merton, R. K. (1957a). *Social Theory and Social Structure*. Glencoe: Free Press.

Merton, R. K. (1957b). Introduction: notes on problem-finding in sociology, in R. K. Merton, L. Broom and L. S. Cottrell (eds), *Sociology Today: Problems and Prospects*. New York: Basic Books, pp. ix–xxxiv.

Mill, J. S. (1947 [1843]). *A System of Logic*. London: Longman, Green & Co.

Mills, C. W. (1959). *The Sociological Imagination*. New York: Oxford University Press.

Mohai, P. and Twight, B. W. (1987). Age and environmentalism: an elaboration of the Buttel model using national survey evidence. *Social Science Quarterly* 68: 798–815.

Mulkay, M. (1979). *Science and the Sociology of Knowledge*. London: Allen & Unwin.

Neuman, W. L. (2014). *Social Research Methods: Qualitative and Quantitative Approaches*, 7th edn. Harlow, Essex: Pearson.

Nordhaus, W. D. (2007). Two centuries of productivity growth in computing. *The Journal of Economic History* 67: 128–59.

Ong, B. K. (2012). Grounded theory method (GTM) and the abductive research strategy (ARS): a critical analysis of their differences. *International Journal of Social Research Methodology* 15: 417–32.

Onwuegbuzie, A. J. and Leech, N. L. (2005). On becoming a pragmatic researcher: the importance of combining quantitative and qualitative research methodologies. *International Journal of Social Research Methodology* 8: 375–87.

Outhwaite, W. (1987). *New Philosophies of Social Science: Realism, Hermeneutics and Critical Theory*. London: Macmillan.

Palmer, R. E. (1969). *Hermeneutics: Interpretation Theory in Schleiermacher, Dilthey, Heidegger and Gadamer*. Evanston, IL: Northwestern University Press.

Pawson, R. (1989). *A Measure for Measures: A Manifesto for Empirical Sociology*. London: Routledge.

Pawson, R. (1995). Quality and quantity, agency and structure, mechanism and context, dons and cons. *Bulletin de Methodologie Sociologique* 47: 5–48.

Pawson, R. (1996). Theorizing the interview. *British Journal of Sociology* 47: 295–314.

Pawson, R. (2000). Middle-range realism. *Archives Européennes de Sociologie* 41: 283–325.

Pawson, R. and Tilley, N. (1997). *Realistic Evaluation*. London: Sage.

Plano-Clark, V. and Ivankova, N. V. (2015). *Mixed Methods Research: A Guide to the Field*. Los Angeles: Sage.

Popper, K. R. (1959 [1934]). *The Logic of Scientific Discovery*. London: Hutchinson. (First published in German.)
Popper, K. R. (1961). *The Poverty of Historicism*. London: Routledge & Kegan Paul.
Popper, K. R. (1972). *Conjectures and Refutations*. London: Routledge & Kegan Paul.
Popper, K. R. (1976). The logic of the social sciences, in T. W. Adorno et al., *The Positivist Dispute in German Sociology*, pp. 87–104.
Priest, J. G. (2000). *Managing Investments in Information Systems: Exploring Effective Practice*. Doctoral thesis. Melbourne: RMIT University.
Priest, J. G. (2002). Tools for co-location analysis of texts. *Research in Practice W2002c*. Melbourne: InfoServ.
Priest, J. G. (2008). Leadership reasoning in crises: investigations and findings. *Research in Practice W2008b*. Melbourne: InfoServ.
Priest, J. G. (2009). Leadership reasoning in crises: the role of experience. *Research in Practice W2009a*. Melbourne: InfoServ.
Priest, J. G. and Sarne, G. (2003). Technology enabled business innovation: systematic practical creativity. *Research in Practice W2003d*. Melbourne: InfoServ.
Priest, J. G. and Sarne, G. (2006). Crisis leadership studies: themes and challenges. *Research in Practice W2006c*. Melbourne: InfoServ.
Priest, J. G. and Sarne, G. (2011). Reasoning and wicked problems. *Research in Practice W2011b*. Melbourne: InfoServ.
Priest, J. G. and Trayner, Q. (2004). Strategic innovation and change: what is effective management practice? *Research in Practice W2004a*. Melbourne: InfoServ.
Punch, K. F. (2014). *Introduction to Social Research: Quantitative and Qualitative Approaches*, 3rd edn. Los Angeles: Sage.
Pye, A. (2005). Leadership and organizing: sensemaking in action. *Leadership* 1: 31–50.
Reichenbach, H. (1948). *Experience and Prediction*. Chicago: University of Chicago Press.
Rex, J. (1974). *Sociology and the Demystification of the Modern World*. London: Routledge & Kegan Paul.
Rittel, H. W. J. and Webber, M. M. (1973). Dilemmas in a general theory of planning. *Policy Sciences* 4: 155–69.
Ritzer, G. and Stepnisky, J. (2013) *Sociological Theory*, 9th edn. New York: McGraw-Hill.
Rose, A. (1950). A deductive ideal-type method. *American Journal of Sociology* 56: 35–42.
Samdahl, D. M. and Robertson, R. (1989). Social determinants of environmental concern: specification and test of the model. *Environmental Behavior* 21: 57–81.
Sayer, A. (1992). *Methods in Social Science: A Realist Approach*, 2nd edn. London: Routledge.

Sayer, A. (2000). *Realism and Social Science*. London: Sage.
Schütz, A. (1963a). Concept and theory formation in the social sciences, in M. A. Natanson (ed.), *Philosophy of the Social Sciences*. New York: Random House, pp. 231–49.
Schütz, A. (1963b). Common-sense and scientific interpretation of human action, in M. A. Natanson (ed.). *Philosophy of the Social Sciences*. New York: Random House, pp. 302–46.
Schütz, A. (1964). *Collected Papers*. The Hague: Martinus Nijhoff.
Schütz, A. (1970). Interpretive sociology, in H. R. Wagner (ed.), *Alfred Schütz on Phenomenology and Social Relations*. Chicago: University of Chicago Press, pp. 265–93.
Schütz, A. (1976). *The Phenomenology of the Social World*. London: Heinemann.
Seale, C. (1999). *The Quality of Qualitative Research*. London: Sage.
Smadja, F. (1993). Retrieving collocations from text: Xtract. *Computational Linguistics* 19: 43–177.
Smith, K. and Hancock, P. A. (1995). Situation awareness is adaptive externally directed consciousness. *Human Factors* 37: 137–48.
Stacy, S. J. G. (1983). *Limitations of Ageing: Old People and the Caring Professions*. PhD thesis, Monash University, Melbourne.
Stockman, N. (1983). *Antipositivist Theories of the Sciences*. Dordrecht: Reidel.
Strauss, A. (1987). *Qualitative Analysis for Social Scientists*. Cambridge: Cambridge University Press.
Strauss, A. and Corbin, J. (1998). *Basics of Qualitative Research: Techniques and Procedures for Developing Grounded Theory*, 2nd edn. Thousand Oaks: Sage.
Tashakkori, A. and Teddlie, C. (1998). *Mixed Methodology: Combining Qualitative and Quantitative Approaches*. Thousand Oaks: Sage.
Tashakkori, A., and Teddlie, C. (eds). (2010). *Sage Handbook of Mixed Methods in Social and Behavioral Research*. Thousand Oaks: Sage.
Teague, B., McLeod R. and Pascoe, S. (2010a). *2009 Victorian Bushfires Royal Commission: Final Report Summary*. Melbourne: VBRC.
Teague, B., McLeod, R. and Pascoe, S. (2010b). The Kilmore East Fire, *2009 Victorian Bushfires Royal Commission Final Report*. Vol/Ch 1(5). Melbourne: VBRC, pp. 70–92.
Teddlie, C. and Tashakkori, A. (2009). *Foundations of Mixed Methods Research: Integrating Quantitative and Qualitative Approaches in the Social and Behavioral Sciences*. Thousand Oaks: Sage.
Thompson, K. (1982). *Emile Durkheim*. London: Tavistock/Chichester: Ellis Horwood.
Van Liere, K. D. and Dunlap, R. E. (1980). Social bases of environmental concern; a review of hypotheses, explanations and empirical evidence. *Public Opinion Quarterly* 44: 181–97.
VFBV (2010). *VFBV Response to Counsel Assisting's Submission on Systemic*

Issues — Training Incident Controllers, in 2009. Bushfires Royal Commission Submission.

Von Wright, G. H. (1971). *Explanation and Understanding.* London: Routledge & Kegan Paul.

Watkins, J. W. N. (1953). Ideal types and historical explanation, in H. Feigl and M. Brodbeck (eds), *Readings in the Philosophy of Science.* New York: Appleton-Century-Crofts, pp. 723–43.

Weber, M. (1947). *The Theory of Social and Economic Organization,* trans. A. M. Henderson and Talcott Parsons; ed. and introduction by Talcott Parsons. New York: Oxford University Press.

Weber, M. (1958 [1904–5]). *The Protestant Ethic and the Spirit of Capitalism,* trans. T. Parsons. New York: Scribner.

Weick, K. E., Sutcliffe, K. M. and Obstfeld, D. (2005). Organizing and the process of sensemaking. *Organization Science* 16: 409–25.

Whewell, W. (1847). *The Philosophy of Inductive Sciences,* 2 vols. London: Parker.

Winch, P. (1958). *The Idea of Social Science.* London: Routledge & Kegan Paul.

Index

Note: Where major concepts occur in many places, and there is a primary discussion of them, the page(s) are shown in italics.

Abbagano, N. 55
abductive logic *see* logic(s) of inquiry
abstract analysis 140
abstracted categories/types 36, 117, 119–23, 133, 143, 147–8
abstracting/ion(s) 12, 13, 46, 251
accounts
  everyday *see* everyday accounts
  participants' *see* everyday accounts
  researcher's *see* researchers' accounts
  social scientific *see* social scientific accounts
action
  directives 94, 155
  orientations 204, 206
actions
  first-responder 80–1, 85, 90, 140–1, 206
  leader's(s') 83–4, 87, 88–9, 91–2, 94–6, 156–7, 226, 227
  meanings and reasons 46, 85, 88–9, 95, 179, 190, 212–13
  social actor's 46, 100–1, 107, 113, 175–6, 179, 190–1, 192, 200
Adorno, T. W. 64
AFAC (Australian Fire Authorities Council) 253
agency, human *see* human agency
agency experience *see* experience, agency
Albert, H. 64
Alexander, J. C. 64
Alldred, P. 12

analysing data *see* data analysis
analysis, macro/meso/micro 217–18
analytic induction 38
approaches to social inquiry/social research 11, 18–19, 20, 21
Arcury, T. E. 74
argument
  deductive *see* deductive argument
  theoretical *see* theoretical argument
association(s)/relationship(s)
  between concepts 13, 14, 25, 37, 45, 61, 66–7, 68–70, 72–3, 74, 78–9, 88, 91, 98, 176, 195–7, 199–200, 205, 206, 209, 218, 226, 251–2, 255
  between typologies 117, 119–20, 122–4, 131, 133, 135, 137–8, 140, 143, 149–51, 159–61, 227
assumptions 30–1, 33, 38, 39
  epistemological *see* epistemological assumptions
  ontological *see* ontological assumptions
  philosophical *see* philosophical assumptions

Bacon, F. 54
Bannister, A. J. 82, 89
Barnes, B. 8, 70
Baronov, D. 11
Barton, A. 105
Bartsch, S. 123
Bauman, Z. 99
Bearman, C. 83

Becker, H. 99, 104, 105, 108–11, 125, 254
Benton, T. 170–71, 186, 194
Berger, P. L. 180, 184
Bhaskar, R. 54–5, 64, 169, 170–1, 173, 174, 176–8, 179, 180–2, 183, 184–5, 186, 193, 194
Blaikie, N. 2, 7–8, 10, 11, 12, 18, 31, 33, 36, 38, 52, 55, 62, 63, 64, 70, 72–4, 100, 115, 124, 125, 168, 169, 170, 171, 174, 183, 186, 193, 197–8, 232, 233, 244, 246, 251, 252, 253, 254, 255, 256
Blocker, T. J. 197
BOTM*line* ™ 137
bottom-up research 4, 16, 33, 124, 221, 247
braided work 134–5, 138
braiding 134, 138, 211, 212
Brannen, J. 20
Brinkmann, S. 132
Bryant, A. 124
Bryant, C. G. A. 55, 64, 70
Bryman, A. 19, 20
bureaucrat(ic) 104, 144, 155
bureaucrat type 155–65

case studies 36
Catton, W. R. 74
causal
 explanation(s) 101–2, 113, 170, 176, 187, 196, 252
 mechanism(s) 30, 36, 46, 169, 171, *187–93*, 196, 198–201, 205, *207–19*, 228, 243
 model(s) 189–91, 192, 217–18, 219
causality, generative and successive views of 175–6
Chalmers, A. F. 64, 70
Charmaz, K. 124
chief type 156–65
choice
 influences on 238–43
 of research paradigm 2–4, *9–22*, 23–4, 44, 66–7, 224–5, 226
Christianson, E. H. 74
co-construct/ing 133
co-frequencies 123, 151–2, 157, 160, 162–3, 255
cognitive
 activity 160, 176
 equipment/capacities 180, 241
 processes 95, 190, 191, 212, 213
 resources 180, 182, 190, 191, 212, 213
 structure 180
Collier, A. 171
collocation 123
Comte, A. 54, 104, 170
concepts
 associations between *see* associations between concepts
 everyday *see* everyday concepts/constructs
 formal definitions of *66–9*, 80, 92, 94–6
 operational definitions of 34, 36, *66–70*, 76, 80, 89, 90, 92, 94–6, 97–8, 201
 pairs of *see* pairs of concepts
 role of 34–5
 sensitizing 32, 35
 social scientific *see* social scientific concepts
 technical *see* technical concepts/constructs
conflict theory 20
confounding factors/variables 122, 131, 162, 196, 207, 218
Conklin, J.
constructionism, social 31, 104
constructionist 176, 180, 237
construction(s)
 of mechanisms 34, 189, 231
 of models 47
 of types/typologies 109, 204
 social/social actors' 16, 89, 121, 227
 sociological 16
constructs
 first-order 112, 114, 117, 119–21, 123, 143
 second-order 112, 114, 120, 123, 150
context(s) 8, 11, 13, 30–1, 37–9, 46, 68–9, 91, 167, *174–6*, 187–90, 198–203, 205–12
co-occurrence(s) 123, 151–3, 161, 218, 254
Corbin, J. 124
correspondence, one-to-one 21, 34, 54, 221
corroborate/ion *see* theory corroboration
co-validate 133, 212
counter-intuitive 39, 66, 193, 219, 252
creativity 231
 in modelling mechanisms 32, 37, 47, 174, 188, 190, 198, 228, 231

Index

in theory construction 3, 4, 14, 32, 37, 47, 67, 117–18, 120, 164–6, 230–1, 233, 237–8
Creswell, J. W. 17, 20
critical rationalism 11, 62
Critical Realism
  constructionist *see* constructionist
  structuralist *see* structuralist
Critical Realist
  characteristic steps of paradigm 187–93
  limitations of paradigm 186
  paradigm 13, 20–1, 25–38, 167, *168–94*, 237, 238
  research 46–7, 195–219, 225, 228
critical theory 11, 21, 71, 126, 182–4, 194
critic's standpoint 184–5
critique(s) 7, 64, 70–1, 100, 113, 124, 125, 167, 172–3, 183, *184–5*, 256
Cruz, M. G. 82, 89

Dahrendorf, R. 64
data
  analysis 2, 8, 10, 12, 20, 22, 25, *37–8*, 65, 97–8, 117, 118–21, 123, 132–5, 142–67, 192–3, 213–15, 217–18
  collection 2, 8, 10, 22, 25, 36–7, 43, 59, 64–7, 98, 133–4, 224–5
  deconstructing 120–2, 123, 147–8, 238
  forms of 36
  generalizing from 2, 12, 14–15, 33, 38, 43, 62, 221
  generation 2, 8, 10, 22, 25, 37, 65, 118–19, 132–3, 142–3
  interpret/ation 11, 67, 69, 97, 167, *191–3*, 218
  kinds of 8, 36
  primary 36, 43, 87, 119, 142, 192, 214, 218
  for proxy variables 66, 68–9, 90, 92, 95, 97–8, 211, 252
  reconstructing 121–3, 147–8, 238
  secondary 36, 42–3, 87, 119, 142, 192
  selection of 8, 36–7
  sources of 8, 36, 69, 90–1, 117, 119, 214
  tertiary 36, 119, 142
  types of 36, 37, 215–16
  use of 35–6
decision making *see* leader's(s') decision making

deconstruction/ing 120–3, 124, 140, 147–8, 238
  everyday typifications 122
  of meanings 120–3, 140, 147
deductive
  argument 35, 45, 46, 59, 61, 66, 67, 75, 88, 176
  logic *see* logic(s) of inquiry
  theory/ies 56, 59, 60–1, 67, 68, 73, 80, 196, 224, 231, 237
Deese, J. E. 123
definitions
  formal *see* formal definitions
  operational *see* operational definitions
Denzin, N. K. 19
depth realism/ist 31, 177
description(s) 1–3, 9, 13, 14, 25, 33, 39, 43, 55, 65–6, 86, 104–5, 110, 114, 117, 122–3, 133, 171, 174, 179–80, 185, 190, 205–6, 220–1, 226, 242, 254
  rich *see* thick description
  thick *see* thick description
design, research *see* research design
dialogic method 233–7
dialogues in social research 115, 203, 231–3, 237, 256
Dilthey, W. 100
domains of reality
  actual 178, 191, 212
  empirical 178, 191, 212
  real 178
dominant logic 13–14, 22, 121, 124, 213
double hermeneutic 232
Douglas, J. 58
duality of structures 115, 175, 180
Duberley, J. 70
Dunlap, R. E. 73, 74, 197
Durkheim, E. 11, 54, 56, 57–9, 67, 68, 104, 170, 172, 176

Eckberg, D. L. 197
effective/ness
  first-responder 80–2, 139, 140–1, 165, 204, 207, 215–16, 227
  investment management 128, 130, 133–4, 138
  leadership responses 80, 84, 86–9, 91–2, 95–6, 98, 149, 151, 153–4, 161–4, 167, 204–5, 206–8, 211, 226–7
egoistic suicide *see* suicide, egoistic

Index

emancipation(ory) 21, 171, 172–3, 182–5, 187
emotional reasoning resource 95, 191–2, 212–13, 215, 216
Endsley, M. R. 83, 86
environmentalism 14, 195–200
episodes, social *see* social episodes
epistemological assumptions 9, 10–12, 14–16, 30–1
  constructionism 31, 104
  falsificationism 31, 60
  neo-realism 31, 182
ethnomethodology/ists 11, 38, 100, 113, 115
ethogenic approach 178–80, 193
events
  associations/conjunctions/uniformities/regularities between 60, 102, 171, 175, 252
  sequence of 66, 67, 102, 175
everyday
  accounts 12, 13, 32, 116–17, 123–4, 179, 192–3, 202, 213–17
  concepts/constructs 34, 36, 37, 96, 234, 248
  knowledge 112
  language 62, 104, 120
  meaning(s) 34, 121–2, 148
  ontologies 181
  social constructions 16
  typifications 30, *46*, *111–12*, *119–23*, 125, 133, *143–8*, 233, 235, 236
  understanding 37
evidence
  for existence of a mechanism 12, 30–2, 34, 36, 37, 47, 173–4, 177, 189–91, 205, 207–8, 212–3, 214, 216, 218–19, 225, 228, 237
  for (dis)confirm/ing 32, 46, 47, 60, 61, 64, 66, 97, 121, 124, 191–3, 213–4, 216, 249
exchange theory 20
experience 252
  agency-based/institutional 83–4, 85, 86, *91–8*, 140–7, 164, 206–7, 214–5, 217–8, 226–7
  communicative 183, 231
  leader's(s') 80, 83–4, 139, 151, 154, 206, 214, 218
  lived/life 15, 30, 33, 41, 56, 59, 62, 75, 84, 85, 88, 91–2, 140–6, 178, 204, 206, 214–5, 226

  other/external/informal/broader 80, 83–6, *87–98*, 139, 141–7, 151, 163–4, 204, 206–7, 208–9, 211–12, 214–5, 216, 217–8, 226–7
  researcher's 234–8, 240–1
  sense 183, 231
  verified by 54
experiential influence(s), typology(types) of
explanation(s) 1–3, 7, 9, 13, 14, 34, 35; *see also* understanding
explanatory mechanism(s) *see* mechanism(s) explanatory
exploring 35, 116, 119, 140, 141, 227

Fallding, H. 105, 154
feminism 11, 105, 185
Feyerabend, P. K. 63
Feynman, R. 174
findings 8, *9–11*, *38–9*, 98, 125, 138, 164–5, 167
fire-response 83, 142, 206, 215, 218
formal definition(s) 66, 92, 94–6
formally define 68
foundations
  methodological 7, 22, 172
  philosophical 7, 17, 22, 63
Fox, N. J. 12
Frankfurt school 183
Friedricks, R. W. 8

Gadamer, H.-G. 100, 232
Garfinkel, H. 38, 104, 113, 115, 126
generalizing/ation(s) 2, 12, 14–15, 25, 33, *38*, 43, 54–5, *60–2*, 70, 102, 108–10
generating knowledge *see* knowledge, generating new
generative view of causality *see* causality
Giddens, A. 64, 99, 100, 101, 105, 113–14, 115, 125, 126, 175, 180, 182, 184, 185, 198, 232
Giedymin, J. 55
Glaser, B. 124
Gould, J. S. 82, 89
Greene, J. C. 20, 21
Grimes, M. D. 74
grounded theory 124–5
Grunwald, J. 83
Guba, E. G. 8

Habermas, J. 64, 183, 185, 231, 233
Hacking, I. 55

Index

Halfpenny, P. 64
Hallebone, E. xv, 19
Hammersley, M. 169
Hancock, P. A. 83, 86
Hardy, T. 255
Harré, R. 170, 171, 174, 175, 176, 178–82, 186, 192, 193–4, 198, 213, 238
Hayes, P. 83
Heidegger, M. 100
Hempel, C. G. 56, 105, 174
hermeneutic circle 116, 232
hermeneutics 11, 12, 99, 100, 114, 126, 183, 186, 217, *232–3*
Hertz, R. 132
Hindess, B. 64
Hollis, J. J. 82, 89
Homans, G. C. 56, 58, 67, 68
Honnold, J. A. 74, 75
'how' research questions *see* research questions
human agency 115, 175, 180, 182, 198
Hume, D. 54, 175
Hurley, R. J. 82, 89
Husserl, E. 100
Hyde, M. 98
hypothes/is/es/izing 13, *34–7*, 45–6, 56, *74–5*, 92, 96, 109, 112, 201–3, 230
  micro/mini 34, 35, 235
  tentative 45, 58
  testing 13, 35–7, 64, 75, 78–9, *91–7*, 123, 224–5
hypothetical
  meaning 101
  model (of a mechanism) 34–5, 37, 46, 47, 174, 198, 200–1, 202–3, 231, 237

ideal types *see* types, ideal/pure
identity, leader's *see* leader's(s') identity
imagination, theoretical *see* theoretical imagination
imagining a mechanism 37, 198, 204
Imber, J. B. 132
impact of leader's actions *see* effectiveness
inductive logic *see* logic(s) of inquiry
InfoServ *see* www.InfoServ.com.au
innovator type 155–65
insider stance 33
insight, leader's 167, 204, 206, 208–11, 216

integrity of the phenomenon 38
intellectual puzzles *see* puzzles, intellectual/explanatory
interpretation(s)
  causal 102
  of data 69, 97, 117–8, 191–3, 211
  of evidence 191–2
  of findings 11, 239
  of observations 55, 60, 62
  researcher's 16, 67, 177
  social actors' 15, 31, 32, 34, 46, 100, 103, 232
  of texts 99
interpretive
  sociology 113–14, 126, 170
  understanding 101–2
Interpretive
  characteristic steps of paradigm 116–24
  limitations of paradigm 114–15
  paradigm 13, 20, 21, 25–38, 46, 65, *99–125*, 181, 186–8, 213, 231–7, 238, 254
  research *127–67*, 224–5, 226–8
interpretivism 11, 12, 17–18, 20, 21, 111, 113–14, 169, 171, 183
intuition, role of 174, 230
iterative cycles 118, 119, 125, 143
iterative processes/iteration(s) 32, 34, 37, 46, 67, 109, 116, 117, 123, 132, 136, 139, 142, 190
Ivankova, N. V. 20

Johnson, P. 70

Kaplan, D. 19
Keat, R. 55, 64, 70, 170–1, 186, 194
King, A. 186
know-how *see* leader's(s') know-how
knowledge
  adequate 1
  advancing 10, 130
  everyday 112
  gap in 128
  generating new 9, 14, 18–22, 55–60, 62, 222
  intransitive/ient dimension of 177, 186–7
  logic of 230
  psychology of 230
  relative 185
  scientific 53–6, 230

knowledge (*cont.*)
  social scientific 16, 62–3, 104, 112, 177, 235
  tacit 131, 178
  tentative 31, 62
  transitive/sient dimension of 177, 186–7
  universal 64
  verifiable 103
Kolakowski, L. 55
Kuhn, T. S. 8–9, 62–3, 70
Kvale, S. 132

Lakatos, I. 8, 63, 64
language
  everyday/participants' 34, 38, 62, 104, 117, 120, 179, 234
  limitations of 56
  as medium of social interaction 103, 114
  ordinary 100
  researcher's 120, 124, 134
  scientific 54, 62
  social scientific/technical 104
Lassman, P. 113
law(s)
  causal 18
  general 60
  scientific 56, 60
  universal 54, 56
Layder, D. 1, 171, 186, 251
Lazarsfeld, P. F. 105
leader's(s')
  actions *80–92*, 94–6, 141, 156–7, 225–7
  decision making 81–2, 84–9, 94–5, 139, 143, 149–51, 153–7, 166, 204, 206, 208, 210–17, 227
  experience *see* experience, agency-based/institutional; experience, other/external/informal/broader
  identity/ies 84, *86–9*, 91–2, 94–5, 143, 150–1, 153–4, 204, 206, 227, 253
  insight 166, 204, 206, 208–11, 216
  interpretation 206, 208–11, 216
  know-how 82, 84, 85, 88, 93, 95, 128, 130, 131, 146, 150, 166, *204–11*, 216; *see also* wisdom
  orientation(s) 85, 94, *153–64*, 204
  reasoning 81, 83, 85, *87–92*, 94–6, 141, 143, 151, 153, 164, 166, 208–13, 216–19, 226–7, 256
  repertoire *see* repertoire(s)

response/s 82–4, 86, 154, 159–67, 204–7
sense making 81–2, *85–9*, 95, 139, 143, 150, 151, 153–7, 204, 206, 208, 210–12, 214–17, 227
wisdom 166, 204, 208–11
Leech, N. L. 20
left-brain 134–7
limitations
  of senses 30, 60
  of a study 39, 189
limitations of paradigms 22
  Critical Realist 118, 186
  Interpretive 114–15
  Neo-Positive 62–4
Lincoln, Y. S. 8, 19
linear processes 32, 116
literature
  review 31–2, 65, 74–5, 129–31, 141, 188, 197, 208
  as source of ideas 31, 65, 87, 116, 188–9, 190, 208, 226–7, 232
logic
  of discovery 63, 67, 174, 182, 183, 230
  dominant *see* dominant logic
logic(s) of inquiry 2, 3, 8, *12–15*, 19–22, 24, 33–4, 39, 60, 100, 125, 220, 230–1
  abductive/ion *12–15*, 19, 30, 33, 34–5, 37, 42, 46, 120–4, 131, 132, 147–9, 170, 213, 221, 231, 235, 237, 243
  deductive/ion *12–15*, 19, 33, 35, 42, 45–6, 54–6, *57–9*, *60–2*, 64, 66–8, 70, 73, 75, 80, 88, 100, 121, 169, 176, 196, 213, 224, 230–1, 237, 243, 251, 252, 254
  inductive/ion *12–15*, 19, 25, 30, 33, 38, 43, 54–8, 61–2, 64, 70, 102, 119, 121, 124, 169–70, 213, 221, 230–1, 243, 251
  retroductive/ion *12–15*, 19, 34, 42, 173–4, 197, 203, 231, 243, 254, 255
Loomis, C. P. 105
Lowe, G. D. 74
Luckmann, T. 180

Mannheim, K. 74
Marsden-Smedley, J. 98
Martindale, D. 104, 105
Marx, K. 11, 170. 172–3, 180, 183
Marxist/ism 20, 171, 184

Index

Masterman, M. 8
maverick theory 80, 87, 89–91, 94, 96, 98, 139, 226
maverick type 155–65
McCarthy, T. 185
McKinney, J. C. 105
McLeod, R. 82, 85, 89, 90, 141
McStay, J. R. 197
meaning
  of action and social action 18, 46, *100–3*, 108, 111, 113, 115, 186, 251, 253
  attributed by social actors 111, 113, 115
  attributed by social scientists 111–12, 235
  context of 112
  deconstruct/ed/ing/ion 120–3, 140, 147, 238
  everyday 34, 118, 121, 143, 147
  frames of 114
  shared 8, 13, 34–5, 183
  socially constructed 18, 46
  subjective *100–3*, 105, 108, 111, 179, 183, 206, 209, 213–4, 232–3
  of texts 232–3
  of theoretical concepts 66–9, 88–90, 134–7
mechanism(s), explanatory/generative/hypothetical/causal 12, 13, 30, 31, 32, 34–7, 46, 138, 169, 170–1, *173–82*, *187–93*, 196, 198–203, 205, *207–19*, 225, 228, 231, 237, 243
Medewar, P. B. 174, 230, 231
member checking 38, 46; *see also* co-validate
Merton, R. K. 7, 56, 58–9, 67, 176
methodological foundations 7–15
methods
  choice of 6–7, 9
  mixed *see* mixed methods
  quantitative *see* quantitative methods
  qualitative *see* qualitative methods
  research *see* research methods
middle-range
  theory 79, 176
  realism 176, 194
Mill, J. S. 54
Mills, C. W. 74, 75
Mitchell, R. G. 124
mixed methods 7, 12, 17, *20–1*, 221, 226, 256

Mohai, P. 74–5
model/ling a regularity 13, 25, 32, 34, 35, 37, 46, 208–9, 212–13
models of explanation
  deductive 61
  pattern 60–1, 64, 102. 175
models of
  mechanisms *173–4*, 180, 188–93, 193, 198, 202–3, 216–19; *see also* causal model(s)
  cognitive resources/structures 180
monologues 231–3, 237, 256
motive(s) 13, 46, *102*, 111, 176
Mulkay, M. 64
multi/ple paradigm(s) 10, 11, 22, 40, 43, 79, 203, 220–8, 233
  in parallel and sequence 4, 222–3
Musgrave, A. 63

Neo-Positive
  characteristic steps of paradigm 65–70
  limitations of paradigm 62–4
  paradigm 20, 25–38, 53–70
  research 40, 45–6, 57–9, 72–98
Neuman, W. L. 18–19
nominal values/variables 96

objective/objectivity 10, 15, 38, 55, 62–3, 99–101, 103, 106, 107, 112, 124, 172, 186
observation(s) 31, 34, *53–6*, *60–2*, 102, 108–9, 169, 171, 177–8, 183, 185, 231, 238, 252
observed
  mechanism(s) 173–5
  patterns/regularities 34, 35, 169, 179, 182, 190, 198, 200, 254
observer 33, 111–12, 115, 177–8
Obstfeld, D. 83, 86
Omodei, M. 83
Ong, B. K. 124
ontological assumptions *8–12*, 14–15, 17, 19, 20, *30–1*, 52, 56, 59–60, 64–7, 103–4, 115, 124, 126, 168–9, 176–9, 181–3, 186–7, 207, 222, 238, 239, 243, 251
  cautious realist 60
  depth realist 182, 207
  idealist 103
ontological depth 177–8, 187
Onwuegbuzie, A. J. 20
operational definitions 80, 89, 92, 94–6

operationalizing concepts *see* proxy variables
ordinal categories/variables 96
orientation(s)
 action 204, 206, 214–15, 217
 communal 88, 164
 institutional 85, 163–4
 leader's(s') *see* leader's(s') orientation(s)
origins of paradigms
 Critical Realism 170–1
 Interpretivism 100–3
 Neo-Positivism 54–5, 70
outcome(s)
 of critique 185
 of a regularity 176, 189–90, 198–9, 200–2
 of human agency 180
 response 81–2, 84, *88–9*, 96–7, 139, 140, 155, 160–1, 163–4, 204–6, 208–9, 212, 214–5, 225–7
Outhwaite, W. 54, 71, 171, 177, 194
outsider stance 33

paradigm(s)
 boundaries 238
 choice *see* choice of research paradigm
 research *see* research paradigms
 multi/ple *see* multi/ple paradigm(s)
 rivalry 20
 role of 2, 9, 13, 17, 22
Pascoe, S. 82, 85, 89, 90, 141
pairs
 of cases 163
 of concepts 69, 75
 of statements 226
 of types 135, 138
participants' accounts *see* everyday accounts
pattern model of explanation *see* explanation(s)
patterns
 in findings/evidence 129, 193
 observed 13–15, 25, 30, 36, 55, 60–1, 65–7, 74, 97, 103, 171, 179–80, 188, 190, 213, 251, 252, 255
 between types/typologies 123–4, 136, 157
 see also regularities
Pawson, R. 169, 171, 174, 175, 176, 182, 194, 198, 199, 202, 217, 237

phenomenology 100, 113, 126
philosophical, 17
 assumptions, 3, 8, 12, 17, 19, 22, 60, 103–4, 182, 220, 251
 foundations 7–15
 perspectives 9
Pilot, H. 64
Pinhey, T. K. 74
Plano-Clark, V. 17, 20
point(s) of view
 of logics of inquiry 12
 of research paradigm 9, 171, 183, 222
 researchers'/social scientists' 8, 10–11, 16–18, 33, 62, 178–9, 233, 240
 social actors'/participants' *15–17*, 33, 53, 94, 96–7, 150, 210
 of social theories/paradigms 9, 107, 183, 186, 222
 users' 11
 see also worldviews
politician type 150–2, 157, 160–5
Popper, K. R. 54, 55, 56, 62–4, 70, 71, 174, 229–31
population(s) 36–8, 67, 69–70, 78, 90–2, 97–8, 118, 131, 141, 198, 207–8
positivism/ive 20
 classical 11, 20, 53–4, 58–9, 60, 62, 64, 70–1, 99–100, 115, 124, 128, 130, 169–70, 175, 179, 183, 254
 logical 11, 54, 55
 neo- *see* Neo-Positive
 standard view 55, 56, 57, 62, 64, 65, 70–1
postulate of adequacy 113–14
practical/ity/ies
 problems 7, 65
 to use 3, 11, 24, 65, 69, 70, 98, 118, 119, 189, 193, 197, 215, 219
pragmatism 11, 12, 17, 20, 21
prediction(s) from theory 61, 66, 68, 78, 91, 97, 104, 109–10, 112
Priest, J. G. 19, 127, 128, 139, 151, 166, 208, 238
problem *see* research problem
proxy variables 66–9, 90, 92, 95, 97, 252
psychological distance 118
Punch, K. F. 17–18, 19
puzzles, intellectual/scientific/explanatory 7, 63, 196
Pye, A. 86

Index

qualitative
  data 15, 37, 97, 226
  methods 7, 19, 21, 97, 242
  research *18–21*, 105, 222
quantitative
  data 37, 96–7, 226, 251
  methods 7, 14, 19, 21, 30, 37, 65, 97, 105, 115, 242
  research *18–21*, 222
quantitative/qualitative dichotomy 18, 19, 21
questioning in Interpretive research 114, 116, 123, 140, 142, 154, 156–7, 160–4
questions, research *see* research question(s)

realism
  critical *see* Critical Realism
  depth *see* depth realism/ist
  scientific *see* scientific realism
realist
  cautious 30, 60, 169
  interview/ing 202, 237
  ontological assumptions *see* ontological assumptions
reality
  domains of 31, 178
  empirical 110
  external 57, 103, 115, 124, 150, 168, 181, 186
  observ/ed/ing/ation(al) 18, 31, 33, 56, 60, 62, 169, 177–8, 183, 231
  social 2, 9, 30–1, 34, 54, 100, *103–4*, 112, 124, 181–2
  socially constructed 16, 103, 111, 121, 124, 171, 175, 182, 186, 231–2
  view of 15, 151
reasoning 188, 190–1, 193, 198–204, 212–13, 256
  people's/participants'/individuals' 188, 190–1, 192–3, 198–204, 208–9, 212
  resources (processes/contents) 165, 188, 209–13, 217–19
  see also leader's(s') reasoning
reasons, social actors' *see* social actors' reasons
reconstruction/ing 16, 56, 58, 120–4, 147, 230, 235, 238
reflexive cycles 116, 117, 125
reflexive/ity 67, 90, 139, 178, 187–8, 208–9, 234, 236
refute/ation 56, 62, 92, 177

regularity(ies) 13, 14, 25, 30, 32, 34, 35, 36, 37, 42–6, 56, 61–2, 64, 66–9, 102–3, 117, 119–20, 122–3, 169–76, 182, 187–93
relatability 38
reliability 38, 78
repertoire(s)
  leaders' 88, 94, 148–54, 159–60
  choice of 149–50, 154, 204
reporting results/findings 39, 189
research
  bottom-up 4, *16*, 33, 124, 221
  design 3, 10–12, 25, 32, 47, 131, 196, 252
  findings *see* findings
  methods 19–20
  methods texts 1, 6–7, 18
  problem 2–3, 7–10, 15, 17, 22, 24–5, *30–6*, 39, *40–4*, *64–6*, 73, 80, 84–6, 98, 109, 112, 128, 140, 185, 187–8, 196, 203, 206, 220–1, 223, *225–6*, 238–42
  top-down *16*, 33, 124, 221
  topic 2, 40, 252
research paradigms 2–4, 7, *8–12*, 13–15, 17–18, 19–22, 24
  in action 45–7, 72–98, 127–67, 195–219
  choice 3, 8, 13, 15, 17, 19–22, 44, 66, 224–5, 238–42
  Critical Realist *see* Critical Realist research
  differences between 4, *25–39*, 45–7
  Interpretive *see* Interpretive research
  limitations *see* limitations of paradigms
  Neo-Positive *see* Neo-Positive research
  origins of *see* origins of paradigms
research question(s) 2, *7–11*, 12–15, 22, 24–5, 30, 39, 40, 42–4, 69, 79, 86–8, 125, 129–31, 138, 139–41, *154–67*, 187–8, *220–5*, 226–8, 238–43, 254
  and the research problem 22, 24, 42–4, 73, 86, 221, 223
  examples of 14–15, 42, 44, 61, 73, 130, 139, 141, 154, 167, 196, 205, 223–5, 226–8
  'how' 7, 187, 188, 228
  types of 7
  'what' 7, *13–15*, 25, 31, 42, 66, 82, 86, 122–5, 127, 130, 138, 140, 151, 154, 157, 159, 187–8, 220–2, 227, 243

research question(s) (*cont.*)
'why' 3, 7, *13–15*, 30, 32, 35, 42, 46, 60–1, 66, 82, 86–8, 117, 120, 122–5, 130–1, 140, 159–61, 164, 167, 187–8, 203, 220–2, 223, 226–8, 243
researcher's(s')
accounts *see* social scientific accounts
stance *16–17*, 33
worldview 31
resources *see* cognitive resources; leader's(s') reasoning; reasoning resources
response
effectiveness 81, 84, 87, 89, 96, 98, 139, 160–1, 164–5, 206–7, 215–6, 226
outcome 88–9, 91, 160–1, 163–4, 206, 209, 212
retroductive logic *see* logic(s) of inquiry
Rex, J. 99, 105, 113, 115, 126, 253, 254
rich description *see* thick description
right-brain 134–7
Rittel, H. W. J. 81
Ritzer, G. 11
road maps *23–39*
Robertson, R. 79
role
choices 217
identity/ies 83, 89, 94, 143, 150–1, 153–4, 156–7, 204, 253
Rose, A. 105

Samdahl, D. M. 75
sample(s)
non-probability 36–7
populations and 118, 141–2
probability 36, 38, 69, 73
purposive 124, 131
response 97
sampling 36–7
Sarne, G. 139, 151, 166, 208, 238
Sayer, A. 171, 184–5, 194
Schleiermacher, D. 100, 232
Schütz, A. 38, 99, 100, 101, 104, 105, 108, 111–12, 113–14, 115, 126, 238, 253, 254
scientific
community/ies 8, 63
inquiry 183, 230
knowledge 53, 55, 56, 62, 63, 112, 230
language 54, 62
law(s) 56, 60
method 17, 53, 59, 169

puzzle(s)/problem(s) 63, 112, 185
realism 12, 21, 169, 177
revolutions 63
Seale, C. 124
Secord, P. F. 170, 171, 179, 192, 194, 213
selection of data sources *see* data, selection of
sense making 81, 82, 85–9, 95, 139, 143, 150–1, 153–7, 204, 206, 208, 210–12, 214–17, 227
sensitizing concepts 32, 35, 201
sequence of events *see* events
sexual abuse 40–7, 221, 223–5, 251
significance, test *see* tests of significance
Sims, N. C. 82, 89
Smadja, F. 123
Smith, K. 83, 86
social
context(s) 31, 37–8, 46, 61, 69, 79, 107, 198
episodes 180, 182
problem(s) 3, 25, 64, 112, 241, 243
social actors'
accounts *see* everyday accounts
actions/activities 175, 192, 213
cognitive activity/resources 176, 182, 192
interpretations 31, 34, 103, 213
meanings 13, 101, 103, 107, 111, 183
motives 13
ontological assumptions 181
reasons 46, 202, 203
resources 46
tacit knowledge 178, 183
typifications 30, 46, 111–13
understanding 113, 114–15
worldviews *see* worldviews
social constructions *see* construction(s)
social constructivist 20
social scientific/researcher's
accounts 12–13, 16, 34, 35, 38, 104, 232, 234
concepts 35, 36, 37, 123, 247, 248
explanation 103
knowledge 16, 104, 177, 185, 235
language 104
meaning 122
ontologies 181
typifications 30, 32, 46, 125, 233, 235, 236, 247
understanding 33–4

social structures 46, 115, 172–3, *180–2*, 186–7, 198
  macro 113, 180–1
  micro 181
social theory 12, 70, 140, 171, 180, 194, 242
socially constructed
  meaning 18
  reality 103, 124
  social structures 171, 175, 186
  typifications 111
  world 182
space and time *see* time and space limitations
Spencer, H. 104
Stacy, S. J. G. 233, 254
stance(s), researcher's *see* researcher's stance
standpoint, critic's 184–5
starting point(s) 12, 25, 32, 61, 64, 169, 171, 243
status 95–6
  of a generalization 55
  of research findings 38
  of scientific knowledge 56, 63
  of a scientific law 56
  of social structures 172, 182, 187
  of a theory 45
Stepnisky, J. 11
Stockman, N. 55, 64, 186
Strauss, A. 124
structural-functionalism 20
structuralist 176, 180, 182, 237
structuration theory 11, 12, 115
structure(s)
  cognitive 180
  duality of *see* duality of structures
  historical 113, 115
  macro 181
  mechanism's 208–12
  micro 181
  social *see* social structures
  subjective meaning 100, 105, 121, 148
  underlying 12, 31, 169–71, 178, 182, 185, 191
  see also mechanisms
successionist view of causality *see* causality, generative and successive views of
suicide, egoistic 56, 58, 67, 176
Sullivan, A. L. 82, 89
survivor type 156–7, 163

Sutcliffe, K. M. 83, 86
symbolic interactionism 20, 100
synthesizing types 121, 147–8, 149–51

Tashakkori, A. 20
Teague, B. 82, 85, 89, 90, 141
Teddlie, C. 20
tentative theory *see* theory, tentative
technical
  accounts 13
  concepts/constructs 123, 138; *see also* social scientific concepts
  language 104
  meanings 89, 121–2, 147
tests of significance 37–8
theme(s) 65–7, 97, 118, 120–1, 129, 142, 147, 157, 236
theoretical
  argument 67, 87–8
  ideas 31, 35, 46, 58, 114, 174, 188–9, 237
  imagination 3, 67, 117–18, 120, 164–5, 174, 188, 190, 204, 228, *229–31*, 237–8; *see also* creativity
  perspectives 9, 11, 20
theorize(ing) 14, 59, 64, 67, 108, 116–18, 122–4, 140, *159–67*, 186, 213, 224
  deductive 59, 67, 224
  interpretive 116–18, 123, 124, 131, 160, 213
theory
  construction/ed/ing 4, 12, 58, 64, 67–8, 69–70, 86, 87–9, 107, *159–67*, *229–37*; *see also* theory development; theory generation/ing
  corroboration 37, 45, 56, 66, 68–9, 75, 92, 97, 226
  deductive *see* deductive theory/ies
  development 4, 32, 45, 58, 67, 70, 73, *87–9*, 105, 119, 122–4, 139, 143, 153–4, 161, 164; *see also* theory construction/ed/ing; theory generation
  existing 34, 64, 66, 69, 70, 164–5, 231, 237–8
  generation/ing 14, *46*, 113–14, 117, 120, *122–4*, 227, 230–2, 235–6, 243, 25; *see also* theory construction/ed/ing
  grounded *see* grounded theory
  middle-range *see* middle-range theory
  new 31, 32, 34, 45, 64
  role of 35
  social *see* social theory

theory (*cont.*)
  tentative 3, 56, 62, 66, 67, 86, 119, 133, 139, 140, 143, 161, 164, 167, 191–2
  testing 12–13, *30–7*, 45–6, 56, 59, 60–4, 66, *67–70*, 73, 75–6, 78–9, 80, *89–98*, 109–10, 112, 122–3, 173, 224–5, 226, 228, 243
theory-laden 177
thick description 132
Thompson, K. 58
Tilley, N. 169, 171, 175, 194, 198–9, 202
time and space limitations 175, 177
Tonnies, F. 104
top-down research 16, 33, 124, 221, 245
transferability 38
Trayner, Q. 151
triangulation 7, 222, 256
truth
  absolute 10, 56, 63
  consensus view of 185
  correspondence theory of 54
  relative 10, 63
Twight, B. W. 74–5
types
  abstracted 117, 119–20, 133, 143, 147
  of experience 92–8
  generating/developing 37, 111–12, *119–25*, *143–67*, 231, 233–7
  ideal/pure *102–8*, 111–13, 238, 254
  pairs of *see* pairs of types
  of reasoning 200; *see also* reasoning; leader's(s') reasoning
  reconstructing 121–3, 149, 238
  of resources 210–11
  synthesizing *see* synthesizing types
typification(s)
  everyday/social actors' 30, *46*, 102, *111–12*, 117, *119–25*, 133, *143–8*, 233–7
  paradigms as 12, 18, 81, 238
  social scientific 13, 30, 32, 38, *46*, 112, 115, 117, 120, *122–5*, *233–7*
typology/ies
  associations between 117, 119, 122–4, 130–1, 133, 143, 153, 156, 159–67, 227, 254
  of braided work 133–8
  constructed/ive *108–11*, 125, 147, 254
  construction/generation of 109, 117, 120–2, 130, 143–59

of experience-based influences 149–54, 204, 218
of leaders' orientations 153–64, 204, 217
role of 105
use of 104

understanding
  interpretive 101–2
  social scientific 9, 16, *33–7*, 115, 117, 120, 121–2, 133, 143, 159, 162, 200–1, 205, 209, 210, 213, 226–8
  of texts 232–3
  types of 102
  see also explanation(s)
universal law(s) *see* laws
Urry, J. 55, 64, 70, 170, 186, 194

validity 38
van Liere, K. D. 74
variable(s) 14
  nominal *see* nominal values/variables
  ordinal *see* ordinal categories/variables
  proxy *see* operationalizing concepts; proxy variables;
VBRC (Victorian Bushfires Royal Commission) 85, 90

Watkins, J. W. N. 105
Webber, M. M. 81
Weber, M. 11–12, 99, 101–3, 104–5, 106–8, 111, 113, 125, 126, 170, 171, 172, 238, 251, 253, 254
Weick, K. E. 83, 86
'what' research questions *see* research question(s)
Whewell, W. 54
'why' research questions *see* research questions(s)
wicked problem(s) 81, 86, 207, 227
WIKID*way*™ 166, 208, 209, 212
wisdom 167, 204, 206, *208–11*, 216; *see also* leader's(s') know-how
worldviews *15–18*
  pragmatic 17, 20
  researchers' 17–18, 22, 31
  social actors' 15–17, 22, 210
www.InfoServ.com.au xv, 4, 5, 82, 118, 122, 137, 139, 208, 238, 255